IMMIGRATION

A CIVIL RIGHTS ISSUE FOR THE AMERICAS

Edited by

Susanne Jonas

and

Suzie Dod Thomas

A Scholarly Resources Inc. Imprint
Wilmington, Delaware

Scholarly Resources Inc.
104 Greenhill Avenue
Wilmington, DE 19805-1897

Library of Congress Cataloging-in-Publication Data

Immigration : a civil rights issue for the Americas / edited by Susanne Jonas
 and Suzanne Dod Thomas.
    p.   cm.
   Includes bibliographical references.
   ISBN 0-8420-2775-0 (pbk.)
    1. United States—Emigration and immigration—Government policy.
2. United States—Emigration and immigration—Social aspects. 3. Emigration
and immigration—Social aspects. 4. Immigrants—Government policy—
United States. 5. Immigrants—Civil rights. I. Jonas, Susanne, 1941–
II. Thomas, Suzanne Dod.
JV6483.I553   1999
325.73—dc21   98-37844
                                          CIP

Contents

Introduction

Susanne Jonas, Suzie Dod Thomas, and John Isbister

The shock was undeniable. On the morning of November 9, 1994, we awoke to the news that 60 percent of the California voters around us believed that immigrant school children who could not produce the proper documentation concerning their legal status should be excluded from public schools and turned in to the INS. That was one of the landslide "messages" of Proposition 187 in California, the nation's first immigration war zone of the 1990s. In 1996, again in California, the world witnessed the videotaped beatings of undocumented immigrants fleeing INS agents in Riverside. In 1997, scholars and human rights groups in Houston documented over a thousand deaths of people attempting to cross the border from Mexico. Were these anomalies or logical outcomes of the criminalization of legally vulnerable undocumented immigrants as people without rights? Even the *New York Times* (which considers itself a voice of moderation) routinely reports on immigration using the discourse of "illegal aliens."

Although most of Proposition 187 is on its way to being declared unconstitutional, it succeeded in "sending a message" to Washington, and in the years that followed, many of its provisions were taken up by other states and by the U.S. Congress. When the 1996 Immigration Reform and Immigrant Responsibility Act was first introduced, it provided for a major reduction in the number of authorized immigrants. Although this provision was eventually removed from the act— because of pressure from a strange combination of corporations and immigrant advocacy groups—a series of punitive measures against undocumented immigrants remained, including the removal of most of their rights of judicial appeal, a major increase in Border Patrol staffing and funding for a massive fence along parts of the Mexican border and other high-tech means of interdiction. The Anti-Terrorism Act, hurriedly passed so that the President could sign it on the first anniversary of the Oklahoma City bombing, provided for summary deportation, without right of appeal, of undocumented immigrants—this in spite of the fact that no immigrants, undocumented or authorized, had any connection whatsoever to the Oklahoma City bombing. Despite the fact that this borders on a violation of due process, it remains on the books.

SUSANNE JONAS and SUZIE DOD THOMAS are members of the Editorial Board of *Social Justice* (P.O. Box 40601, San Francisco, CA 94140).

The 1996 Welfare Reform Act went so far as to eliminate Supplementary Security Income (SSI) and food stamps to elderly and disabled *legal* immigrants. In 1997, President Clinton did succeed in softening the SSI provision (but not the food stamp cutoff) so that it does not apply to immigrants whose status was affirmed before August 22, 1996, the date of the welfare act. This softening, while welcome, will become less relevant over time, since all new immigrants will be excluded from benefits. Finally, in the worst display of immigration as a political football and a relic of the Cold War, Nicaraguan Contras in the U.S.—but not Guatemalan or Salvadoran asylum seekers—were slated for outright amnesty in the "Relief to Victims of Communism" Act of 1997.

The tide of political opinion in the country has moved sharply against immigrants in the 1990s, although not completely against immigration. The debate over the 1996 Immigration Act was revealing on this distinction. The Congress decided not to reduce the number of authorized immigrants. In effect, it also decided not to reduce the number of undocumented immigrants in the country. Although in the end the act focused primarily on the undocumented, it directed all the new resources toward the patrol of the border—a strategy that has proven completely ineffective at stopping the growth of the undocumented population—and none at enforcement of sanctions against employers who hire the undocumented. Since undocumented immigrants enter the country overwhelmingly for the purpose of finding work, employer sanctions would be the only serious way to reduce their number. In effect, then, the Congress made it clear that it does not want to reduce the number of immigrants in the country—whether undocumented or authorized—but that it is completely committed to reducing and even in some cases eliminating their rights. The Congress seems to be pro-immigration but anti-immigrant. Taken together, what the most recent acts indicate is that the representatives of the American people want a low-paid, compliant and easily exploitable immigrant labor force, with no basic democratic rights.

In the years since the Proposition 187 shock, a major national debate has been building over immigration. For the most part, however, it is a debate among advocates of immigration "reform," that is, people who are anti-immigrant and anti-immigration: What are the most effective ways to exclude immigrants of color from the U.S., and to punish those who are here? Should AFDC, Medicare and housing assistance be denied only to undocumented immigrants or to all noncitizens? Should the long-standing principle of admitting immigrants to reunite families be jettisoned? How can exclusionary legislation be passed, while at the same time permitting exceptions for specific categories of skilled labor needed by high-tech corporations? Should asylum appeals be virtually eliminated? Should the children of undocumented immigrants be barred from the public school system, in violation of a 1982 Supreme Court ruling? Should the 14th Amendment of the U.S. Constitution be repealed, in order to deny citizenship to children born in the

U.S. of undocumented parents? These are among the measures receiving serious consideration in Congress.

At a time when immigrants—primarily Latin American and Asian—are once again being blamed for the problems experienced by U.S.-born working people, we are also seeing intensified right-wing and racist attacks on affirmative action and welfare. There is a larger process of demonizing the most vulnerable victims of economic restructuring—Latino immigrants and African-American welfare mothers, among others. In this climate, there has been little room for intervention in the public debate by progressive voices.

Even among progressives, or those who have traditionally thought of themselves as progressives, there are many dilemmas and divisions over immigration. A 1994 California initiative for comprehensive Canadian-style health care insurance would not have covered undocumented immigrants had it been passed. Most troublesome have been the debates over the impact of new immigrants on job opportunities and the availability of services to disadvantaged communities, including African-American and older immigrant communities. In spite of a great deal of economic research showing the contrary, some progressives and representatives of disadvantaged communities are worried that immigration takes away jobs and reduces the wages of low-income Americans. Economic restructuring and, above all, corporate downsizing, in which large numbers of people see their job prospects and living standards decline, have given rise to a widespread politics of insecurity. Working-class communities of color are among those facing conflicts over these issues because they apparently do not all share the same short-range interests and their underlying common interests are less visible. What does the word "progressive" mean in relation to immigration, when some long-standing civil rights activists, even such a heroine as the late Barbara Jordan, have espoused a crackdown on "illegal aliens"?

The answers are not simple: the issues need to be aired. Yet few spaces exist in which to air them. It is our objective in this volume to provide a space for discussion and debate. Out of these discussions, we hope, can emerge a progressive agenda on immigration. What does it mean to move toward a "progressive agenda" on an issue where progressives do not all agree with each other? One premise, we suggest, is that concerns about human rights, civil rights, democracy, participation, economic rights, and social equity are legitimate starting points for the discussion—and that this is the case even in an era of economic crisis, restructuring and downsizing.

This premise is grounded, we believe, in contemporary realities. Despite the most immediately visible concerns about job displacement, for example, economic restructuring and corporate downsizing have also created some spaces where "interests" and rights converge for many different communities. To put it another way, immigrant bashing has political and economic "spread effects" that reach far beyond immigrants of color. When proposals to repeal the 14th Amendment of the Constitution are being seriously considered, it is evident that a broader threat to democracy itself has arisen. If the anti-immigrant tide and the attacks on entitlements are not stemmed, they will continue to spread beyond undocumented immigrants to affect permanent legal residents as well. We could face a scenario in which the lowest sectors of the work force are largely composed of noncitizens with no suffrage and limited (or no) access to social welfare. If the political, economic, and social rights and anti-discrimination protections won by U.S. workers and people of color during the 20th century are restricted to citizens, those democratic gains themselves stand to be reversed, leaving the entire U.S. working class even more vulnerable to assaults by transnational capital in the 21st century.

As we take on these issues in the late 1990s, perhaps our own history can guide us. Before the 1960s, African Americans in the south lived amid a white population that regarded them as having no rights. Yet out of the depths of their anger and despair was born the Civil Rights Movement that won important legal protections and recognition of their rights as human beings. They learned to focus and channel their anger by building a vast social movement—as we must do now. In today's world, a civil rights movement must deal with the reality of globalization, and must therefore adopt an internationalist orientation toward domestic problems. Central to the agenda of a new civil rights movement should be the rights of migrants, workers as well as refugees, who move across borders.

We are beginning to see a few encouraging signs. The organized labor movement in the U.S., the AFL-CIO, which has traditionally excluded new immigrants, is for the first time recognizing that its own future is intimately tied to the future of (largely Latino and Asian) immigrant sectors of the work force and has begun a serious campaign for organizing immigrant workers in some key sectors of production and services. A pioneering example is the multi-union Los Angeles Manufacturing Action Project. This is not only a fight for the "social citizenship" rights of immigrant workers but also potentially a path toward revitalization of the labor movement itself, building on the life experiences, knowledge, and energies that immigrants bring with them. Campaigns around concrete issues, such as universal enforcement of minimum wages and other labor standards, could also unite immigrants with other sectors of the work force, providing an alternative to the divisive politics of insecurity.

Another source of hope comes from the growing awareness within Latino communities that, amid often divergent interests, there are points of unity in the defense of immigrant rights. In addition, immigrant rights advocates are finding some support in other communities of color. It is to be hoped that we are seeing an incipient revival of the best that is in our tradition from the Civil Rights Movements of the 1960s. To mention only a few examples: Los Angeles and other major American cities have seen massive demonstrations in defense of immigrants. Public service workers throughout California pledged not to comply with the provisions of Proposition 187 if it remained in effect. Texas has seen "Border Justice" campaigns at many points along its border with Mexico. Latino youth in many cities and states have shown great energy and creativity in organizing against attacks on immigrant rights. A coalition of Latino organizations marched on Washington, D.C., on October 12, 1996, *Día de la Raza*, in defense of the rights of immigrants and Latinos generally. Citizenship and voter registration drives have been mounted throughout the country.

A great deal more remains to be done, however. In 1990, after a decade of negotiation, the U.N. General Assembly adopted the International Convention on the Protection of the Rights of All Migrant Workers and Members of Their Families, a comprehensive charter which, if put into force by the world's countries, would go a long way toward protecting the human and civil rights of millions of migrants. To go into force, however, it requires ratification by twenty states. To date it has received less than half that number of ratifications, and none from Europe, Canada or the United States, the principal immigrant-receiving areas of the world.

Resolving the complex issues relating to the rights of migrants requires the best efforts not only of advocates and activists, but also of scholars and researchers. As one prominent U.S. scholar put it in speaking of Latin American and Latino Studies, research must "catch up with the immigration backlash" in order to affect public debate over the issue. One of our goals in this book is to close the gap between progressive movements and progressive scholars. We hope that the articles in this volume will enrich the public debate by describing the implications of the complex global processes that are redefining the parameters of state sovereignty and state control over borders. Although such analyses do not translate easily into sound bytes, they deal with realities that are transforming the lives of immigrants and non-immigrants alike in the Americas in the 21st century.

We open this volume with a portrait drawn from the daily life of a recent Latin American immigrant to the U.S. J.C. Malone's "Riding the Endless Immigration Roller Coaster (A True Story)" is an experience-based story by a professional journalist and writer who emigrated from the Dominican Republic to Michigan. This poignant tale of his job-search odyssey is a testament to the human toll of the process, caused by anti-immigrant sentiments in the receiving society and by the particularities of U.S. racism—even in the case of immigrants who bring great human and social resources. He also adds touches of humor to this story of the sacrifices made by entire generations of immigrants so that their children may live the "American Dream."

In "Beyond Sovereignty: Immigration Policy Making Today," Saskia Sassen argues that the demands of globalization of capital have created changes in the state, relativizing its autonomy and regulatory capacities. Drawing on examples from around the globe (Western Europe and Japan as well as the U.S.), she lays bare the dynamics shaping immigration and refugee processes and the links between the policies of receiving countries, the needs of capital, and the state's foreign policy objectives. Her analysis reveals how the state has attempted to single out the individual and the border as sites for regulation. She argues, however, that the cross-border movements of people are embedded in larger global factors that constrain policymakers, even against their will. As a result of these processes, the state itself is less monolithic; policy becomes the terrain for competing political pressures, opening up spaces for new agendas on immigration.

In "The Battle for the Border: Notes on Autonomous Migration, Transnational Communities, and the State," Néstor Rodríguez redefines the battle as more than a simple struggle to stem the tide of undocumented migration. The late 20th century has inaugurated a new age of capitalist development; just as capital has developed new resources for its functioning, many working-class communities in peripheral regions of the world economy have, in effect, broadened their base for survival across nation-state boundaries, through autonomous undocumented migration. This process has led to the creation of transnational communities that recompose the contours of class structures and class relations through self-activity and the use of capital's new communications and transportation technologies. After tracing the state's strategies against autonomous migration, he questions the need for the continuing existence of rigid nation-state boundaries. The author concludes that the battle for the border will become a war for the border, as new institutional actors wear down nation-state boundaries. Migrants, both legal and undocumented, will continue to play a major role in this development, since the purpose of the battle for the border is not to end labor migration but to terminate its autonomous origin.

Juan Vicente Palerm's essay, "The Expansion of California Agriculture and the Rise of Peasant-Worker Communities," presents a compelling, empirically based analysis which demonstrates that current realities belie the politically motivated goals of the authors of Proposition 187 in California, as well as similar initiatives in other states and in the U.S. Congress. Until we face up to the facts— the centrality of immigrant labor and of binational peasant-worker communities in Mexico and California to the economies of states such as California—immigration policies inspired by fear, ignorance and stereotypes are likely to displace rational policies. Such an outcome is detrimental to American society as a whole, because it not only violates basic values of democracy and human rights, but also flies in the face of basic trends in our changing economy.

In "Gender and International Labor Migration: A Networks Approach," Linda Miller Matthei highlights the increasing importance of women as actors in the migration process. Contrary to long-held assumptions in migration research that males are the primary migrants, she argues that there is substantial (although fragmentary) evidence that both migrant and nonmigrant women are actively involved in and central to building and maintaining the transnational networks that link migrant sending and receiving societies. She examines the contributions of world-systems analysis in bringing to light the significant economic role that female labor migrants play in the U.S. economy. Yet theoretical models that purport to explain household strategies do not fully account for women's role in migration. She argues for an analytical approach that is more socially and culturally grounded and focuses on migration as a gendered process of transnational network building. In her view, the notion of migration as a process of network building illuminates factors such as access to employment and settlement through social networks and the persistence of transnational ties.

In raising the question, "Are Immigration Controls Ethical?" John Isbister challenges Americans to reflect on the ethics involved in immigration issues. "Ethics" is not to be confused with interests. If we look only at interests, some Americans benefit, while others can be negatively affected by immigration. Ethics, by contrast, implies a focus on the equal moral worth of all people. This is the context for his examination of basic American precepts and his theoretical evaluation of open borders versus immigration controls. He concludes by proposing an ethically defensible immigration policy based on equal moral worth of all human beings, worldwide; from this perspective, he raises provocative questions about the propensity of U.S. citizens to defend their standard of living through support of restrictionist immigration policies.

In "Rethinking Immigration Policy and Citizenship in the Americas: A Regional Framework," Susanne Jonas addresses the multiple cross-border realities affecting U.S. immigration policies as well as their political consequences throughout the Americas. Using a multidisciplinary approach, she lays out the need for a regional framework as the context for a discussion of existing versus alternative policies. Existing U.S. "national security"-based immigration policies are of questionable effectiveness; in addition, they have antidemocratic and destabilizing effects in various sites throughout the hemisphere, including the U.S. An alternative set of policies—more in tune with current economic realities and stated U.S. political goals of promoting democracy and stability—would be based on a cross-border reconceptualization of citizenship and would recognize the accountability of states to civil society across borders and at borders. She also questions the immigration-related effects of U.S.-promoted neoliberal economic policies in the hemisphere. Finally, an alternative immigration policy would take a positive view of and build upon the transnational networks and practices initiated by immigrants.

The next two articles address the challenging issues of intergroup relations within and among communities of color in dealing with immigration. The strength of these articles is that, rather than generalizing about the "impact of immigration," they present specific community experiences that demonstrate the complexity and variety of everyday relations, ranging from competition to collaboration. In the first of these articles, "Chinese Suburban Immigration and Political Diversity in Monterey Park, California," John Horton uses ethnographic interviews, exit polls and census data to research the ethnic transformation of Monterey Park (a suburb of Los Angeles), occasioned by the influx of Chinese immigrants and the ensuing economic, social and political transformations as well as dislocation. In spite of these dislocations, some unity has been forged in a diverse community around common interests—as illustrated by the story of how the community united against a card club that wealthy Chinese and old-time white sectors of the power structure wanted to build, against the wishes of the Latino and Chinese communities. He describes the players, their positions, their strategies and the outcome in a way that suggests how diverse communities can unite around concrete interests.

The second case study is Néstor Rodríguez's "U.S. Immigration and Inter-group Relations in the Late 20th Century: African Americans and Latinos." In this article, Rodríguez focuses on the arena of intergroup relations between African Americans and Latinos from the perspective of Latino immigration. He begins by locating the arena of intergroup relations within larger structural processes related to global change and immigration. Utilizing findings from recent intergroup surveys and ongoing ethnographic research in the Houston area, he goes on to argue that contrary to some expectations, tensions and community instability are not the only resulting relations between African Americans and Latinos in cities experiencing high immigration. He makes the case for varied modes of Latino/African-American intergroup reactions, and presents Houston as a positive counter-example to other situations, such as inner Los Angeles, which have experienced high levels of tension resulting in part from (or attributed to) immigration.

In "Treacherous Waters in Turbulent Times: Navigating the Recent Sea Change in U.S. Immigration Policy and Attitudes," Lowell Sachs presents the view from Washington—the political pressures shaping immigration policies and debates in Congress. Now that immigrants are viewed as a liability, he discusses the effort in Congress to "pull up the welcome mat and shut the door." The author outlines the major pieces of legislation currently being considered in Congress. He demonstrates the ways in which politicians have exploited the nation's fears about the economy, crime, drugs and other such issues in garnering support for them-selves and their positions in Congress. What began as an attack on undocumented immigration has turned into calls for lower quotas, elimination of family reunifi-cation principles, and curtailment of services for legal immigrants.

"For an Immigration Policy Based on Human Rights," by David Bacon, builds on the author's grass-roots immigrant advocacy experience to counter the attack on the rights of undocumented immigrants. The author addresses the thorny issue of financial costs versus contributions made by undocumented immigrants to the system, exposing who pays and who benefits, and the ways in which the undocu-mented are particularly exploited because of their vulnerable legal status. After focusing on the politically expedient strategies of the Democratic Party and the Clinton administration, he traces the complex evolution of the AFL-CIO's position on undocumented immigration, particularly in the context of a changing global economy and the North American Free Trade Agreement (NAFTA). The author describes a plethora of new and exciting immigrant labor-organizing initiatives, revealing the potential for immigrant workers to revitalize and strengthen the U.S. labor movement as a whole. He calls for a policy based on respect for human rights, as defined in the 1990 U.N. International Convention on the Protection of the Rights of All Migrant Workers and Members of Their Families. In the author's words, "Immigration is a relationship between countries, forged by people passing back and forth. The problems which this movement poses cannot be solved by the actions of one country alone . . . [but] must find global solutions. . . ."

In "Right-Wing Politics and the Anti-Immigration Cause," Sara Diamond outlines the complexities of the right's positions, including the fault lines within the right *vis-à-vis* immigration policy. She points out the contradictions and strange bedfellows generated by the immigration issue in relation to the right's broader goals. During the Proposition 187 campaign in California, for example, the Christian right-wing coalition was not vocal, and more generally, the Christian right has downplayed the issue of immigration in order to avoid appearing racist at a time when it was making inroads into communities of color. This stands in sharp contrast to the position of the "paleoconservatives" and Pat Buchanan, who equate nationality with cultural/ethnic characteristics—the crude implication being that the government's role should be to preserve the white power structure. Unlike these paleoconservatives, the Christian Right has adopted a more moderate posture on immigration in order to win converts (especially from communities of color) to its "core issues," against abortion and homosexuality.

Michael Welch focuses on "The Immigration Crisis: Detention as an Emerging Mechanism of Social Control." Detaining large numbers of undocumented immigrants is a relatively recent development in INS policy. Until the 1980s, only those deemed likely to flee and hide or who posed a security risk were detained. Since that time, political shifts have fundamentally altered immigration policy, resulting in greater reliance on detention. Welch examines the major changes in detention policy and outlines some of the injustices taking place in this increasingly repressive arena. When INS policy is viewed in the context of "the new penology," such policy can be understood as an important mechanism of social control.

Taken together, these articles suggest how much research and organizing remain to be done. We hope that this collection will contribute to the insertion of progressive voices into the public debates about immigration. We also hope that the alternative approaches in this volume will broaden the parameters of debate, so that it is no longer simply among restrictionists, but, as it ought to be, a discussion about what kind of society the U.S. will be in the 21st century.

Riding the Endless Immigration Roller Coaster (A True Story)

J.C. Malone

M Y BROTHER AND I WERE TRAPPED AND HOPELESS, WITH THE SENSATION THAT takes over after finding out that there is no mobility for you, even though you have all that it takes to keep moving. Quite often we pay no attention to life's daily routines, but on that day they struck me in the face and turned the street corner into a giant screen where my present was explained and my future was unveiled by the past.

"Don't you remember," my brother asked me, "how when we were kids, people used to harass us because we spoke a different language?"

We were stuck in a traffic jam on a Friday afternoon during rush hour. Due to a blackout, the street lights on five consecutive busy corners were out. There were hundreds of cars, bumper to bumper, covering a few miles in different directions. The air was sultry, filled with fumes from the vehicles, where angry motorists were honking their horns, yelling, and insulting each other with all kinds of racial slurs.

"Black immigrant descendants have no future here. Perhaps our ancestors belonged to an African nomadic clan. I am going to honor that tradition, by getting out of this country," my brother added while I listened silently. He vented his frustration about the lack of social and economic mobility. He was convinced that the college would never change his part-time job as a professor into a full-time position. He was also angry at the bank where he worked as a senior employee; they never offered him any of the management positions that had come up over the past few months.

It took us about three hours to get out of the jam. A few weeks later he quit both jobs and I dropped him at the airport. "Some day you'll find out that there is no future for us here. When that happens, remember that you can count on me, I hope to be established by then," he told me before crossing the immigration gate on his way to the U.S.

In regard to the lack of social and economic mobility, he had a point. I was in charge of the business section of a daily newspaper, but they never gave me the position of editor, nor did they pay me the salary, even though I did the job.

J.C. MALONE (P.O. Box 7491, Grand Rapids, MI 49510–7491; e-mail: Maro4@aol.com) is a free-lance writer. His editorial comments are published by the Spanish newspapers of *The Miami Herald, L.A. Times*, and *The Chicago Tribune*. In English, he writes for *The Grand Rapids Press* and has a syndicated column with Hispanic Link, a Washington, D.C., syndicated service.

1

Nevertheless, it was kind of normal for me. I grew up seeing my dad in his deputy management position, doing his own work and that of his manager, who only showed up on payday. His boss' commitment to the job was so strong that he even got to the office late on that day. In that case, he would visit dad at home to pick up his cash.

My dad was a British citizen, just like Prime Minister John Majors. In fact, my dad and Alexander Hamilton were born in the same place, on the British island of Nevis. He was, nevertheless, Black and poor, a migrant farm worker who migrated to the Dominican Republic, across the border from Haiti. He was chasing the Dominicans' bitter sugar industry, which bloomed after the end of the First European War in 1918.

My brother was right. The Dominican Republic — the birthplace of the first "Americans," if we accept that definition for those descendants of Europe, Africa, and Asia born in the new continent — is not good to Black immigrants and their offspring. The European extermination of the continent's Native American population started there in the early 16th century. The African slave trade on the continent also started there.

Less than two years after my brother's departure, my situation at the paper became unbearable. A business editor who knew nothing about the job was hired, and I had to literally train him to be my boss. He quit afterward, but I still didn't get the position. Instead, I was assigned to write a story that would have caused the downfall of a huge corporation that had grown as fast as the head of foam on a beer poured quickly into a glass. That emporium had strong political and military connections.

"That's not an assignment, that's an order for you to commit *hara-kiri*," said a friend of mine. By keeping up with my assignment, I could have counted on one thing for sure: a few bullets in the head, leaving my daughters with nothing. The paper didn't provide life insurance.

In those days, the government lacked the money to pay the country's oil bill. We had no gas for cars or cooking and no electricity or water supply for homes. I spent an entire day in line waiting to put gas in my car and then burned a few gallons searching for the bag of charcoal my family needed to cook a meal. This went on for several months, while I was also trying to come up with a TV production. I had plenty of time, good credit, and some savings. In those days, I often received letters from my brother, who insistently asked me to come to Grand Rapids, Michigan, to put together a Spanish newspaper as a family business.

I thought, "A family business in the U.S.? What a pilgrim idea!" My marriage had crashed into divorce and the TV station never bothered to answer my request, despite having open space available.

As my savings started to dissipate, my stress level increased. Other than my daughters, I had few personal ties to hold onto. My brother's proposition became attractive; it was a way out. No longer would I have to stand by watching as business and political leaders carried out scams on each other, while agreeing upon ways to fleece the whole country. I wouldn't have to continue working as a journalist, prostituting my intelligence to factions that would never represent my personal or social class interests, let alone the general weal.

I could no longer provide for my daughters, so I sold my car, gave the money to my former wife, and bought a ticket to the U.S. That was how I made the decision to leave the Dominican Republic. I thought the Dominican Republic wasn't good for a Black immigrant descendant, that I would find better opportunities in the U.S., all the while ignoring that the story could repeat itself. The Dominican system spit me out. I flew to New York City one morning in December 1990, with no other pretensions than to help my brother and to try to get a job so as to resettle with my girls.

By six o'clock that afternoon, I was in the middle of the Times' Square Station "rush hour." In my right hand I carried a suitcase, in my left a briefcase, and a bag full of books hung on my shoulder. As I walked, I felt squeezed in the middle of the lonely rushing crowd. The trains' clatter, voices, musicians, beggars, and speakers announcing departures filled the air. Passing through a gate, I was pregnant with my own hopes and illusions. But I became distracted when the bag on my shoulder got stuck and tore. The books tumbled out and scattered across the floor. I dove after them, crawling between the passing legs. There, I got a bottom-up view of many Americans and also noticed the diversity of the national shoe market.

I felt the silent and indifferent cruelty that those legs symbolized as the shoes steamrolled across my hands. One pair stood in front of my eyes and I looked up to see a woman with big eyes and black hair. She smiled at me with a mixed expression of sympathy and pity. She shrugged her shoulders and waved her hands, signaling for me to hurry up and gather my stuff. Then she marched away.

It took me about 10 minutes to get the books together. They were more or less OK, with one exception — my most cherished novel. For the longest time, I had held on to her, like a first love. She accompanied me from my early adolescence. Her once elegant hard cover was broken and her pages had fanned out across the floor. Those feet of rushing commuters destroyed one of my most beloved books without noticing or caring.

I got up slowly, uncertain about what to do about my book. I decided to leave her there and turned to go. A voice stopped me: "Hey, you can't leave it there." It was a cop. "There's a trash can," he commanded, pointing with his right hand to the corner. I knelt, picked her up, and walked slowly in his direction, as in a funeral procession. I placed her in the can and saw the title for the last time: *Good Morning Sadness* by Françoise Sagan.

I dove back into the crowd, going up and down stairs, crossing gates and bridges to finally arrive at the Port Authority. There I boarded the bus to Grand Rapids, Michigan. On the bus I felt relief from the previous incident and the situation I had left at home. The gas crisis, indeed, worsened as President Bush and Saddam Hussein were preparing to fight for Kuwait's oil.

Then I thought about life's irony. It was December 16. On that day the year before, I was in the Winter Garden Theater in downtown New York City, attending the play *Cats*, Andrew Lloyd Webber's musical version of T.S. Eliot's *Old Possum's Book of Practical Cats*. Afterwards, I went to the Village to have drinks and listen to the music. That was the last time I had seen my brother, because I had sent him a ticket to visit me. Now I was on this bus with a ticket he had sent me, in the middle of my trip into the unknown, the other side of the United States, the immigration process.

When the bus pulled off the highway at the exit, a billboard with Santa and his reindeer welcomed me to Grand Rapids. My brother and his family picked me up at the station and drove me to their apartment. We had dinner and some drinks, and caught up with each other for the year apart. I then understood why he had insisted that I come and put a newspaper together with him as a family business. After two years of cleaning toilets and doing janitorial chores in a hotel, his self-esteem was very low and he had $2,000 in savings. Yet he had the idea of a business and now a brother who could flesh it out and bring it to life. That was my mission.

By that time, the churches in Grand Rapids numbered 604 — more than the gas stations and bars combined. They were spread around a downtown area filled with square buildings, which might well be an indication of the mentality of those who control the city.

"You just have to concentrate on the business and don't worry about anything. Here you'll have a roof over your head and food on the table. I will keep working in the hotel. This business will take me out of that place and will prevent you from doing the same work," my brother told me with a smile, trying to disguise the depressed expression on his face. The next day before going to work, he dropped me off at the public library and I started gathering information about the city.

Putting together a newspaper by yourself in a city where you don't know anyone isn't an easy job, but I puttered along with the project. I worked day and night, deciding who to interview, conducting interviews, taking pictures, writing stories, doing the typesetting and graphic design, helping my brother sell the ads, and then distributing the paper. This routine continued for over a year, but as the paper started picking up financially, my relationship with my brother started going down the drain.

By mid-spring my former wife arrived. She had quit her oncology nursing job in the Dominican Republic once the country's situation had deteriorated. She got a job in a sweat shop sewing sports apparel, and in November we sent for our daughters.

The cold November air announced the beginning of winter just as my relationship with my brother overheated. I had to get out of his house with my kids and their mother. The first snow fall my daughters experienced was through the window of a friend's dance studio where we slept that first night. By the next morning, homeless and with no source of income, I found myself sledding through the icy Grand Rapids streets in an old Honda Civic without heat and with bald tires. That was my own car in the nonstop immigration roller coaster that had taken my dad to the Dominican Republic and brought me to the U.S.

Between the beginning of November and the December holidays, we lived in five different places. I began searching for a job and a warm place to shelter my kids from the Michigan winter's rage. My strongest asset for the job market was the Spanish language. By now I had over 12 years of professional experience in writing, editing, and teaching. Locally, there were a few publishers that produced Spanish titles for bookstores around Latin America, many colleges that taught Spanish, and huge corporations that translate their product literature into Spanish. "There should be a place for me here," I told myself, and started my search.

Because he knew nothing about the media business, my brother still needed me to keep the paper running. He offered me a few dollars that I badly needed and I spent the rest of the winter fulfilling that hunger contract while I searched for another job. In the middle of that fight, with winter refusing to let the spring push it aside, I got my first job interview. It was on a Thursday morning in the Spanish department of a local publishing house.

Sledding over the icy streets, I slipped into the interview, convinced that my skills and experience would be enough for me to get the job. My future depended on this new window of opportunity. That mood prevailed as I reached the World Mission of the Christian Reformed Church in North America, which owns the publishing house. Never mind that this Dutch-originated Calvinist sect is similar to the one responsible for the development of apartheid in South Africa. I refused to be a realist, though, since I couldn't afford to be pessimistic. Locally, this church has more power than the Catholic Church in Latin America.

A tall and thin middle-aged blond man received me. He had a hard expression on his face and gentle manners. He gave me a tour of a room with bookshelves and showed me the Spanish titles they had published. We entered his office, which had just enough light for him to work and see a poster of John Calvin and other religious decorations on the walls. He praised my credentials as we sat down and he asked about my religious life.

"Daddy was a Pentecostal minister," I answered proudly.

"We have that in common," he added. "My dad was a minister, as was my grandfather in Holland." I crossed my legs and continued the conversation.

"My granddad was also a minister, but mom was not quite a religious person; she had a different lifestyle."

Visibly surprised, he asked: "Different lifestyle? How was that? What do you mean?"

I cleared my throat. "Well, let's see if I can explain it better for you. On the weekends, for example, my dad used to go to church and my mom to the bar."

He rubbed his hands, leaned over the desk, cleared his throat a few times, and looked at me the way one examines a bug. With visible discomfort, he asked: "What kind of minister was your dad? How did he give his wife that kind of freedom?"

"Daddy had a strong faith in God. He believed that if God wanted Mom to act differently, he would have made her change her behavior. Being her husband, he thought, gave him no right to impose creeds and lifestyles on her, because God never uses his power to impose. He set us free. They had an excellent relationship; I never saw them fighting."

He leaned back in his seat, loosened his tie a bit — the office wasn't hot — and passed his hands over his hair. Then he offered me candy from the jar on the desk. With a forced smile he talked about work.

"Generally, church members from South America do our Spanish work. If we need you, I'll let you know." The interview was over. Here, as an immigrant, I wouldn't have taken a job away from Americans. The ones doing the work didn't even bother to immigrate to the U.S.

By the time I was back in my car sledding through the streets, I knew that he wouldn't call me. "There should be other options," I consoled myself, trying to avoid going back home in a depressed mood. I spent the spring dropping resumes and cover letters into the mail, and answering the local newspaper "help wanted" ads, but all I received in the mail were utility, phone, hospital, and sundry other bills.

For the *Cinco de Mayo* celebration, the formerly family business newspaper got plenty of ads. The paper was growing, but my relationship with my brother, now the sole owner, was going under. Money was coming in and my brother had his share of the "American Dream." He didn't need me anymore. Indeed, he hired someone else and fired me from my own project.

I spent the rest of spring doing translations and free-lancing as a graphic designer to supplement my former wife's income to support the kids. In the summer, the local newspaper printed a story about a publisher who proudly explained that while living in Spain, he had violated laws prohibiting his Protestant religion. Back in Grand Rapids, he was running his family publishing house with big sales in the Spanish market. I mailed him my resume, followed up with a phone call, and set up an appointment.

That day was muggy, characteristic of the kind of angry summer that burns the forest. My car didn't have air conditioning, so I arrived almost melting in sweat. The receptionist informed him that I was there and asked me to go in. He was tall and semi-bald. Of the few remaining hairs, the gray ones had almost completely seized control of his head. His face was friendly and relaxed and he had a simple and direct manner. We spoke in Spanish and English. He expressed interest in my credentials and asked just one question: "Is your experience based only on secular publications?" My positive answer ended the interview without promise.

I then approached Grand Rapids Community College and talked to the chairperson of the Foreign Language Department. She suggested that I send my resume and a cover letter. I did. Three years later, I still haven't received an answer and she hasn't returned my repeated phone calls.

When fall came, my optimism and hopes were traveling in the same direction as the leaves, rendering me as defenseless and naked as a tree exposed to the upcoming winter's rage. I couldn't give up. A year had already passed since my daughters' arrival, and I had nothing to offer them but my bare hands and my naked heart and soul. I had it all there for them, standing as still as I could. My former wife and I did everything we could, within our limitations, to offer them a home and the sense of being part of a happy family. With our mutual frustration with a shattered relationship, we slept together head to toe every night for quite some time. Despite hating the dysfunctional lover of the past, we developed a bond that often arises among human beings who share adversity.

That fall I finally landed a job using my basic journalistic skills. As a reporter, I took pen and notebook in hand, approached people, introduced myself, and interviewed them about their preferences. Then I used a computer to process the information. Yet I wasn't wearing a suit and tie. Instead of a press pass on my chest, I donned a different sign: Spectrum Lanes. I had become a waiter in a bowling alley.

Reporters and waiters have similarities. If the former writes something incorrectly, he must make a correction the next day. If the latter doesn't listen carefully and writes down incorrect information, he must take the plate back to the kitchen for corrections. Twice each week I waited on 500 female bowlers. There was warmth and joviality. I had fun, made friendships, and some money, but bowlers don't tip very well and the money wasn't adequate even for a simple lifestyle.

I kept up my job hunt because waitering didn't solve my financial and personal problems. Bad news never comes alone. There were serious problems with my kids. They kept getting sick as the weather changed. The mailman visited religiously with his sadistic smile, bearing all sorts of bills.

By the end of fall, a friend told me about a possible opening in the Spanish Department at Calvin College, the intellectual arm of the Christian Reformed Church. The letters and phone conversations with the person in charge were very polite. Although praising my credentials, she let me know that they wouldn't hire me. She told me that the Grand Rapids Baptist College was about to open a Spanish section and suggested I apply there. She wished me luck.

The Michigan winter returned, threatening to freeze my soul; the sunshine faded from view and with it my hopes of finding a better job. Following the instructions from the "job hunting manuals" I had read, I got the name of the Baptist College "contact person." I called to find out if we had something in common. This person was in charge of the college's radio station; of course, I started my journalistic career in radio. I was invited to tour the station and talk about the possibility of a job.

I rushed out into a mild winter morning, brightened by shy sunshine over snow. The "contact person" was a young white male with freckles and a well-kept beard. We conversed politely for half an hour while touring the radio station. He then tried to introduce personal and religious topics. By now I knew better than to allow that to happen again and instead turned the conversation to professional subjects. He confirmed that an opening was soon available and assured me that I had excellent qualifications. Besides my language skills, they could use my journalistic experience. He gave me the name of a new "contact person," whom I, again, would need to provide with a resume and cover letter.

Within two weeks I received two letters from the college. The second one said: "Enclosed you will find a faculty data sheet and a doctrinal statement of the college. I would encourage you to read the doctrinal statement and lifestyle expectations appended to the data sheet. All faculty hired are expected to be in agreement with these beliefs and standards. In order to receive further consideration for the position, please fill out the data form and forward it to...." One of the documents was a kind of contract. Signing it would mean that I accepted all their doctrinal principles, that I agreed to live according to their philosophy, and that I accepted all the doctrinal statements as absolutely true — my own beliefs had no importance at all.

The form requesting personal and professional information had a section titled "church affiliation." Among other questions, they asked: "Do you or your spouse ever use intoxicating beverages, tobacco, profanity, engage in dancing, gambling, movie theater attendance? __Yes __No." That was not all. Further down was this statement: "If yes, please explain." I couldn't explain that my country is defined by our National Poet as a place located in an "unbelievable archipelago of sugar and alcohol."

Oh, the Baptists! They are so clear and precise. They expected me to attend church and participate in its activities. If my "pastor" had any complaint about me, my job would be in danger. They expected me to quit being myself in order to get the job. So much for that! At times, I believe I wasted that opportunity to get a job and save my soul.

One afternoon that winter I came home upset and yelled at everything and everyone. Tons of bills mounted up daily and my earnings were insufficient to survive. It was the kind of day in which you shake your fist in the air and yell at the roof, the sky, heaven, or whatever is up there. I found one of my daughters trying to eat a roach. My first reaction was to keep yelling. The second was to run toward her. My former wife and partner in the struggle reached her first and removed the little roach from her mouth.

I read mixed messages in her sweet and frightened little eyes. "Daddy, why did you do that to me? Why are you upset at me?" The other expression was from a cold and hungry child. Her eyes calmed me down and my anger faded away. I picked her up, hugged her tight to my chest and cried in silence for a few minutes. I then gave her to her mom, who was standing nearby and holding us.

"We need to move from here," I said while getting ready to go to the bowling alley, preparing to smile and make jokes to my customers, so they would tip me well.

That evening at work, I was waiting on a male customer who came to wait for his league. He was drunk. Suddenly, the guy stood and started yelling at me, saying that I had stolen $10.00 from him. He yelled at the top of his lungs and half the people in the bowling alley watched as he approached me with the clear intention of knocking me down. A few coworkers and bowlers stopped him. I had to sit down with my supervisor and count all my money to demonstrate that until that moment, I had only made $3.00 in tips.

I thought about quitting, but the images of my daughter that afternoon were too vivid and raw in my mind. I held back. When that customer left, I noticed that he had only bitten off a few pieces of his steak. I had to put the leftovers in the trash, while my daughter was hungry enough to eat a roach.

The following morning, I woke up with Sagan's novel title, *Good Morning Sadness*, on my mind. We had no food in the cupboards. My three daughters, my former wife, and I ended up in a church food line. A tall, white male received us. He asked us to pray. Then we had to stand in silence for a minute of thankful meditation while watching the dark ceiling. He said God was up there. Too bad it was so dark I couldn't see him. The man then gave us two grocery bags filled with quite dated food.

That day it occurred to me that charity is perhaps nothing other than a subliminal stage of prostitution of the commandment "love one another." It seems to me that those with the power to make major donations could use that power to make changes in society that would end the need for charity. I might not understand the concept of giving in this post-industrial society, but I don't remember my dad's church making that kind of donations.

First, they were too poor to afford them. Equally important, I think they approached it differently. I have vivid childhood memories of a beggar standing at the door while we were having lunch in the dining room. My dad would get up from his chair, walk to the door, and bring him in. My dad would sit the visitor in his own chair and give him his own meal. When that happened, the whole family would stop eating and watch the visitor satisfy his starving stomach. He would usually eat it all and we would have to take some food out of each plate to make up a plate of food for my dad. This happened more times than I can count.

In Grand Rapids, I felt surrounded and was on the verge of surrendering to various problems. We had to move from that roach-infested house and found a cozy little apartment. But the landlord didn't tell me that it was inhabited. I figured it out after turning off the lights at bedtime. The floor started moving and making noise. When we turned the light on again, the whole floor was covered with roaches. We moved several times in an attempt to escape the roaches, but it was impossible; they controlled that entire area in town. For a moment, I thought that my whole mission in life was to kill roaches. We had a real territorial war, in which the weapons industry, in this case the roach spray makers, got a fairly good cut from my defense budget.

One night I went to bed with roaches on my mind. They were all I had; I saw them everywhere and thought about ways of getting rid of them without spending money or smashing them with my shoes. That night I dreamed about my mother and her cruel treatment of roaches: she let them starve to death. "I started out with that method," I told her in my dream, "but it doesn't work very well because they seem to live upstairs." She asked me to get help from my neighbor. I thought about calling him and organizing an action plan with tactics and strategies against the roaches. That was impossible because he was too busy, with people coming and going from his place all the time. He never used the front door. He always received his visitors through the back door. Many times we couldn't sleep because of loud business discussions and disagreement in his apartment.

At that moment I felt as though I had become an American cockroach. My family and I were starving in a house that was full of roaches and smelled of bug spray. Winter had become a long, dark tunnel for me. The sunshine had disappeared and many problems arose from various directions.

In a parent-teacher conference, I was told that my daughters had "Attention Deficit Disorder, speech problems, and very strange social behavior." They suggested a "Special Education Program for them" to me. That was one more reason for us to move, to change school districts, because the girls had their own version of what was going on at school: they complained about their fellow students and the teachers.

"The kids make fun of us, Dad. They say we are ugly and stupid. And the teachers don't take enough time to explain the lessons to us."

We moved as only an immigrant can and changed school districts, too. The problem continued. Nowhere did the teachers take the time to figure out that the kids were still learning English, struggling with a new language.

While dealing with this, I continued my job search and tried to get one at the public library. I called a friend who works there and stopped by to explain my situation. Francesca, a short young woman with dark hair, was in love in those days — glowing, happy, loving, and feeling loved. She treated me sweetly, informed me that by spring there would be openings, and promised to send me the information.

As the snow began to melt with the first sunshine, her letter arrived. Spring was here again and its creative and hopeful energy, I thought, would fertilize the desert of my sterile struggle. I discovered that part of the season's enchantment had to do with the joy of surviving the winter. The gray winter days faded away. I could see the sun every day and listen to the birds singing in the green trees.

As I opened Francesca's letter, I sensed positive energy issuing from the envelope. Once again, my resume and cover letter were in the mail. The response was quick and precise. I had to take a typing test. That was no problem. The library would be a good place to work. They don't pay the best wages, but it would be part-time work and that would give me more time to write.

Another letter informed me of the day and time for a written test. I arrived 15 minutes early and waited in a big room with a few Caucasian women of different ages. A short woman who looked like one of Botello's sculptures walked into the room to administer the test. Her androgynous look, with a tailored jacket, signaled that she was "dressed for success" and was trying to break the "glass ceiling." The test was tucked under one arm. It was simple: 50 questions, mostly English grammar, were to be answered in 15 minutes. It was copyrighted in 1957. I wasn't even born then! My prospects were few.

Everything turned out the way I anticipated. They didn't hire me. I wrote to the "business manager" explaining what had happened. I pointed out that the test's 1957 date not only was before my birth, but it also predated the 1964 Civil Rights Act. No answer. When I go to the library now, I see those who "passed" the test at the checkout counter. They put rubber stamps on the books stating the return date. That's their basic job, but I wasn't qualified to do it.

Soon thereafter, a friend connected me with one of Amway's corporate lawyers. The company produces Spanish literature for its merchandise. At its office, I found another middle-aged white male with an abundant mix of gray and blond hair. He seemed humane, kind, and very gentle. We talked for a while and he checked my resume. Then he promised to recommend me to Amway. He believed the company could use my experience and skills.

I left his office full of hope. Two weeks later the mail brought a letter from Amway. There was currently no opening, but they promised to keep my information in their "active file," whatever that means. I never heard from them again, even though I called a zillion times.

Later on, Rich — very rich — De Vos, the more liberal of the Amway owners (God knows, I don't pretend to offend him by calling him liberal), published his book, *Compassionate Capitalism*. There he tried to "humanize" capitalism with charity and giving more people the opportunity to sell Amway products.

The local paper reviewed the book as Mr. De Vos' "legacy." I picked it up in the public library, read it, and wrote an article about it for a Spanish magazine in Miami. Somewhat later, a physician friend of mine told me on the phone that Amway distributors had attempted to involve him in the business in the Dominican Republic. Among the documents they used was my article about Mr. De Vos' philosophy and wealth.

I wrote to Amway's public relations department and told the story. I sent them a copy of the article, and told them that I was available if they needed to use my skills for translation or any other job. They never answered me. I don't know why.

In my article, I didn't say anything against Mr. De Vos. I didn't even say that he might have forgotten to quote Kahlil Gibran's *The Prophet* while talking about "giving."

The end of winter also meant the end of the bowling season. I was, again, without income. Searching for a new job, I received a morning of training to become a cabby. One suggestion made with total solemnity by my trainer was: "Never get out of the cab, for any reason, because only inside here can you listen to God."

"What exactly are you talking about?" I asked him with surprise. He was staring at the radio, the source of the dispatcher's voice.

"People call him dispatcher," he said, "but in all reality, that guy's name is God. He is the one who knows where the good runs are and decides who gets them. For me, that's the way the business works and I make money. I hope it works for you," he added with a smile, pushing up his glasses with the back of his hand.

I followed his instructions the best I could and between four in the afternoon and midnight, I didn't get out of the cab. I had already drunk a few bottles of juice and the water I had brought along. While counting my money I figured that the "God of the Cabbies" hadn't helped me very much. I didn't have enough money to pay for the cab lease, which cabbies call OPS, whatever that means. I needed to get some liquid out of my system, but the gas station on the corner refused to let anyone into their bathroom after dark due to high crime in the area.

I rushed down a dark street and found some bushes very close to the railroad tracks. While standing there taking care of my needs, I noticed some lights flashing behind me. It was a cop. I was engaged in a very serious violation called "public urination." The officer let me know that he could arrest me due to such an infraction, and he called his supervisor for consultation. He made me feel that I was very deep in hot guacamole dip.

There I was, with two officers, each costing the taxpayers around $100,000 a year, discussing my future. They took about 15 minutes checking out my driving records and perhaps consulting their chief. I mean, it was a very delicate matter, a major moral offense. My anxiety increased a lot during this waiting period. For a moment I thought they were going to have me deported. The thought of being deported to the Dominican Republic because of "public urination" worried me. Perhaps the reporter covering the airport wouldn't include my name in his story.

The cops returned with good news. They wouldn't arrest me, even though they should. They were extremely helpful and only gave me an $80.00 fine. After eight hours of work I hadn't earned a penny for myself. I wanted to yell at them, but I couldn't. I was grateful that they hadn't arrested me even though the fine increased my budget deficit. I owed both the cab company and the city.

"I forgot to tell you to take an empty milk jug with you into the cab for those cases. I am sorry about that," said my trainer when I told him my story the next day.

I had to appear before a judge, a large African American male, who offered me two options: "You can either plead guilty to public urination and pay an $80.00 fine or you are going to trial." I couldn't refuse the bargain. We negotiated payment arrangements, just as tax collectors might do with first-time delinquent offenders.

After a few weeks, the God of the Cabbies answered my prayers and I was able to make enough money to feed my kids, avoid hunger lines, and afford to pay tuition for them at a private school. The new school teaches Spanish once a week. My kids became proud of their language and all the previous troubled diagnoses faded away. They were doing just fine. I also made enough money to abandon the losing war against the roaches and moved to a place where my mom's technique worked very well.

From my cab I had the opportunity to see U.S. society from "inside," in a kind of closed-circuit vision. I learned a few things. The struggle of inner-city dwellers, for instance, was no different from mine. Inner-city problems are solvable if we can recover a sense of brotherhood among human beings. There is no difference between poor babies in the African American and Hispanic ghettos, and those we have in Latin America. Their runny noses are the way in which their souls bleed due to the ancestral inequalities in which they happened to be born. In their eyes you can see a glint of hope for a better life. Here, as over there, the doctors can keep their noses dry, but who will heal their wounded souls?

I learned that poverty in Latin America is a less painful experience. Down there we know that we don't live in one of the richest societies ever known. We don't have to witness the opulence evident in the U.S., while living below the poverty level. I learned that while chasing money here, people miss the healing power of the fall morning breeze. I learned that each flower blooming in the spring is nothing but the renaissance of new hopes and dreams for the poor, the oppressed ones; and that regardless of whether the summer burns them, they will bloom again the following spring. You can exploit and oppress an entire population all the time, but there is no way of killing their hopes for brotherhood, regardless of their color or social or economic level.

All the money in the world wouldn't pay for what I have learned in the immigration process. I have learned to be grateful to the society that has painfully given me all this knowledge. Each lesson has been as harsh as ripping skin. Grand Rapids showed me that immigrating is like being born again. Nothing that you were previously matters here. No one believes you. Very few respect you. In most cases, they don't even pay attention to you, because you speak with a strange accent. You have to start from below zero. Nothing that you have known, none of your previous parameters, have importance anymore.

I grew up with a sense of intrinsic value as a person. Mom and Dad made me believe that I had personal worth. I used to believe that I had value because of who I am. Here I learned that you have value because of what you have. I have nothing. I couldn't understand how a society that is filled with so many smiling faces, with loving and caring people, can be so mean to their fellow humans. For a moment I doubted that Walt Whitman and T.S. Eliot's poetry came from this place.

In the process, I had to relearn how to speak, read, and write, to drive in the snow, and to dress according to the weather. I had to learn how to walk on ice without falling and breaking my back, while wrapped up in a coat just like the sculptures Christo wraps.

Above all, immigration taught me that I am stronger than I thought I was. I stood with pride through the whole process. I starved and suffered, but my soul, heart, mind, and body survived for me to get my share of the American Dream of freedom.

I am using my share to express my thoughts and feelings. My hope is that they will help us remember that we are all members of the human family. It's a very dysfunctional family, I know, but all of us are entitled to equal rights, regardless of our nationalities, race, gender, sexual orientation, or religious affiliation. At least, that's the way in which it was written in the religious scriptures and in the gospel of this country: the U.S. Constitution.

Now I look back and see my brother running his newspaper, my kids are doing fine in school, while I am writing for a few newspapers across the country and doing some translations. It seems like a Steven Spielberg "happy ending," but until now I hadn't gotten a job.

After all, I know that I'm not a "good immigrant." I don't have Arnold Schwarzenegger's biceps and I don't work in movies that promote violence and glorify weapons. I'm only an ignorant and ignored immigrant, in a country that seems to have forgotten that in the beginning they were nothing but immigrants. I don't know where the whole experience will take my daughters. Does anyone know where you can end up riding a nonstop roller coaster? I did learn an American expression that defines part of society's attitude toward the experiences of people like me: "who cares?"

Beyond Sovereignty:
Immigration Policy Making Today

Saskia Sassen

THE INTERACTION BETWEEN THE DENATIONALIZING OF KEY ECONOMIC INSTITUTIONS and spaces, on the one hand, and the renationalizing of politics on the other provides one of the main contexts for immigration policy and practice today. We see a growing consensus in the community of states to lift border controls for the flow of capital, information, services, and more broadly, to further globalization. Yet when it comes to immigrants and refugees, whether in North America, Western Europe, or Japan, we see the national state claiming all its old splendor and asserting its sovereign right to control its borders, a right that is a matter of consensus in the community of states.

What does it mean for the state to relinquish sovereignty in some realms and to continue to be sovereign in others? If we accept, as I do, that the state itself has been transformed by its participation in the implementation of laws and regulations necessary for economic globalization, we must accept as a possibility that sovereignty itself has been transformed. Elsewhere (1996b) I have argued that exclusive territoriality — a marking feature of the modern state — is being destabilized by economic globalization and that we are seeing the elements of a process of denationalization of national territory, though in a highly specialized institutional and functional way. Further, the particular combination of power and legitimacy we call sovereignty, which has over the last century become almost synonymous with the national state, is today being partly unbundled, redistributed onto other entities, particularly supranational organizations, international agreements on human rights, and the new emergent private international legal regime for business transactions (*Ibid.*). With all of this happening, what does it mean to assert, as is repeatedly done in the immigration literature, that the state has exclusive authority over the entry of non-nationals? Is the character of that exclusive authority today the same as it was before the current phase of globalization and the ascendance of human rights as a nonstate-centered form of legitimate power?[1]

SASKIA SASSEN is a Professor in the Department of Urban Planning at Columbia University, New York, NY 10027. Her most recent books are *Cities in a World Economy* (Pine Forge/Sage, 1994) and the just completed *Immigrants and Refugees: A European Dilemma* (Fischer Verlag in Germany, 1996). She has begun a new five-year research project on "Governance and Accountability in a World Economy." This article is an extract from a book being prepared for the Twentieth Century Fund, *Immigration Policy in a World Economy*. The author thanks the Fund for its support.

My analysis focuses largely on immigration in the highly developed receiving countries. I use the notion of immigration policy rather broadly to refer to a wide range of distinct national policies. I should note that it is often difficult to distinguish immigrants and refugees. Yet there is (still) a separate regime for refugees in all these countries. Indeed, there is an international regime for refugees, something that can hardly be said for immigration. The focus in this brief essay is on the constraints faced by the state in highly developed countries in the making of immigration policy today.[2]

The Border and the Individual as Regulatory Sites

In my reading there is a fundamental framework that roots all the country-specific immigration policies of the developed world in a common set of conceptions about the role of the state and of national borders. The purpose here is not to minimize the many differences in national policies, but to underline the growing convergence in various aspects of immigration policy and practice.[3]

First, the sovereignty of the state and border control, whether land borders, airports, or consulates in sending countries, lie at the heart of the regulatory effort. Second, immigration policy is shaped by an understanding of immigration as the consequence of the individual actions of emigrants; the receiving country is taken as a passive agent, one not implicated in the process of emigration. In refugee policy, in contrast, there is a recognition of other factors, beyond the control of individuals, as leading to outflows.[4] Two fundamental traits of immigration policy are, then, that it singles out the border and the individual as the sites for regulatory enforcement.

The sovereignty of the state when it comes to power over entry is well established by treaty law and constitutionally. The Convention of The Hague of 1930 asserted the right of the state to grant citizenship; the 1952 Convention on Refugees, which asserted that the right to leave is a universal right, remained silent on the right to entry — better silence than evident contradiction. (As is well known, the status of refugees and their right not to be forcibly returned are established in international law, but there is no corresponding right of asylum; such right is at the discretion of a receiving state.)

There are various human rights declarations and conventions that urge states to grant asylum on humanitarian grounds, but they all recognize the absolute discretion of states in this matter.[5] A few states, notably Austria and Germany, give those formally recognized as refugees a legal right to asylum — though this is under revision. More recently, the various agreements toward the formation of the European Union (EU) keep asserting the right of the state to control who can enter. This is quite a contrast with the assertions in the General Agreement on Tariffs and Trade (GATT), North American Free Trade Agreement (NAFTA), and the EU about the need to lift state controls over borders when it comes to the flow of capital, information, services, and state controls over the domestic financial markets.

On the matter of the individual as a site for enforcement, two different operational logics are becoming evident. One of these logics — the one embedded in immigration policy — places exclusive responsibility for the immigration process on the individual, and hence makes of the individual the site for the exercise of the state's authority. There is a strong tendency in immigration policy in developed countries to reduce the process to the actions of individuals. The individual is the site for accountability and for enforcement. Yet it is now increasingly being recognized that international migrations are embedded in larger geopolitical and transnational economic dynamics. The worldwide evidence shows rather clearly that there is considerable patterning in the geography of migrations, and that the major receiving countries tend to get immigrants from their zones of influence. This holds for countries as diverse as the U.S., France, or Japan. Immigration is at least partly an outcome of the actions of the governments and major private economic actors in receiving countries. Economic internationalization and the geopolitics resulting from older colonial patterns suggest that the responsibility for immigration may not be exclusively the immigrant's. Analytically, these conditions only can enter into theorizations about the state and immigration when we suspend the proposition implicit in much immigration analysis — that immigration is the result of individual action. In the other logic, that embedded in human rights agreements, the individual emerges as a site for contesting the authority (sovereignty) of the state because s/he is the site for human rights. (For a detailed analysis of the interaction of these two logics, see Sassen, 1996b.)

Beyond Sovereignty: Constraints on States' Policy Making

When it comes to immigration policy, states under the rule of law increasingly confront a range of rights and obligations, pressures from both inside and outside, from universal human rights to not-so-universal ethnic lobbies. The overall effect is to constrain the sovereignty of the state and to undermine old notions about immigration control.

We see emerging a de facto regime, centered in international agreements and conventions as well as in various rights gained by immigrants, that limits the state's role in controlling immigration. An example of such an agreement is the International Convention adopted by the General Assembly of the United Nations (U.N.) on December 18, 1990, on the protection of the rights of all migrant workers and members of their families (Resolution 45/158). (See, e.g., Hollifield, 1992; Baubock, 1994; Sassen, 1996b: Part Three.) Further, there is a set of rights of resident immigrants widely upheld by legal authorities. We have also seen the gradual expansion over the last three decades of civil and social rights to marginal populations, whether women, ethnic minorities, or immigrants and refugees.

The extension of rights, which has taken place mostly through the judiciary, has confronted states with a number of constraints in the area of immigration and refugee policy. For instance, there have been attempts by the legislatures in France and Germany to limit family reunification, which were blocked by administrative and constitutional courts on the grounds that such restrictions would violate international agreements. The courts have also regularly supported a combination of rights of resident immigrants that have the effect of limiting the government's power over resident immigrants. Similarly, such courts have limited the ability of governments to restrict or stop asylum seekers from entering the country.[6]

Finally, the numbers and kinds of political actors involved in immigration policy debates and policy making in Western Europe, North America, and Japan are far greater than they were two decades ago: the EU, anti-immigrant parties, vast networks of organizations in Europe and North America that often represent immigrants, or claim to do so, and fight for immigrant rights, immigrant associations and immigrant politicians, mostly in the second generation, and, especially in the U.S., so-called ethnic lobbies.[7] The policy process for immigration is no longer confined to a narrow governmental arena of ministerial and administrative interaction. Public opinion and public political debate have become part of the arena wherein immigration policy is shaped.[8] Whole parties position themselves politically in terms of their stand on immigration, especially in some of the European countries.

These developments are particularly evident in the EU.[9] Europe's single market program has had a powerful impact in raising the prominence of various issues associated with free circulation of people as an essential element in creating a frontier-free community; the European Community (EC) institutions lacked the legal competence to deal with many of these issues, but had to begin to address them. Gradually, EC institutions have wound up more deeply involved with visa policy, family reunification, and migration policy — all formerly exclusively in the domain of the individual national states. National governments resisted EC involvement in these once exclusively national domains. Yet now both legal and practical issues have made such involvement acceptable and inevitable, notwithstanding many public pronouncements to the contrary. There is now growing recognition of the need for an EC-wide immigration policy, something denied for a long time by individual states.

In the case of the U.S., the combination of forces at the governmental level is quite different, although it has similar general implications about the state's constraints in immigration policy making. Immigration policy in the U.S. today is largely debated and shaped by Congress, and hence is highly public and subject to a vast multiplicity of local interests, notably ethnic lobbies.[10] We know well how very sensitive members of Congress are to the demographics of their districts. This has made it a very public process, quite different from other processes of policy making.[11]

The fact that immigration in the U.S. has historically been the preserve of the federal government, particularly Congress, assumes new meaning in today's context of radical devolution — the return of powers to the states.[12] There is now an emerging conflict between several state governments and the federal government around the particular issue of federal mandates concerning immigrants — such as access to public health care and schools — without mandatory federal funding. Thus, states with disproportionate shares of immigrants are asserting that they are disproportionately burdened by the putative costs of immigration. The costs of immigration are an area of great debate and wide ranging estimates.[13] At the heart of this conflict is the fact that the federal government sets policy, but does not assume responsibility, financial or otherwise, for the implementation of many key aspects of immigration policy. The conflict is illustrated by the notorious case of the State of California and its $377 million lawsuit against the federal government. The radical devolution under way now will further accentuate some of these divisions.

The Substance of State Control over Immigration

One of the questions raised by these developments concerns the nature of the control by the state in regulating immigration. The question here is not so much how effective a state's control over its borders is — we know it is never absolute. The question concerns rather the substantive nature of state control over immigration given international human rights agreements, the extension of various social and political rights to resident immigrants over the last 20 years, and the multiplication of political actors involved with the immigration question.

There is the matter of the unintended consequences of policies, whether immigration policies as such or other kinds of policies that affect immigration. For instance, the 1965 U.S. Immigration Act had consequences not intended or foreseen by its framers (Reimers, 1983; Briggs, 1994); it was generally expected that it would bring in more of the nationalities already present in the country, i.e., Europeans, given its emphasis on family reunion. Other kinds of unintended consequences are related to the internationalization of production and foreign aid (Sassen, 1988; *Journal für Entwicklungspolitik*, 1995; Bonacich et al., 1995). These often turned out to have unexpected impacts on immigration. Similar unintended consequences have been associated with military aid and subsequent refugee flows, e.g., El Salvador in the decade of the 1980s (Mahler, 1995; Jonas, 1991). Although immigration policy has rarely been an explicit, formal component of the foreign policy apparatus in the U.S., the latter has had significant impacts on immigration besides the well-established fact of refugee flows from Indochina. If one were to be discreet, one would say that foreign aid has rarely deterred emigration.[14]

Domestic U.S. policies with a foreign, overseas impacts have also contributed to promoting emigration to the U.S. There is the notorious sugar price support provision of the early 1980s: tax payers paid three billion dollars annually to support the price of sugar for U.S. producers. This kept Caribbean Basin countries out of the competition and resulted in a loss of 400,000 jobs there from 1982 to 1988; for example, the Dominican Republic lost three-quarters of its sugar export quota in less than a decade. The 1980s was also an era of large increases in immigration from that region.

A second type of condition that illuminates the substantive nature of the control by states over immigration is a twist on the zero sum argument. Recent history shows that if a government closes one kind of entry category, another one will have a rise in numbers. A variant on this dynamic is that if a government has, for instance, a very liberal policy on asylum, public opinion may turn against all asylum seekers and close up the country totally; this in turn is likely to promote an increase in irregular entries.[15]

A third set of conditions can be seen as reducing the autonomy of the state in controlling immigration. Large-scale international migrations are embedded in rather complex economic, social, and ethnic networks. They are highly conditioned and structured flows. States may insist on treating immigration as the aggregate outcome of individual actions and as distinct and autonomous from other major geopolitical and transnational processes. Yet they cannot escape the consequences of those larger dynamics and of their insistence on isolating the immigration policy question.

These constraints on the state's capacity to control immigration should not be seen as a control crisis. This type of analysis opens up the immigration policy question beyond the familiar range of the border and the individual as the sites for regulatory enforcement. It signals that international migrations are partly embedded in conditions produced by economic internationalization both in sending and receiving areas. Although a national state may have the power to write the text of an immigration policy, it is likely to be dealing with a complex, deeply embedded and transnational process that it can only partly address or regulate through immigration policy as conventionally understood.[16]

Although the state continues to play the most important role in immigration policy making and implementation, the state itself has been transformed by the growth of a global economic system and other transnational processes. These have brought yet another set of conditions to bear on the state's regulatory role. One particular aspect of this development is of significance to the role of the state in immigration policy making and implementation: the state in all the highly developed countries (and in many of the developing countries) has participated in the implementation of a global economic system and in furthering a consensus around the pursuit of this objective. This participation has transformed the state itself, affected the power of different agencies within it, and has furthered the internationalization of the interstate system. It is thus no longer sufficient simply to examine the role of the state in migration policy design and implementation; it is also necessary to examine the transformation of the state itself and what that can entail for migration policy and the regulation of migration flows and settlement. For the purposes of immigration policy analyses, it is becoming important to factor in these transformations of the state and the interstate system precisely because the state is a major actor in immigration policy and regulation.[17]

Implications for Immigration Policy

Today we can see in all highly developed countries a combination of drives to create border-free economic spaces and drives for renewed border-control to keep immigrants and refugees out. The juxtaposition between these two dynamics provides one of the principal contexts in which today's efforts to stop immigration assume their distinct meaning.

Current immigration policy in developed countries is increasingly at odds with other major policy frameworks in the international system and with the growth of global economic integration. There are, one could say, two major epistemic communities — one concerning the flow of capital and information, the other immigration. Both of these epistemic communities are international and both enjoy widespread consensus in the community of states.

There are strategic sites where it becomes clear that the existence of two very different regimes for the circulation of capital and the circulation of immigrants poses problems that cannot be solved through the old rules of the game, where the facts of transnationalization weigh in on the state's decisions regarding immigration. For instance, there is the need to create special regimes for the circulation of service workers within GATT and NAFTA as part of the further internationalization of trade and investment in services (see Sassen, in progress). This regime for the circulation of service workers has been uncoupled from any notion of migration; yet it represents a version of temporary labor migration. It is a regime for labor mobility that is in good part under the oversight of entities that are quite autonomous from the government.[18] This points to an institutional reshuffling of some of the components of sovereign power over entry and can be seen as an extension of the general set of processes whereby state sovereignty is partly being decentered onto other non– or quasi-governmental entities for the governance of the global economy.

These developments have the effect of reducing the autonomy of the state in immigration policy making and multiplying the sectors within the state that are addressing immigration policy and therewith multiplying the room for conflicts within the state. The assertion that the state is in charge of immigration policy is less and less helpful. Policy making regarding international issues can engage very different parts of the government. Though the state itself has been transformed by its participation in the global economy, it has of course never been a homogeneous actor. It is constituted through multiple agencies and social forces. Indeed, it could be said (*cf.* Mitchell, 1989) that although the state has central control over immigration policy, the work of exercising that claimed power often begins with a limited contest between the state and interested social forces. These interest groups include agribusiness, manufacturing, humanitarian groups, unions, ethnic organizations, and "zero population growth" efforts. Today we need to add to this the fact that the hierarchies of power and influence within the state are being reconfigured by the furthering of economic globalization.[19]

The conditions within which immigration policy is being made and implemented today range from the pressures of economic globalization and its implications for the role of the state to international agreements on human rights. The institutional setting within which immigration policy is being made and implemented ranges from national states and local states to supranational organizations.

NOTES

1.   Immigration can then be seen as a strategic research site for the examination of the relation between the idea of sovereignty over borders and the constraints states encounter in the design and implementation of actual policy on the matter.

2.   The subject of the transformation of the state itself as a consequence of its participation in the implementation of global economic systems cannot be addressed here. See Sassen (1996b). For good recent reviews of what globalization has actually meant, see, e.g., Briggs, *Competition and Change* (1995), Rosen and McFadyen (1995), Mittelman (1996), and Knox and Taylor (1995).

3.   There is a vast and rich scholarly literature that documents and interprets the specificity and distinctiveness of immigration policy in highly developed countries (e.g., Weil, 1991; Cornelius, Hollifield, and Martin, 1994; Weiner, 1995; Soysal, 1994; Thranhardt, 1993; Bade, 1992, to mention just a few). As a body this literature allows us to see the many differences among these countries. See also Shank (1994) for an examination of Japan.

4.   Refugee policy in some countries does lift the burden of immigration from the immigrant's shoulders. U.S. refugee policy, particularly for the case of Indochinese refugees, does acknowledge partial responsibility on the part of the government. Clearly, in the case of economic migrations, such responsibility is far more difficult to establish, and by its nature far more indirect.

5.   One important exception is *The 1969 Convention on Refugee Problems in Africa* adopted by the Organization of African States, which includes the right to entry.

6.   These efforts that mix the conventions on universal human rights and national judiciaries assume many different forms. Some of the instances in the U.S. are the sanctuary movement in the 1980s, which sought to establish protected areas, typically in churches, for refugees from Central America; judicial battles, such as those around the status of Salvadorans granted indefinite stays, though formally defined as illegal; the fight for the rights of detained Haitians in an earlier wave of boat lifts. It is clear that notwithstanding the lack of an enforcement apparatus, human rights considerations limit the discretion of states in how they treat non-nationals on their territory. It is also worth noting in this regard that U.N. High Commission on Refugees is the only U.N. agency with a universally conceded right of access to a country.

7.   Although these developments are well known for the cases of Europe and North America, there is not much general awareness of the fact that we are seeing incipient forms in Japan as well. For instance, in Japan today we see a strong group of human rights advocates for immigrants, efforts by non-official unions to organize undocumented immigrant workers, and organizations working on behalf of immigrants that receive funding from individuals or government institutions in sending countries (e.g., the Thai Ambassador to Japan announced in October 1995 that his government will

give a total of 2.5 million baht, about U.S.$100,000, to five civic groups that assist Thai migrant workers, especially undocumented ones; see *Japan Times*, October 18, 1995).

8.   Further, the growth of immigration, refugee flows, ethnicity, and regionalism raises questions about the accepted notion of citizenship in contemporary nation-states and hence about the formal structures for accountability. My research on the international circulation of capital and labor has raised questions for me on the meaning of such concepts as national economy and national work force under conditions of growing internationalization of capital and the growing presence of immigrant workers in major industrial countries. Furthermore, the rise of ethnicity in the U.S. and in Europe among a mobile work force raises questions about the content of the concept of nation-based citizenship. The portability of national *identity* raises questions about the bonds with other countries, or localities within them, and the resurgence of ethnic regionalism creates barriers to the political incorporation of new immigrants. (See, e.g., Soysal, 1995; Baubock, 1994; Sassen, 1996a.)

9.   There is a large and rich literature on the development of immigration policy at the European level; please refer to footnote 2 for a few citations. Longer bibliographies and analyses on the particular angle under discussion here — limitations on the autonomy of the state in making immigration policy — can also be found in Sassen (1996b, forthcoming).

10.   Jurisdiction over immigration matters in the U.S. Congress lies with the Judiciary Committee, not with the Foreign Affairs Committee as might have been the case. Congressional intent on immigration is often at odds with the foreign affairs priorities of the executive. There is a certain policy making tug of war (Mitchell, 1989). It has not always been this way. In the late 1940s and 1950s, there was great concern with how immigration policy could be used to advance foreign policy objectives. The history of which government agency was responsible for immigration is rather interesting. Earlier, when the Department of Labor (DOL) was created in 1914, it received the responsibility for immigration policy. In June 1933, President Roosevelt combined functions into the Immigration and Naturalization Service within DOL. The advent of World War II brought a shift in the administrative responsibility for the country's immigration policy: in 1940, President Roosevelt recommended that it be shifted to the Department of Justice, because of the supposed political threat represented by immigrants from enemy countries. This was meant to last for the duration of the war and then INS was to be returned to the DOL. Yet it never was. It also meant that immigration wound up in Congress in committees traditionally reserved for lawyers, as are the Senate and House Judiciary Committees. It has been said that this is why immigration law is so complicated (and, I would add, so centered on the legalities of entry and so unconcerned with broader issues).

11.   There are diverse social forces shaping the role of the state depending on the matter at hand. Thus, in the early 1980's bank crisis, for instance, the players were few and well coordinated; the state basically relinquished the organizing capacity to the banks, the IMF, and a few other actors. It was all very discreet, indeed so discreet that if you look closely the government was hardly a player in that crisis. This is quite a contrast with the deliberations around the passing of the 1986 Immigration and Reform Control Act — which was a sort of national brawl. In trade liberalization discussions, there are often multiple players, and the executive may or may not relinquish powers to Congress.

12.   Aman, Jr. (1995) has noted that although political and constitutional arguments for reallocating federal power to the states are not new, the recent reemergence of the Tenth Amendment as a politically viable and popular guideline is a major political shift since the New Deal in the relations between the federal government and the states.

13.   The latest study by the Washington-based Urban Institute found that immigrants contribute $30 billion more in taxes than they take in services.

14.   Take El Salvador in the 1980s: billions of dollars in aid poured in, and hundreds of thousands of Salvadorans poured out as U.S. aid raised the effectiveness of El Salvador's military control and aggression against its own people. The Philippines, a country that received massive aid and has had high emigration, is similar. In both cases it was foreign aid dictated by security issues. Emigration resulting from U.S. economic and political interventions is evident in the Dominican emigration in the 1960s and in the emigration from India and Pakistan to the U.S. — with the latter two associated also

with security aid from the U.S. (I have long argued as a scholar that policymakers should have migration impact statements attached to various policies.)

15.   Increasingly, unilateral policy by a major immigration country is problematic. One of the dramatic examples was that of Germany, which began to receive massive numbers of entrants as the other European states gradually tightened their policies and Germany kept its very liberal asylum policy. Another case is the importance for the EC today that the Mediterranean countries — Italy, Spain, and Portugal — control their borders regarding non-EC entrants.

16.   On a somewhat related matter, it seems to me that the sense of an immigration control crisis that prevails today in many of the highly developed countries is in some ways unwarranted, even though states have less control than they would like because immigration is caught in a web of other dynamics. When we look at the characteristics of immigrations over time and across the world, it is clear that these are highly patterned flows, embedded in other dynamics that contain equilibrating mechanisms, and have a duration (many immigrations have lasted for 50 years and then come to an end). There is more return migration than we generally realize (e.g., Soviet engineers and intellectuals who went back to Moscow from Israel, or Mexicans who returned after becoming legal residents through the IRCA amnesty program, feeling that now they could circulate between the two countries). We also know from earlier historical periods, when there were no controls, that most people did not leave poorer areas to go to richer ones, even though there were plenty of such differences in Europe within somewhat reasonable travel distances (Sassen, 1996a, in progress).

17.   Crucial here are the changed articulation of the public functions of the state with major economic sectors and the displacement of what were once governmental functions onto non– or quasi-governmental entities (Sassen, 1996b).

18.   Another instance of the impact of globalization on governmental policy making can be seen in Japan's new immigration law that was passed in 1990 (actually an amendment of an earlier law on the entry and exit of aliens). This legislation opened the country to several categories of highly specialized professionals with a Western background (e.g., experts in international finance, in Western-style accounting, in Western medicine, etc.) in recognition of the growing internationalization of the professional world in Japan; it made the entry of what is referred to as "simple labor" illegal (Sassen, 1993). This can be read as importing "Western human capital" and closing borders to immigrants.

19.   For instance, an item on internal changes in the state that may have impacts on immigration policy is the ascendance of so-called soft security issues. According to some observers, recent government reorganization in the Departments of State, Defense, and the CIA reflects an implicit redefinition of national security.

REFERENCES

Aman, Jr., Alfred C.
     1995   "A Global Perspective on Current Regulatory Reform: Rejection, Relocation,
                        or Reinvention?" Indiana Journal of Global Legal Studies 2: 429–464.
Bade, Klaus J. (ed.)
     1992   *Deutsche im Ausland, Fremde in Deutschland: Migration in Geschichte und
                        Gegenwart.* Munich: C.H. Beck Verlag.
Baubock, Rainer
     1994   Transnational Citizenship: Membership and Rights in International Migration.
                        Aldershot, England: Edward Elgar.
Bohning, W.R. and M.L. Schloeter-Paredes (eds.)
     1994   Aid in Place of Migration. Geneva: International Labor Office.
Bonacich, Edna, Lucie Cheng, Norma Chinchilla, Nora Hamilton, and Paul Ong (eds.)
     1994   Global Production: The Apparel Industry in the Pacific Rim. Philadelphia:
                        Temple University Press.

Bose, Christine E. and Edna Acosta-Belen (eds.)
1995   Women in the Latin American Development Process. Philadelphia: Temple
            University Press.
Briggs, J.
1994   *Competition and Change. The Journal of Global Business and Political
            Economy* 1,1. Harwood Academic Publishers.
Cornelius, Wayne A., Philip L. Martin, and James F. Hollifield (eds.)
1994   Controlling Immigration. A Global Perspective. Stanford: Stanford University
            Press.
Hollifield, James F.
1992   Immigrants, Markets, and States. Cambridge, Mass: Harvard University Press.
Hugo, Graeme
1995   "Indonesia's Migration Transition." *Journal für Entwicklungspolitik* 11,3:
            285–309.
Jonas, Susanne
1991   The Battle for Guatemala. Boulder, Colorado: Westview.
Journal für Entwicklungspolitik
1995   *Schwerpunkt: Migration*. Special Issue on Migration. Vol. 11, No. 3.
            Frankfurt: Brandes and Apsel Verlag.
Knox, Paul L. and Peter J. Taylor (eds.)
1995   World Cities in a World-System. Cambridge, U.K.: Cambridge University Press.
Mahler, Sarah
1995   American Dreaming: Immigrant Life on the Margins. Princeton, N.J.:
            Princeton University Press.
Massey, Douglas S., Joaquin Arango, Graeme Hugo, Ali Kouaouci, Adela Pellegrino, and J.
Edward Taylor
1993   "Theories of International Migration: A Review and Appraisal." Population
            and Development Review 19,3: 431–466.
Mitchell, Christopher
1989   "International Migration, International Relations and Foreign Policy."
            International Migration Review (Fall).
Mittelman, James (ed.)
1996   Yearbook of International Political Economy. Volume 9. Boulder, Colorado:
            Lynne Reiner Publishers.
Reimers, David M.
1983   "An Unintended Reform: The 1965 Immigration Act and Third World
            Immigration to the U.S." Journal of American Ethnic History 3 (Fall): 9–28.
Rosen, Fred and Deidre McFadyen (eds.)
1995   Free Trade and Economic Restructuring in Latin America. A NACLA Reader.
            New York: Monthly Review Press.
Sassen, Saskia
1997   Immigration Policy in a Global Economy. (In progress.) Under preparation for
            The Twentieth Century Fund.
1996a   Immigrants and Refugees: A European Dilemma? Frankfurt: Fischer Verlag.
1996b   On Governing the Global Economy. The 1995 Leonard Hastings Schoff
            Memorial Lectures delivered at Columbia University, to be published by
            Columbia University Press.
1993   "The Impact of Economic Internationalization on Migration: Comparing the
            U.S. and Japan." International Migration 31,1.
Shank, Gregory (ed.)
1994   Japan Enters the 21st Century. A Special Issue of Social Justice. Vol. 21,
            No. 2 (Summer).
Soysal, Yasmin
1994   Limits of Citizenship. Chicago: University of Chicago Press.
Thranhardt, Dietrich (ed.)
1992   Europe: A New Immigration Continent. Hamburg: Lit Verlag.

Weil, Patrick
    1991   *La France et ses étrangers*. Paris: Calmann-Levy.
Weiner, Myron
    1995   The Global Migration Crisis. New York: Harper Collins.
Zolberg, Aristide R.
    1990   "The Roots of U.S. Refugee Policy." R. Tucker, Charles B. Keely, and
                    Wrigley (eds.), Immigration and U.S. Foreign Policy. Boulder, Col.: Westview
                    Press.

The Battle for the Border: Notes on Autonomous Migration, Transnational Communities, and the State

Néstor Rodríguez

Introduction

T HE GLOBAL LANDSCAPE IN THE LATE 20TH CENTURY PRESENTS A DRAMATIC SOCIO-geographical picture: the movement across world regions of billions of capital investment dollars and of millions of people, and concerted attempts to facilitate the former and restrict the latter. Capital, in its various forms, e.g., corporations and financial funds, circulates among core countries and peripheral regions of the world economy. In the former setting, international funds finance such enterprises as real-estate development, service industries, and stock and money markets. In the latter, it gravitates to a host of financial and production activities, including banking, mining, manufacturing, and the exploitation of natural resources. Numerous international economic agreements (GATT, NAFTA, EC, etc.)[1] emerge to facilitate the transnational movement of capital. Two agreements (the EC and NAFTA) attempt to establish regional economic communities with few or no restrictions on the transnational movement of capital. Human movements across nation-state borders are just as dynamic: 100 million people relocate across the world regions of Eastern and Western Europe, Asia, Africa, Latin America and the Caribbean, and North America (*Migration World*, 1994).

For some, this global scene represents a fundamental change threatening the established world system of nation-states. Among the most urgent issues listed by the vocal leaders of those concerned with these dynamics are the relocation of jobs to less-developed countries and the loss of control over national borders. In the United States, dramatic measures are being implemented to halt the immigration of people who enter the country without papers (the "illegal aliens"). In

NÉSTOR RODRÍGUEZ is an associate professor in the Department of Sociology at the University of Houston and the director of the university's Center for Immigration, 492 PGH, College of Social Science, University of Houston, TX 77204–3472, (713) 743–3946. He has conducted research in the areas of Mexican and Central American immigration and settlement and on evolving inter-group relations in new immigrant communities in the Houston area, as well as on historical urban specialization in the world economy. His present research focuses on the growth of transnational communities among migrant populations. The author is grateful to Rosa Dávila, Tatcho Mindiola, and Michael A. Olivas for their comments on an earlier draft of this article.

workplaces, these measures include the enactment of federal regulations to create a new worker status of "authorized worker," pilot projects to verify authorized-worker status through centralized computer data in Washington, D.C., and pilot projects to draw on the collaborative support of employers in replacing unauthorized workers with authorized workers. At the U.S.-Mexico border, the measures include a large increase in the number of U.S. border agents, a human fence of Border Patrol agents in El Paso, construction projects to erect fences, ditches, walls, and other physical barriers, and calls by visiting political candidates for the deployment of U.S. troops. In California, voters approved a referendum to exclude undocumented residents from public-supported services, and in other regions of the country, county and city officials acted to rid undocumented immigrants from public social welfare programs. Across the country the anti-immigrant mood raises the issues of the need for a national identification card and the denial of citizenship to U.S.-born children of undocumented parents.[2]

These attempts to halt undocumented immigration and to curtail legal immigration I refer to as "the battle for the border." On the U.S. government side, the principal actors include the large bureaucracies of the Immigration and Naturalization Service, the Border Patrol, the National Security Council Working Group on Illegal Immigration, units of the National Guard and Army Reserves, well-financed special-interest groups and think tanks, and university scientists developing new border surveillance technology. On the migrants' side, the principal actors include men, women, and children from mainly working-class backgrounds with little education and income, as well as persons fleeing political persecution. The migrants' side also includes smugglers, who often share a social background with the immigrants they bring, and sometimes employers. Before it became illegal in 1986 to hire undocumented workers, big and small employers played a major role in attracting these migrants.

The battle for the border is more than just a struggle to "stem the tide" of an undocumented migrant wave; the battle for the border is fundamentally about social-historical development. It is about the changing significance of nation-states in the global order, and thus of the changing relevance of nation-state boundaries. It is a struggle to maintain nation-state borders in a global context made increasingly fluid by the heightened transnational migration of capital and labor. Although the nation-state system expedited the political-administrative consolidation of the world economy in an earlier era (Cohen, 1987), by the late 20th century the presence of multinational capital and international labor has increasingly countered this function.

Globalization has usually been conceptualized in terms of capital's ability to mobilize and integrate economic resources and activities among different world regions (e.g., see Dicken, 1992). However, the autonomous social action of working-class and peasant communities in developing countries also has significantly increased transnational development. Autonomous international migration organized by workers, their families, and communities has significantly challenged the status of the U.S.-Mexico border by making it increasingly irrelevant. By the late 20th century, large numbers of migrants had constructed transnational communities between U.S. settlement areas and places of origin back home (e.g., see Hagan, 1994). In many ways, these transnational structures functioned as if the border did not exist. The battle for the border, which will eventually be lost, is thus a reaction to this worker-led transnational sociospatial reconfiguration. The battle for the border is more than just a move to control illegal immigration; it is a struggle to resist attempts by working-class communities in peripheral countries to spatially reorganize their base of social reproduction in the global landscape. This attempted change by foreign working-class communities seriously challenges the established stratified sociospatial global order.

In the sections below I discuss the battle for the border in the southern United States from three perspectives. The first involves what I term "autonomous migration," that is, the movement of peoples into the U.S. independent of state authorization and regulation. The second concerns the growth of transnational communities, which circulate resources between migrant points of destination and origin for social reproduction. The third is the reaction of the state to reinsert the border as a meaningful divide in community lives. I end the article with critical remarks concerning social-scientific research on undocumented migration and with comments regarding the prospects of the battle for the border.

Autonomous International Migration

By "autonomous international migration" I mean international migration organized by workers, their families, and communities independent of intergovernmental agreements. It is the movement of people across nation-state borders outside state regulations. Autonomous migration means that working-class communities in peripheral countries have developed their own policies of international employment independent of interstate planning. As such, autonomous international migration can be considered to be state-free migration, i.e., a process that decenters the state as the regulator of human movements across international boundaries. Through autonomous migration undocumented workers themselves have created a guestworker program, which many U.S. employers have supported.

It is important to understand that autonomous migration means more than unauthorized ("illegal") border crossings: it means a community strategy implemented, developed, and sustained with the support of institutions, including formal ones, at the migrants' points of origin and U.S. points of destination. Precisely because core institutions (legal, religious, local governmental, etc.) support this migratory strategy, undocumented migrants do not perceive its moral significance as deviant. Migrants may see their autonomous migration as extralegal, but not necessarily as criminal. (Thus, while some migrants may use the Spanish term *ilegal* to refer to an undocumented worker, they never use the term "criminal.") It is also important to understand that migrant communities do not formally acknowledge autonomous migration as policy; this policy is neither written in any legal document nor declared by any official. It emerges as popular policy as families and other community institutions adopt autonomous migration as an approved course of action for social reproduction.[3]

Autonomy as Self-Activity

While the concept of autonomy as self-activity can be traced back to Marx' writing in *Capital*, several unorthodox Marxist groups have used the concept since the 1930s to analyze the former Soviet bureaucracy and workers' autonomous struggles against unions and the Communist Party (Cleaver, 1979). From the 1930s to the 1950s, C.L.R. James and Raya Dunayevskaya in the Johnson-Forest Tendency movement used the concept to analyze autonomous labor struggles in the United States, including independent black struggles, and in the Soviet Union. From 1949 to 1967, Cornelius Castoriadis and Claude Lefort, founders of a French revolutionary group and journal called *Socialisme ou Barbarie*, also used the concept to critique the Soviet bureaucracy and reified concepts of orthodox Marxism. Since the early 1970s, several Italian Marxist theorists (e.g., Mario Tronti, Toni Negri, and Sergio Bologna, Franco Piperno, and Oreste Scalzone), working together in the group and magazine *Potere Operaio* (*Workers' Power*), have used the concept to analyze independent and spontaneous worker struggles in Italian northern factories (Cleaver, 1979). According to these theorists, these worker struggles, which involve many migrants from southern Italy, are waged not only against capital, but also against their "official" organizations, i.e., the Communist Party and unions. In the late 1970s and 1980s, Harry Cleaver and several co-analysts in the United States used the concept of autonomy to analyze workplace struggles of Latino immigrant workers, and, more recently, the Zapatista revolt in the southern Mexican region of Chiapas.[4]

In an essay entitled "The Return of Politics," Lotringer describes the growth of autonomous struggle among Italian working-class groups as a characteristic of postindustrial social conflict in which the division between the factory and society is increasingly disappearing. Lotringer's comments on the Italian Autonomy movement characterize some of the basic features of autonomous struggles:

> Autonomy is a "body without organs of politics, anti-hierarchic, anti-dialectic, anti-representative. It is not only a political project (*sic*), it is a project for existence" (Lotringer and Marazzi, 1980: 8).

To paraphrase at the level of workers' struggles, the workers' self-activity is not channeled through political parties; it challenges the hierarchies of organizational labor, refuses to follow capital's plans for (dialectical) development, and seeks to express its own voice. The purpose of the workers' self-activity is survival.

Some comparisons between Lotringer's characterization and autonomous migration are obvious: undocumented migrants are not organized into political groups,[5] they contradict capital's global stratification, they articulate their own international policy, and their purpose is survival. Autonomy, according to Lotringer (1980), refuses to separate economics from politics, and politics from existence. From the perspective of the many large and culturally dynamic Latino migrant settlements in the United States (e.g., see, Pedraza and Rumbaut, 1996: Chapters 25–28), one can observe that undocumented migrants refuse to separate economics from community, and community from ethnicity.

Though autonomy as self-activity has been analyzed mainly in the form of industrial worker struggles, it is also present in other arenas of social life. In Latin American rural areas, for example, landless peasants have a history of autonomously taking over plots of land for farming (e.g., see Foley, 1991), and in Latin American cities, poor working-class people have created shantytowns of *callampas, favelas, pueblos jóvenes*, and *villas miserias* through autonomous invasions of land for self-built housing (Green, 1991). Lúcio Kowarick describes the conditions that lead to autonomous, sudden eruptions for improved neighborhood services among shantytown residents in São Paulo:

> These movements [are] nurtured by a series of social bonds forged in neighborhood interactions, in the common experience of living in neglected districts, in the delays in public transportation, in accidents, illness, and floods... (Kowarick, 1994: 37).

For Kowarick (1994), "micromovements" among shantytown residents occur when, under certain circumstances, subjective accumulated experiences link conflicts and demands.

Autonomous Migration as Human Agency

It is one thing to argue that marginalized populations participate collectively in independent and spontaneous demands for change, but it is quite another to posit that these activities constitute social forces that are altering or even restructuring global structural arrangements. Yet, the latter is precisely the basis for my thesis of the battle for the border, that is, that autonomous migration has recomposed the settlement space of communities in peripheral countries in a manner that pays little heed to the nation-state divide. This has occurred not only through the migration of millions of undocumented migrants, but also through these migrants' development or fortification of community structures that transcend the border and at various levels (social, cultural, economic, etc.) unite U.S. settlement areas with communities of origin back home. From this perspective, the state's battle for the border concerns more than controlling the border — *it is about maintaining a border.*

Studies of social change that remain wedded to the structural level of impersonal forces have often failed to recognize the transformative power of human agency by ordinary men and women, including undocumented immigrants. At the structural level, according to Michael Peter Smith (1989), the social actions and struggles of ordinary men and women remain invisible as mediums as well as outcomes of social structures. Smith comments on the human dimension of structural change as follows:

> Although impersonal conditions constitute the historical context within which people act, people are not merely passive recipients of these structural economic and political conditions. They are creators of meaning, which is also a wellspring of human action and historic change (Smith, 1989: 355).

Commenting on the unrecognized condition of this human role, Smith states:

> [S]cant attention has been paid to the varieties of agency exercised by popular classes and to the dynamics of their resistance to dominant structural tendencies in the larger political economy (*Ibid.*).

Smith's words are a late 20th century restatement of what unorthodox Marxists had earlier termed autonomous struggles. This is illustrated by Cleaver's comments on studies of worker autonomy by Italian New Left theorists:

> From the study of the reality of autonomy among rank-and-file workers...they were able to articulate with new sharpness and depth the position that the working-class is not a passive, reactive victim...and that its ultimate power to overthrow capital is grounded in its existing power to initiate struggle and to force capital to reorganize and develop itself (Cleaver, 1979: 52).

Cleaver points out, however, that studies that remain confined to the "economic" sphere are sure to miss the major social conflicts that affect societal change through other arenas. When social scientists and political groups do recognize social struggles in other arenas (e.g., shantytown housing), there is often a tendency to devalue these conflicts as mere appendages to workplace movements (Kowarick, 1994).

From the perspective of autonomous migration, human agency means more than the formation of undocumented work forces. As undocumented migrants participate in activities of the larger immigrant community, it also means the development of community forces that, while marginally situated, eventually affect core institutional sectors in mainstream society. This includes various examples, such as political activism to counter proposed restrictions against immigrant populations and the organizing of soccer leagues that socially appropriate and culturally recompose public spaces in many U.S. cities. In some cases, the migrants' impact of human agency is mediated by mainstream institutions. For example, constituting a large consumer market, undocumented migrants also have attracted considerable attention from mainstream businesses. In some cases, the Spanish-language and Latin themes used in the advertising by these businesses have substantially restructured the symbolic aspect of social environments previously regulated by the dominant culture.

Viewing autonomous migration as a source of human agency contradicts the perception of undocumented migrants as a docile, job-happy, helpless population. Instead, from the perspective of human agency, undocumented migrants take on the role of historical actors restructuring sociospatial contours across global regions. Several conditions are at the base of this social action. One condition, undocumented status itself, seemingly affects this social action in opposite ways. On the one hand, the restrictions of undocumented status motivate undocumented migrants to implement survival strategies that through social networks recompose work forces and settlement spaces (Hagan, 1994). On the other hand, undocumented status keeps many migrants unattached from bureaucratic systems, allowing them short-term benefits to maneuver and survive with greater ease. The benefits of this include entering the country without state approval, locating jobs without applying for worker certification, and in some cases circumventing income-tax systems to keep a greater share of their usually low incomes.

The human agency associated with the autonomous migration of undocumented migrants is reminiscent of the experiences of earlier U.S. immigrants, who arrived and adjusted with little state intervention. Describing the rise of mass immigration from Europe in the 1815 to 1860 period, Maldwyn Allen Jones (1992) concludes,

> The mass immigration of the nineteenth century originated as a self-directed, unassisted movement.... Here lies a key to the patterns both of distribution and of adjustment. That immigrants moved entirely as individuals or in family groups, that they received virtually no aid or direction, and that they were subject to control neither by European nor by American agencies or governments would largely determine their destination in the New World and the nature of their reaction to it (Jones, 1992: 98–99).

As Jones describes (1992: Chapter 6), nativistic movements soon emerged to counter the large-scale immigration patterns of the mid-1800s. The tactics used by these movements to discredit new European immigrants were fairly similar to today's methods.

A variety of immigrant characteristics, e.g., racial, linguistic, and religious, have been associated with the rise of anti-immigrant movements, but it is also the rise of immigrant settlement space that draws heated controversy as it forms the basis for the growth of immigrant communities. In attacks against new Irish immigrants in the 1830s and 1840s, for example, nativist Protestants entered Irish districts to burn down Catholic religious centers (*Ibid.*).

Transnational Communities

In the late 20th century, many new immigrant settlement spaces in the United States, as well as in other countries, have developed into transnational communities. These communities span between the migrants' settlement spaces in the U.S. and their communities of origin. Transnational communities maintain constant interaction across nation-state boundaries. Containing a host of formal and informal sectors, transnational communities are products of human agency. Many transnational communities were developed mainly by autonomous migration before the enactment of the Immigration Reform and Control Act (IRCA) of 1986. These communities play a major role in facilitating the migration, settlement, and survival of many undocumented persons who enter the U.S. In many ways, transnational communities carry out functions of social reproduction across international boundaries as if these boundaries did not exist (see Goldring, 1995; Smith, 1994; and Kearney, 1991).

Transnational communities challenge the relevancy of the border because they constitute an alternative to a state-supported global order of nation-state divisions that attempts to correlate national space with race and ethnicity. For Michael Kearney (1991: 54, 55), today's transnational communities, and the transnational age in general, represent a passing beyond the "modern age" in which forms of "organization and identity...are not constrained by national boundaries." Kearney also refers to this phase as a post-national age.

What also should be recognized about the transnational age from the perspective of transnational communities is the role of self-activity by mainly low-income migrants. While broad economic and political forces pressured populations to migrate, the social and individual actions of migrants, however, played a central role in building transnational communities. This involved developing neighborhoods, creating formal and informal organizations, opening ethnic businesses, and establishing linkages with institutions in the larger society, e.g., labor markets and school systems. It was a phenomenal task, considering that before the enactment of IRCA these processes were accomplished mostly by migrants who not only lacked legal immigrant status, but often also faced heated opposition from established residents (e.g., see Rodríguez and Hagan, 1992). The intensification of opposition, such as through Proposition 187, in the 1990s further turned some transnational community settings in the United States into contested terrains.

To be sure, through their promotion of technological development in transportation and communication, two economic sets of mainstream actors in the U.S. also played a major role in the emergence of transnational communities. One set consisted of highway construction firms that lobbied aggressively to promote government expenditures on highway development. A result, initially promoted as a national defense weapon, was the interstate highway system of over 45,000 miles built at a cost of over $129 billion (Koch and Ostrowidzki, 1995). Interstates and other superhighway systems developed over the last 40 years greatly facilitated travel not only for U.S. citizens, but also for newcomers. The ability to journey on a single highway for hundreds of miles through unknown areas greatly facilitates travel for many new immigrants seeking to reach distant destinations. Texas' well-developed highway system, the largest in the country, no doubt played a major role in attracting the many Mexican bus lines that now transport thousands of migrants yearly between Texas cities and Mexican localities.

While superhighways improved the ability to travel, high-tech electronic systems revolutionized the ability to communicate, greatly enhancing transborder telecommunication in transnational communities. Along with jet travel, high-tech communication enabled transnational community members to substantially transcend the spatial separation between communities of origin back home and immigrant settlement areas in the United States. Many migrants in transnational communities now enjoy same-day, if not instant, communication with family members back home, even in some of the most remote areas of Latin America (Rodríguez, 1995b). Indeed, in some cases migrants stay continually in touch with friends and relatives as they make their way to the United States through Central America and Mexico. Also, after entering the country, new Latino migrants are able to continue viewing their favorite television programs through international Spanish-language television systems and thus maintain a cultural continuity with communities back home. For Mexican migrants, two mega-wattage radio stations, one in Monterrey and one in San Luis Potosí, provide continuous evening and early morning musical and news programs reaching from southern Mexico to the U.S. interior.

The actions of several members of a Maya immigrant group in Houston demonstrated how migrants can appropriate high-tech telecommunication technology to strengthen transnational community ties and maintain traditional practices. Using two fax machines, one in a migrant's home in Houston and the other in the group's Guatemalan home *municipio* of San Cristóbal Totonicapán, members of the Maya group organized an elaborate *quinceañera* celebration for a family member back home. Through faxes sent between Houston and the *municipio*, families in both settings were recruited to participate in the event's religious ceremony and to assist in preparing a feast for several hundred invited guests. The migrant organizers of the event used faxes not only to recruit families, but also to select traditional background motifs and to schedule payments for ceremonial materials and food supplies.

The use of high-tech communication in transnational communities will continue to increase substantially in the 1990s, since telecommunication companies are investing billions of dollars to expand their operations in the United States and

abroad (see *CWA News*, 1993). In some Latin American countries, telecommunication companies are among the fastest growing industries and have greatly
enhanced the capacity of the local communities' residents to communicate with
relatives abroad. In Mexico, for example, the ratio of telephones per 100 population increased from 5.4 in 1976 to 9.6 in 1986, a 78% increase (U.S. Bureau of the
Census, 1992; 1978).

In addition to providing a host of functions for social reproduction among
migrant households in the United States and in communities of origin, transnational
communities also constitute a social political space (Smith, 1994), enabling the
transnational circulation of migrant struggles in various relational spheres.
Nagengast and Kearney (1990), for example, report the formation of a pan-Mixtec
transnational association developed by Mixtec migrants to defend themselves in
California and Oregon on issues regarding discrimination, exploitation, health,
and human rights. The Mixtecs, who migrate from Oaxaca, also meet with
Mexican officials on the U.S. side of the border to discuss abuses Mixtecs face as
indigenous communities in Mexico. Conflict between Sprint Long Distance and
Latino telemarketers in the San Francisco area showed another political dimension
of transnational communities. When Sprint fired 235 Latino telemarketers in its
San Francisco facility in July 1994 for demanding a union election, a Mexican
telecom union offered to care for telemarketers' families that lived in Mexico until
the case was reviewed by U.S. authorities (*CWA News*, 1994). The Mexican union
also obtained the Mexican government's commitment to investigate the firings of
the Latino telemarketers under the NAFTA labor agreement (*CWA News*, 1996).

At another level, transnational communities represent political space for
gender relations. To the extent that female migrants use transnational communities
to leave traditional gender roles back home and seek self-defined opportunities
through their migrant roles, it is possible to conceptualize transnational communities as a means of empowerment for some women (e.g., see Hondagneu-Sotelo,
1994). Of course, this opportunity may vary among migrant women according to
factors such as age and marital status. Undoubtedly, however, for many women,
whether migrant or abandoned wives back home, the transnational community
remains one more social structure exploited by men.[6]

Finally, transnational communities, as outcomes of human agency, represent
the lengthy struggles by migrant workers to reunite with their families and
communities, against the designs of an international capitalist system that values
foreign migrant labor but provides no assistance for its maintenance and reproduction (see de Brunhoff, 1978; Burawoy, 1976). The Bracero Program, which
imported five million Mexican farm workers from 1942 to 1964, epitomized this
labor system (see Garcia, 1980; Olivas, 1990). Organized through the state, the
program yearly imported thousands of Mexican workers for seasonal work in the
fields of U.S. agribusiness. When the *braceros* completed the harvest, they were
sent back to Mexico until the next season. *Braceros*, all men, were not allowed to

bring their families to the United States. The poor communities from which the *braceros* originated bore all the costs of developing and reproducing this migrant labor force (Burawoy, 1976). Undocumented Latino immigration since the late 1960s, in which whole families migrate and community structures are extended north of the U.S.-Mexican border, represents a different system of migrant labor. It is a system of autonomous migration where working-class migrants themselves determine which resources for the social reproduction of their families and communities are brought to the United States and which resources are maintained back home.

State Strategies Against Autonomous Migration

The state in capitalist society is not a monolithic institution mindlessly following the plans of capital. On many social issues, various agencies of the state may offer different goals and agendas. In some cases, it is even possible to think of state policies as negotiated outcomes among different state offices (Skocpol, 1985). The operation of the Bracero Program, for example, involved disagreements between the Department of Agriculture, which generally favored it, and the Department of Labor, which at the end worked to curtail the program (see Craig, 1971; see also Calavita, 1992). Yet it is possible, I believe, to conceive of a capitalist state in terms of the tendency of state agencies in capitalist society to work within policy contours that historically have favored the reproduction of the capitalist system. Of particular significance has been the state's role in regulating or attempting to regulate immigrant labor, formally and informally.

I contend that the goal of current state activities to control undocumented immigration goes beyond an attempt to regain control of the border. It is more an attempt to end autonomous migration, which for many years has been a creative power of transnational communities. Stopping the self-directed migration of communities across the border will end the transnational survival strategy for many migrant families who have yet to achieve legal immigrant status. It will also limit the social resources of the many legal immigrant families who have undocumented family members.

Recent state strategies to control autonomous migration have included several approaches. The implementation of IRCA in 1986 had a three-pronged approach: bring undocumented immigrants into the legal system through amnesty and legalization, close the labor market for undocumented labor by prohibiting the hiring of undocumented workers, and increase the number of border enforcement agents (Hagan and Baker, 1993). Although undocumented immigration apparently slowed down for a few years after the passage of IRCA, by 1990 the INS was apprehending as many illegal Latino entrants as it had in pre-IRCA days.[7] IRCA actually strengthened autonomous migration by enlarging, through legalization, the support base consisting of immigrants with legal residence in the United States. The 2.7 million migrants (mainly Mexicans) who were legalized under IRCA made the transnational community stronger for undocumented members by becoming more stable sources of social support (Hagan, 1994).

In the 1990s, the state moved with greater interest to control undocumented immigration by restricting the access of undocumented migrants to the social wage, i.e., the "indirect wage" of public human service programs used mainly by working-class persons (Withorn, 1981; de Brunhoff, 1978). While the federal government moved to restrict undocumented residents from public housing subsidized by the Department of Housing and Urban Development, local governments acted formally or informally to restrict undocumented persons from indigent health and medical care in public institutions (e.g., see Asin, 1995). Many public-supported colleges and universities also acted to exclude undocumented students (Rodríguez, 1994). Although undocumented migrants felt the restrictions, for many it did not represent a dramatic change since they depended on internal survival strategies more than on social wage programs. Indeed, through social networks, transnational communities provided assistance to those in need (Hagan, 1994), though this is not always a given (see Menjívar, forthcoming).

A third state strategy to emerge in the 1990s was to forcefully confront autonomous migration at the border, i.e., to impose physical barriers at the U.S.-Mexico borderline to stop illegal entry. The barriers varied by region, but included barbed wire and steel fences and a human wall of Border Patrol agents in El Paso. More than stopping undocumented entry, the strategy attempted to reimpose the border as a major divide in the lives of transnational Latino working-class people. As such, the strategy became a space war, as the state struggled to politically reinforce international boundary space to restrict the autonomy of foreign migrant labor. Additionally, the U.S. state attempted to deter undocumented Central American immigration by mobilizing the Mexican state to apprehend U.S.-bound Central Americans in Mexico.

Similar to the interdictions of Haitian migrants at sea, the campaign to stop Central American migrants in Mexico reflected, in my view, the U.S. state's desire to avoid legal and political struggles in the United States with activist organizations that work in defense of migrants and political refugees inside and outside transnational communities. Throughout all the major border points and immigrant settlement areas, numerous community-based organizations have developed to take on the state in legal and political struggles on behalf of migrants (Rodríguez and Urrutia-Rojas, 1990). Many of these organizations involve immigrant residents of transnational communities, but some are composed mainly of U.S.-born activists. When community organizations working to protect undocumented Central Americans came together to form the Sanctuary Movement in the 1980s, the state attempted to suppress the movement through its Operation Sojourner, which gathered information to prosecute movement members (Crittenden, 1988). By the mid-1990s, transnational communities contained numerous broad-based organizational networks working to mobilize community sectors on behalf of migrant and refugee rights and against proposed state policies to restrict immigrant populations. One network called for and organized toward a massive immigrant march on Washington on October 12, 1996, the Latin American *Día de la Raza* (Columbus Day). The plan was to recompose immigrant political struggles from the local level to the level of the country.

Even state actors do not think that border enforcement alone is sufficient to control undocumented immigration. In their promotion of NAFTA, Mexican and U.S. state representatives viewed sustained economic growth in Mexico as essential for halting this immigration (Teitelbaum and Weiner, 1995). From the perspective of NAFTA, the state strategy for control of undocumented migration is thus inter-regional development. Yet, the strategy faces very uncertain prospects, even without considering the vacillating conditions of the Mexican economy. NAFTA's long-term success, for example, will require an agricultural restructuring that will undoubtedly release a massive army of rural migrants (Barry, 1995). This scenario, cited by *zapatista* rebels in Chiapas as one reason for their revolt (Ross, 1995), is reminiscent of the rural enclosure movements that accompanied Europe's Industrial Revolution. Displaced from their peasant livelihoods, many of Europe's unemployed rural people made their way to the United States (Jones, 1992). This option remains a viable one for the Mexican case.

Conclusion

The late 20th century has inaugurated a new age of global capitalist development. Just as capital has expanded globally to seek new resources for its existence, many working-class communities in peripheral regions of the world economy have extended their base for survival across nation-state boundaries. They have done so autonomously through undocumented migration. This has created a new transnational person, a person who out of necessity has become very adaptable to new settlement environments (Kearney, 1995). Undocumented migrants have developed transnational communities that recompose the global spatial contours of class structures and class relations. They have accomplished this through self-activity and through capital's developments of new communication and transportation technology. This transnational development seriously challenges the continuing existence of rigid nation-state boundaries.

If the depictions of working-class transnational man and transnational woman sound farfetched, it is because social science has failed to capture the self-activity and human agency of undocumented migrant communities. This failure has resulted from at least two methodological factors. One factor has been the constant use of the individual as the unit of analysis in research of undocumented immigration. At this level, the reconstructive power of undocumented migration is limited to the individual; when the higher aggregate level of the household is used, it is usually examined as a unit struggling for existence and not as a source of structural social change. The resulting picture is one of a victimized population of docile, job-happy migrants in settings where only capital has power and workers passively suffer the consequences. A second factor has been the almost permanent use of the nation-state as the moral unit of analysis (Sjoberg and Vaughan, 1971). What benefits the nation-state is taken as a fixed value, and thus the effects of undocumented migration are measured against the "national interest," not from the standpoint of what benefits migrant communities or humankind in general. As Kearney (1991) maintains, this is an official social science that is dependent on conceptual categories provided by the dominant system and that works in the service of the nation-state. It is also a social science theoretically unprepared to capture important transnational changes in a post-national era.

What does the future of the battle for the border hold? It will continue and more than likely become a war for the border as even more potential institutional actors (e.g., international banks and health-care systems) also wear down nation-state boundaries in search of greater markets. Certainly, migrants, legal and undocumented, will continue to play a major role in this development, as U.S. employers will continue their historical role of attracting migrant labor. This was evidenced by California Governor Pete Wilson's trip to the U.S. Congress, soon after Proposition 187 was passed, to recommend the reintroduction of a *bracero* migrant program. Wilson's recommendation clearly indicated that the purpose of the battle for the border is not to end labor immigration, but to terminate its autonomous origin.

NOTES

1. See Cornelius, Martin, and Hollifield (1994) for a description of the policy context of international migration in different world regions. This context includes the General Agreement on Tariffs and Trade (GATT), the North American Free Trade Agreement (NAFTA), and the European Community (EC).

2. The calls and proposed measures to limit undocumented immigration are listed regularly in major U.S. newspapers. Also, see examples in *Migration World*, a magazine of the Center for Migration Studies in Staten Island, New York.

3. I base these comments on my observations, since 1988, in the Guatemalan highland *municipio* of San Cristóbal Totonicapán (see Rodríguez, 1995a; 1995b). The *municipio* and other surrounding ones in the Guatemalan highlands have sent a large number of undocumented migrants to the United States since the early 1980s.

4. Many papers and publications using an autonomous perspective are listed in Cleaver et al. (1991). Also, see Cleaver (1994).

5. I do not mean to imply that undocumented migrants do not participate in political groupings, which they certainly do. What I mean is that the undocumented have not organized into a formal political group, such as a political party.

6. For example, see "Irma's Story: The Life of an Illegal Alien" in Nathan (1991). For comparative materials from Britain, see Mama's (1993) "Women Abuse in London's Black Communities."

7. See INS apprehension figures in U.S. Bureau of the Census (1994: Table 323). INS apprehension figures are poor indicators for estimating how many migrants enter the country because

nonmigrant factors, e.g., the number of border enforcement agents, affect the number of apprehended entrants. Yet, the trends shown by apprehension statistics may represent changes in actual undocumented migration.

REFERENCES

Asin, Stefanie
  1995   "A New Look at Gold Card Safeguards: Closer Checks Ahead for Hospital District." Houston Chronicle (February 23): A–21.
Barry, Tom
  1995   Zapata's Revenge: Free Trade and the Farm Crisis in Mexico. Boston: South End Press.
Burawoy, Michael
  1976   "The Functions and Reproduction of Migrant Labor: Comparative Material from Southern Africa and the United States." American Journal of Sociology 81,5: 1050–1087.
Calavita, Kitty
  1992   Inside the State: The Bracero Program, Immigration, and the I.N.S. New York: Routledge.
Cleaver, Harry
  1994   "Introduction." In ¡Zapatista!: Documents of the New Mexican Revolution. Brooklyn, New York: Autonomedia: 11–24.
  1979   Reading Capital Politically. Austin, Texas: University of Texas Press.
Cleaver, Harry, Jim Fleming, and Conrad Harold (eds.)
  1991   "Bibliography." Jim Fleming (ed.), Harry Cleaver, Michael Ryan, and Maurizio Viano (trans.), Antonio Negri, Marx Beyond Marx: Lessons on the Grundrisse. Brooklyn, New York: Autonomedia: 222–242.
Cohen, Robin
  1987   "Policing the Frontiers: The State and the Migrant in the International Division of Labor." Jeffrey Henderson and Manuel Castells (eds.), Global Restructuring and Territorial Development. Beverly Hills: Sage: 88–111.
Cornelius, Wayne A., L. Philip Martin, and James F. Hollifield (eds.)
  1994   Controlling Immigration: A Global Perspective. Stanford, Cal.: Stanford University Press.
Craig, Richard B.
  1971   The Bracero Program. Austin, Texas: The University of Texas Press.
Crittenden, Ann
  1988   Sanctuary: A Story of American Conscience and the Law in Collision. New York: Weidenfeld and Nicolson.
CWA News
  1996   "Sprint/La Conexión Familiar Workers Tell of Rights Abuses at International Forum." Vol. 56,3 (March): 12.
  1994   "Sprint Long Distance Shuts Latino Telemarketing Office to Avoid Union Election, Spread Fear." Vol. 54,7 (September): 3.
  1993   Vol. 53,9 (November): 7.
de Brunhoff, Suzanne
  1978   The State, Capital, and Economic Policy. London: Pluto Press.
Dicken, Peter
  1992   Global Shift: The Internationalization of Economic Activity. New York: The Guilford Press, 2nd Edition.
Foley, Michael W.
  1991   "Agenda for Mobilization: The Agrarian Question and Popular Mobilization in Contemporary Mexico." Latin American Review 26,2: 39–74.

Garcia, J.R.
1980   Operation Wetback: The Mass Deportation of Mexican Undocumented
               Workers in 1954. Westport, Conn.: Greenwood Press.
Goldring, Luin
1995   "Blurring Borders: Transnational Community, Status, and Social Change in
               Mexico-U.S. Migration." Paper presented at the 1995 meetings of the
               American Sociological Association, Washington, D.C.
Green, Duncan
1991   Faces of Latin America. London: Latin American Bureau.
Hagan, Jacqueline Maria
1994   Deciding to Be Legal: A Maya Community in Houston. Philadelphia: Temple
               University Press.
Hagan, Jacqueline and Susan Gonzalez Baker
1993   "Implementing the U.S. Legalization Program: The Influence of Immigrant
               Communities and Local Agencies on Immigration Policy Reform." Interna-
               tional Migration Review 27,3 (Fall): 513–537.
Hondagneu-Sotelo, Pierrette
1994   Gendered Transitions: Mexican Experiences of Immigration. Berkeley:
               University of California Press.
Jones, Maldwyn Allen
1992   American Immigration. Chicago: The University of Chicago Press, 2nd Edition.
Kearney, Michael
1995   "Theorizing Transnational Personhood and Community in the Age of Limits."
               Unpublished paper.
1991   "Borders and Boundaries of State and Self at the End of Empire." Journal of
               Historical Sociology 4,1 (March): 52–74.
Koch, Wendy and Vic Ostrowidzki
1995   "Paving a Way of Life: Interstate Highway Revolutionized America, But at
               What Cost?" Houston Chronicle (November 19): A–6.
Kowarick, Lúcio
1994   "Introduction." Lúcio Kowarick (ed.), Social Struggles and the City: The Case
               of São Paulo. New York: Monthly Review Press: 31–40.
Lotringer, Sylvere and Christian Marazzi
1980   "The Return of Politics." Semiotext(e) Italy: Autonomia, Post-Political Politics
               3,3: 8–23.
Mama, Amina
1993   "Woman Abuse in London's Black Communities." Winston James and Clive
               Harris (eds.), Inside Babylon: The Caribbean Diaspora in Britain. London:
               Verso: 97–134.
Menjívar, Cecilia
1996   "Immigrant Kinship Networks: Vietnamese, Salvadorans, and Mexicans in
               Comparative Perspective." Journal of Comparative Family Studies. Forthcom-
               ing.
Migration World
1994   "International Migration Growing in Size and Importance." Vol. 22,4: 3.
Nagengast, Carole and Michael Kearney
1990   "Mixtec Ethnicity: Social Identity, Political Consciousness, and Political
               Activism." Latin American Research Review 25,2, 61–91.
Nathan, Debbie
1991   Women and Other Aliens: Essays from the U.S.-Mexico Border. El Paso,
               Texas: Cinco Punto Press.
Olivas, Michael A.
1990   "The Chronicles, My Grandfather's Stories, and Immigration Law: The Slave
               Traders Chronicle as Racial History." St. Louis University Law Journal 34:
               425–441.

Pedraza, Silvia and Rubén Rumbaut (eds.)
    1996   Origins and Destinies: Immigration, Race, and Ethnicity in America. New York: Wadsworth.

Rodríguez, Néstor
    1995a   "The Real 'New World Order': The Globalization of Racial and Ethnic Relations in the Late Twentieth Century." Michael Peter Smith and Joe R. Feagin (eds.), The Bubbling Cauldron: Race, Ethnicity, and the Urban Crisis. Minneapolis: University of Minnesota Press: 211–225.
    1995b   "Lessons on Survival from Latin America." Forum for Applied Research and Public Policy (Fall): 90–93.

Rodríguez, Néstor and Jacqueline Hagan
    1992   "Apartment Restructuring and Latino Immigrant Tenant Struggles." Comparative Urban and Community Research 4: 164–180.

Rodríguez, Néstor and Ximena Urrutia-Rojas
    1990   "Impact of Recent Refugee Migration to Texas: A Comparison of Southeast Asian and Central American Newcomers." Wayne H. Holtzman and Thomas H. Bornemann (eds.), Mental Health of Immigrants and Refugees. Austin, Texas: Hogg Foundation for Mental Health: 263–278.

Rodríguez, Roberto
    1994   "Central American Students Organize to Be Seen and Heard." Black Issues in Higher Education (April 21): 26–30.

Ross, John
    1995   Rebellion from the Roots: Indian Uprising in Chiapas. Monroe, Maine: Common Courage Press.

Sjoberg, Gideon and Ted R. Vaughan
    1971   "The Sociology of Ethics and the Ethics of Sociology." Edward Tirayakian (ed.), The Phenomenon of Sociology. New York: Appleton-Century-Crafts: 259–276.

Skocpol, Theda
    1985   "Bringing the State Back In: Strategies of Analysis in Current Research." Peter R. Evans, Dietrich Rueschemeyer, and Theda Skocpol (eds.), Bringing the State Back In. Cambridge: Cambridge University Press: 3–43.

Smith, Michael Peter
    1994   "Can You Imagine?: Transnational Migration and the Globalization of Grassroots Politics." Social Text 39 (Summer): 15–33.
    1989   "Urbanism: Medium or Outcome of Human Agency?" Urban Affairs Quarterly 24,3 (March): 353–357.

Teitelbaum, Michael S. and Myron Weiner
    1995   Threatened Peoples, Threatened Borders: World Migration and U.S. Policy. New York: W.W. Norton.

U.S. Bureau of the Census
    1994   Statistical Abstract of the United States: 1994. Washington, D.C.
    1992   Statistical Abstract of the United States: 1992. Washington, D.C.
    1978   Statistical Abstract of the United States: 1978. Washington, D.C.

Withorn, Ann
    1981   "Retreat from the Social Wage: Human Services in the 1980s." Radical America 15,1–2 (Spring): 23–32.

The Expansion of California Agriculture and the Rise of Peasant-Worker Communities*

Juan Vicente Palerm

T he issue of immigration has been catapulted to the forefront of the American imagination in recent years. Immigration, in effect, has become a topic so central to politics that it defines many candidates' aspirations to public office while it makes or breaks their campaigns. As the topic of immigration becomes increasingly politicized, society's already weak ability to examine it objectively and dispassionately is further compromised. The immigration debate is not only highly polarized, but it also has become a "dialogue" between two obtuse, unchanging monologues accented with rhetorical hyperbole. Although there is insufficient factual information regarding the issue to reach firm conclusions—experts, for example, cannot even agree on the numbers involved—both sides have become extremely skillful in collecting, shaping, and brandishing evidence and experts to bolster their positions, especially those that exert the most powerful influence upon public opinion. Once political objectives have been reached, neither thought nor analysis follows.

The losers in this sad state are not only the immigrants themselves who, as a result of inflammatory public debate, are often scapegoated and victimized, but also society as a whole, with its diminished ability to gain a true and objective understanding of the immigration phenomenon and its place in the modern economic and social milieu. The veil of emotion and misinformation obscures an important opportunity to develop and enact appropriate and fair policies that will guide immigration decisions in the long term. Because laws are being adopted and policies established to enact them on the basis of xenophobia and ignorance, we are surely condemned to revisit these issues in the very near future.

*An early version of this essay was presented at the "Del pasado al futuro: Nuevas dimensiones de la integración México-Estados Unidos" conference organized by the Universidad Nacional Autónoma de México, the Universidad Autónoma Metropolitana-Xochimilco, and the University of California, Santa Cruz, in Mexico City, March 17–19, 1997.

JUAN VICENTE PALERM is Professor of Anthropology at the University of California, Riverside, CA 92521, and Director of the University of California Institute for Mexico and the United States (UCMEXUS).

45

Limitations to the Cost/Benefit Approach

One popular approach to the issue at hand—an approach that immediately captured public interest and involvement—is constituted by diverse claims concerning the cost/benefit ratio of immigrants in the national, state, and local economies. Do immigrants come to the United States to work or to partake of generous U.S. public services, including welfare? What do immigrants contribute in terms of payroll, sales, and property and use taxes, and what benefits do they extract from tax-supported infrastructures and services? If only these questions could be firmly answered, the immigration question could be settled on the basis of net economic value alone, without having to consider more complex issues, such as human rights, the American tradition of immigration, labor supply and demand, language, and educational levels. But the approach inherent in these frequently asked questions has contributed to further obfuscation of the issue because there are no established methods of measurement and no appropriate aggregated and disaggregated data with which to address them. There are, in short, no easy, clear-cut answers but plenty of opportunities to launch speculative and conjectural conclusions.

Recent revivals of the cost/benefit approach are especially troublesome because they are in great measure responsible for galvanizing popular support for mean-spirited and probably unconstitutional measures (such as Proposition 187 in California) that fuel anti-immigrant sentiment, promoting xenophobia and divisiveness. In the policy arena, the cost/benefit approach serves to justify boosting the ability of the Immigration and Naturalization Service (INS) to "control" immigration through the militarization of the border; to revise immigration laws in ways that prevent family reunification and, in effect, force families to separate; and to change welfare laws in such a manner that both legal and undocumented immigrants, regardless of need, will be denied basic public services. Aside from the disruptiveness of such measures, they are unlikely to be effective in their purported purpose: to manage immigration.

California Agriculture

The growing presence of immigrant workers in the lowest-paid jobs—but within key industries—of the California economy stand in sharp contrast to the notion that recent immigrants are a burden to the economy (Table 1). Agriculture, with a reported 91% immigrant work force in 1996, is an especially inviting case to review in light of the current immigration debate.

This essay focuses on examination of the immigration phenomenon in the context of one particular branch of the economy, California agriculture. Interestingly, agriculture was one of the few healthy components of the state's economy during the recent recession, and the industry continues to thrive in the current recovery. Immigrant labor appears in great measure to be responsible for a robust and invigorated agricultural economy in California that—in addition to providing affordable food for the American consumer—contributes, with its increasing exports, to an improved national trade balance. These benefits of both domestic and international scope are achieved at a low cost to both the California farmer and the American taxpayer. A focus on California agriculture will reveal and allow us to address a number of little-known and poorly understood developments regarding immigrant farm workers and the communities they have formed.

Table 1. Immigrants in Selected California Industries, 1980–1990

Occupation	1980 %	1990 %
Construction Laborer	20	64
Janitor	26	49
Farm Worker	58	91
Maid/Houseman	34	76
Electronics Assembler	37	60
Household Child Care	20	58
Restaurant Cook	29	69
Gardener	37	66
Drywall Installer	9	48

Sources: California Department of Industrial Relations; *Los Angeles Times*, 1997 (January 13).

Agriculture is, without question, big business in California. In 1996 the farm-gate value of the state's agriculture reached a record $24.5 billion, with an aggregated value exceeding $65 billion. For the past fifty years, California has been the nation's first-ranked agricultural producer, now distantly followed by Texas with only one-half the output. Also in 1996, farm products worth $12 billion were exported from California, representing one-fifth of the nation's agricultural exports. Principal importers of California crops are the Pacific Rim and European nations and NAFTA partners.

California agriculture has maintained a consistent growth rate. Between 1980 and 1994 farm value increased from $13.7 billion to $20.1 billion—nearly 50% (*California Agricultural Statistics*). From 1994 to 1996 the state's farm value grew by $4.4 billion (21.8%) and, based on current figures, state officials expect an additional 8% increase during 1997, raising California's farm output to $27 billion. Because this period is one characterized by low inflation, farm value augmentations represent real growth based on improved crop yields, commodity values, and labor productivity. Completing a picture of growing efficiency and profits, increased crop yields and values occurred at a time when total farm acreage and cost of farm wages declined (Villarejo and Runsten, 1993). Farming in California is changing: production is more intensive, thus creating more value, more jobs, and more income for the state. In a recent public appearance staged to release the state's laudable annual agricultural report, Governor Pete Wilson boasted that "[t]he

California [agriculture] of today is unrecognizable from the one 50 years ago. . . . We have come a remarkable distance in a short period of time" (*Los Angeles Times*, 07–17–97).

California agriculture is, indeed, changing rapidly and in special ways. Above all, California farmers are responding to new market opportunities at home and abroad and to certain economic constraints. On the one hand, farmers are supplying the growing demand for wholesome fruits and vegetables fueled by changes in the increasingly health-conscious American diet and the hunger for off-season specialty products abroad. On the other hand, farmers are eschewing traditional crops that no longer provide acceptable returns, even when they are subsidized by the federal government, and they are making better use of costly resources such as high-value land, water, and energy—that is, California farmers are rapidly abandoning low-value field crops (such as cotton, hay, and cereals) and farming high-value specialty crops (such as broccoli and strawberries), which are more marketable and guarantee a much higher rate of return to investments (Palerm, 1991).

Between 1980 and 1994, for example, the share of the state's farm value attributable to field crops decreased from 28% to 15%, while the share of fruits and vegetables increased from 39% to 48% (*California Agricultural Statistics*). A similar diversion of farm acreage from field crops to fruits and vegetables occurred, a circumstance that helps to explain why farm value swells at the same time that acreage shrinks. The California Institute for Rural Studies, for example, reports that between 1982 and 1992 the total cropland in the state fell by 778,106 acres, while that devoted to vegetables increased by 122,171 acres, and that to orchards by 87,377 acres (*Wall Street Journal* [05–14–97])—that is, nearly one million acres were eliminated from low-value field crop production during the decade. State-of-the-art greenhouses and nurseries devoted to floral products are also a growth industry while livestock, dairy, and poultry—though still a significant part of the state's agricultural economy—are progressively losing ground.

California agriculture is increasingly a high-tech business, requiring sophisticated farming and management skills. The new fruit and vegetable crops are supported and enhanced by cutting-edge technological innovations developed by the University of California. These, among other results, increase yields and diminish risks. New, improved, and bioengineered strawberry plants, for example, have boosted yields from four to nearly forty tons per acre; day-neutral varieties have stretched the harvest season from three to nearly ten months of the year; and frost-free and pest-resistant varieties now defy the cold winter months, insects, and diseases. What was once a high-risk, short-season, scarce but valuable commodity has become a low-risk, long-season, abundant but still high-value commodity (Wells, 1996). The biotechnological transformation of strawberry growing has been replicated for many other California specialty crops, with similar production gains.

The influence of new technology is not limited to the plants themselves. Laser-guided machines level and grade farmland to exact requirements; computer-regulated irrigation systems deliver precisely measured and timed amounts of moisture and nutrients to each plant, vine, or tree; and specially bred insect predators and powerful chemical pesticides contain or eliminate diseases. Moreover, state-of-the-art sorting, packing, cooling, storage, shipping, and processing installations conserve, transform, and otherwise pamper high-value farm commodities until they can be delivered to the consumer. As will be examined later, the only aspect of specialty-crop farming that remains virtually unaffected by modern technology is the labor input, especially during harvest.

California agriculture is highly concentrated, both geographically and in ownership. Of California's fifty-eight counties, fifteen, located primarily in the southern half of the state, generated 97% of the total farm value in 1994, a substantial increase from 1980 when the same counties accounted for 86% of the farm value (*California Agricultural Statistics*). In addition, of approximately 80,000 farms registered in California, the top 8,000 are responsible for nearly 90% of the state's farm value (Martin, 1984:11). California agriculture is both heavily concentrated and capitalized. It is without question the epitome of modern capitalist farming, a model that is as much envied as it is emulated by other U.S. states and many nations of the world.

Agricultural Labor and the Transformation of California Agriculture

Since the late 19th century, California's agricultural industry has been extraordinary in its size, scale, and consistent capability of producing large volumes and a cornucopia of valuable commodities. But today's industry is not business as usual. California agriculture in recent decades has experienced a major transformation that has radically altered farming and the business of farming. To be sure, agriculture in the state has been restructured to meet the challenges and opportunities presented by globalization. Evidence of this change may be observed in the industry's increased ability to export a substantial share of its production and to successfully compete with premium products in the world marketplace. The transformation was accomplished by the combination of both capital-intensive and labor-intensive methods to achieve the reintensification—or hyperintensification—of farming necessary to ensure the production and delivery of premium products that will return a premium price. As a result, California farms and agricultural entrepreneurs have become avid consumers of capital, technology, and labor. Contrary to conventional wisdom, the modernization of California's agricultural production does not entail the replacement of workers with labor-saving machines; rather, the new techniques and crops demand labor's increased involvement. Thus, the reintensification of farming has been accompanied by a social transformation and restructuring of the rural environment.

Since its beginnings, California agriculture has been a heavy user of labor; and, in contrast to the rest of the nation, it has especially relied upon hired rather than family labor. Indeed, family labor on California farms has been declining steadily since 1955, when the Employment Development Department began to collect data, and had shrunk to 60,000 in 1985 (Palerm, 1991:12–13). One author estimates that farmers provide 23% of farm work, while the remaining 77% is supplied by permanent and seasonal hired labor (Martin, 1984:13). Moreover, hired labor on California farms has been made up primarily of immigrant workers. Experts agree that these farms early on created a distinct and separate labor market (McWilliams, 1939, and Fisher, 1953), and at least one claimed that the development of California agriculture was possible only because an inexhaustible supply of immigrant workers was readily available (Fuller, 1940).

Initially, the state's agricultural industry tapped into a diverse assortment of labor pools resulting from successive waves of immigrants (including Chinese, Japanese, Filipino, Mexican, and even bankrupt Depression-era Dust Bowl farmers from Oklahoma, Arkansas, Missouri, and Texas). But since the 1940s, when the Bracero Program was established, California agriculture has specialized in the use of Mexican migrant workers who trekked from their home communities to California but returned to Mexico when their employment contracts expired (Galarza, 1978). After the cancellation of the Bracero Program in 1964, efforts such as immigration control and the introduction of labor-saving farm machinery were undertaken to free California farms from their dependency upon large numbers of hired workers (Runsten, 1981). Although California farms never fully disengaged from an immigrant labor force—Mexicans continued to access farm employment as undocumented workers—the number of laborers employed by these farms initially declined and later stabilized (Mamer and Fuller, 1978:31; Sosnick, 1978:17). It was not until the reintensification of California agriculture in the late 1970s and early 1980s that the numbers of employed immigrant farm workers began to swell, eventually reaching unprecedented proportions. Today, most experts agree that from 700,000 to 1,000,000 individuals are employed by California farms each year (Campos and Kotkin-Jaszi, 1987; Villarejo and Runsten, 1993:21); 90% of these workers are Latinos, the vast majority from Mexico. Yet there is little awareness of this unexpected development and the fact that California's thriving, reintensified, and global agricultural industry completely relies upon Mexican immigrant and migrant labor.

The State of California does not keep or publish good records concerning farm employment. This lack is in part due to the large number of Mexican-origin workers who enter the job market without proper documentation, but also because farm employers do not keep or report complete data. As a result, efforts to measure the farm labor market and the size of the agricultural labor force often employ circuitous and somewhat convoluted methods. This author, for example, estimated the acreage devoted to new specialty crops, for which there are excellent records, and applied well-established man-hour-per-acre work requirements for each crop in order to calculate the considerable size and growth rate of the new farm labor market (Palerm, 1991). In 1987 the state's Employment Development Department (EDD) began to publish fairly reliable farm employment statistics, the EDD's Report 882A, but these were unfortunately and inexplicably discontinued after 1992. The five-year sequence, however, offers a valuable window on the dynamics of the farm labor force at both the state and county levels.

Figure 1 reveals a number of characteristics of the state's farm labor cohort. First and foremost, it is evident that agricultural employment is indeed growing, and in significant numbers. Second, the difference between low-employment (December–February) and high-employment (May–September) seasons is increasing, but, third, the duration of the high-employment season is enlarging as the bell-shaped curve broadens. Thus, although farm employment in California continues to be highly seasonal, the employment period is now longer.

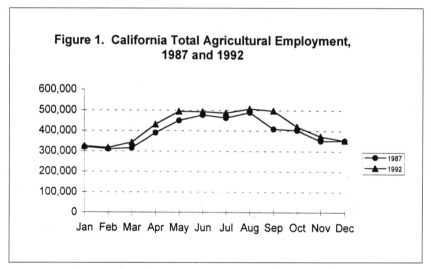

Figure 1. California Total Agricultural Employment, 1987 and 1992

Source: Employment Development Department Report 882A, 1987, 1993.

County-level information is much more pertinent and revealing, particularly when counties especially affected by the reintensification of farming are considered. Figure 2 illustrates that for Santa Barbara County, farm employment is increasing at both the high- and low-employment seasons; in May and June it actually doubled in seven years. The difference between the numbers of workers hired in low- and high-employment seasons has increased dramatically, however. In 1985, 45% more workers were hired in the high-employment season than in the low-employment one, but by 1992, 68% more workers were needed in the high-employment season (Campos and Kotkin-Jasci, 1987). The county's farm employment is equally affected by two major forces: first, the impressive expansion of vegetable crops (broccoli, lettuce, cauliflower, and celery) that are farmed year-round and offer nearly year-round, intermittent employment; and, second, the equally impressive expansion of fruits (strawberries and wine grapes) that are highly seasonal and offer continuous employment during a few months of the year. The two pronounced employment peaks in 1992 in the Santa Barbara figure correspond to the strawberry harvest season (April–June) and the wine-grape harvest (September).

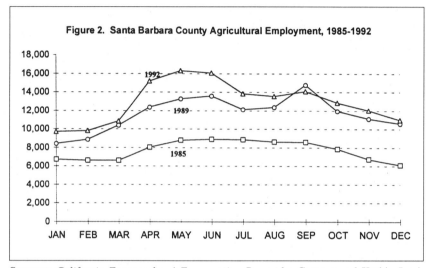

Figure 2. Santa Barbara County Agricultural Employment, 1985-1992

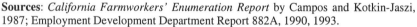

Sources: *California Farmworkers' Enumeration Report* by Campos and Kotkin-Jaszi, 1987; Employment Development Department Report 882A, 1990, 1993.

The recent expansion of labor-intensive strawberry farms in Santa Barbara County—at the expense of a traditional machine-dependent dairy industry—is particularly illustrative of what we have described as the reintensification of farming. Before 1980, Santa Barbara's strawberry farms hardly reached 1,000 acres, and median crop yields were less than ten tons per acre. Some of the best farmland in the county was dedicated to irrigated pasture and alfalfa to support the production of well-established but ailing dairy farms. During the 1990s, strawberries surpassed 5,000 acres, crop yields tripled, and the fruit-bearing season increased from less than five to nearly nine months per year through the introduction of improved plant varieties. Strawberries, while using only 4% of the farmland, became the county's most valuable crop, with an annual value exceeding $80 million and accounting for 18% of the county's total farm value (Palerm, 1994:5).

With the conversion of many acres to strawberry farms, labor requirements increased precipitously. While most farms and dairies, previously encompassing thousands of acres, had been operated by the owners themselves with the support of machinery and the occasional aid of a few hired hands, each acre converted to strawberries occupies at least two full-time workers during the expanded peak harvest season. Santa Barbara strawberry farms employ as many as 10,000 workers at a time to tend and harvest the crop, 90% of them seasonally during the extended harvest, and 10% nearly year-round.

Other fruit and vegetable crops have had similar, though not so dramatic, impacts upon Santa Barbara County farm values and employment over the same time period. Broccoli, for example, the county's second crop in terms of value, doubled acreage to 25,000 and tripled yields, creating a host of new year-round intermittent jobs (Palerm, 1994:4–5). Commercial wine grapes, not previously grown in the area, now occupy 10,000 acres and have created a small number of year-round positions and nearly 3,000 seasonal, one-month harvest jobs (Haley, 1989; Palerm, 1994:9). Altogether, the reintensified agriculture of Santa Barbara County (including over 60,000 acres devoted to vegetables, 10,000 acres to wine grapes, and 5,000 acres to strawberries) currently employs some 23,000 workers: some year-round but intermittently, others seasonally, and a lucky few full-time, year-round. Controlled field observations suggest that 43% of this work force is of Mexican origin and has settled permanently in the area, while the remaining 57% is also Mexican but is present only during the harvest season (Palerm, 1994:11).

California's $24.5 billion—and growing—agricultural industry is responsible for triggering an employment explosion in the countryside, especially in those counties where the reintensification model of agricultural growth and development has been adopted. There are, without question, more farm workers in California today than ever before—nearly twice the number reported at the height of the Bracero Program in the 1950s, before mechanization reduced their numbers. Many of today's farm workers provide menial but not unskilled manual labor, especially during harvest, while others occupy more privileged and better-paid positions as, for example, machine operators, irrigators, and field and labor supervisors. Most of these workers—more than 90%—are of Mexican origin, and nearly one-third are women.

The farm employment boom, in turn, has greatly stimulated immigration and migration practices from Mexico. There are, in effect, two clearly defined outcomes. First, a larger number of migrant farm workers, drawn from an increasingly larger part of Mexico, trek to California seeking seasonal farm jobs and return to their home communities when employment ends. Second, a growing number of former migrant farm workers are settling permanently with their families near farm employment sites due, in great measure, to both increased job opportunities and to extended work seasons that offer year-round or nearly year-round employment. We estimate that approximately one-half of the state's farm labor requirement is supplied by seasonal migrants from Mexico, while the other half is supplied by settled immigrants from the same country.

Migrant Farm Workers

Because migrants have formed an intrinsic part of the California agricultural landscape for such a long time, they (and their life-styles) are better known, studied, and documented than are settled immigrants. Indeed, the better-known experience of the migrants, especially during the Bracero years, has served to construct the stereotypical view of the California farm worker that is increasingly less true to the observable reality of today. There is now, nonetheless, a well-established tradition of migration that links communities and people in rural Mexico with those in agricultural California (Massey et al., 1987; Mines, 1981; Palerm and Urquiola, 1993; López Castro, 1986)—a tradition that is multigenerational, functional, and vibrant. Many communities, as the above-cited scholars have reported, have built extensive networks of kin, friends, and *paisanos* that greatly facilitate and support the movement of people across the border and into the workplace. Over time, sending communities in rural Mexico have become specialized suppliers of labor and dependent upon dollar wage remittances from the United States. The degree to which rural communities and families in, for example, the states of Michoacan, Jalisco, Guanajuato, and Zacatecas have become economically, socially, and culturally dependent upon the California connection is matched only by the degree to which agricultural enterprises and farmers in California have become dependent upon the Mexican connection. These linkages have solidified so as to configure a binational system of agricultural production and reproduction—a system whose separate parts have become functionally interdependent, to the extent that neither can be correctly understood or analyzed without reference to the other (Palerm and Urquiola, 1993:311).

The binational system is changing, however, and some of these changes need to be recognized. First, migrant farm workers are no longer mostly young single males but now include a much more diverse group of people in terms of their age, sex, and marital status. Many married and single women have joined the circular stream, and it is now fairly common to observe whole or partial families traveling and working together. It is certain that the combination of Mexico's domestic problems and California's increased job opportunities is drawing a larger and more diverse group of Mexican migrants from that country's traditional sending communities.

Second, the displacement effect also is drawing a large number of new migrants from Mexican regions and communities that had not previously participated in the circular seasonal movement. Especially noteworthy are the increased numbers of migrants from the southern state of Oaxaca who, in a short time, have not only become a significant part of the agricultural labor force in California (Zabin et al., 1993; Runsten and Kearney, 1994) but also have become serious competitors for the farm jobs traditionally held by migrants from the conventional sending communities. The new Oaxacan migrants, who are extracted mostly from indigenous Mixtec and Zapotec villages, have different and distinct cultural traditions, social organization, and ways of managing their affairs and building their networks. They often are at odds with the traditional mestizo migrants from the central states and have added a new ingredient of conflict and tension within the farmworker population.

Third, although immigrant farm workers who have settled in the California rural environment constitute an important part of the migrant networks by providing support, information, and shelter to the seasonal migrants—especially to kin, friends, and *paisanos*—they are becoming less cooperative as their economic and social lives become more separate and loyalty to their Mexican home communities begins to wane. Settled immigrants, as we will discuss later, are building new but fragile homes and communities in California and often feel threatened by the competitive presence of growing numbers of migrants in already overcrowded homes, overburdened communities, and oversupplied labor markets. As a result, another dimension of tension and conflict is emerging between immigrant and migrant farm workers.

Fourth and foremost, changing U.S. laws and regulations regarding immigration, the growing determination for enforcement, and increasing anti-immigrant and anti-Mexican sentiment all are subjecting the well-established binational system to change (Martin et al., 1995). Although the binational system emerged under the friendly binational agreement of the Bracero Program and matured during the post-Bracero era characterized by "benign neglect" of border issues and calculated tolerance of undocumented farm workers, the system is currently under increased pressure to change. The Immigration Reform and Control Act (IRCA) of 1986 was the first concentrated effort to interrupt the incorporation of undocumented immigrants into the U.S. job market by establishing severe measures that targeted both undocumented aliens and the employers who hire them. But even then, agricultural employers interceded in favor of the migrant farm workers and their own interests and managed to impose three special programs that ensured the continuing protection and flow of migrants to the nation's agricultural fields: the Special Agricultural Workers (SAW) program, the Replenishment Agricultural Workers (RAW) program, and H-2A, a non-immigrant visa program for seasonal farm workers. Since then, however, the tide has turned, and it appears that the country is determined to close the border by erecting greater physical obstacles and implementing special operations designed to impede the easy flow of undocumented migrants, including those who practice circular migration. Thus far, there is little evidence that the increased presence of the INS at the border is reducing the number of migrants who cross it successfully and ultimately enter the farm labor market. But the border crossing has become more expensive and dangerous as undocumented farm workers are forced to contract the services of *coyotes* (unscrupulous guides) and to pass through remote and environmentally hostile terrain. Increased pressure at the border, it seems, is not so much shutting out migrant farm workers as it is shutting them in with increased costs and risks. Once in the United States, these workers are less likely to return home when the usual employment season ends; rather, they may remain from one season to the next and even settle down permanently in the United States and import their families to join them.

In short, increased competition for farm jobs (even with farm employment rising), aging and fraying social networks, and increased hostility and persecution have in recent times made the already hard lives of migrant farm workers even more difficult, uncertain, and insecure. When these difficulties are compounded by increased and more effective border control, we must question the continued survival of the system that has shuttled seasonal farm workers back and forth across the border for fifty years. The demise of this traditional system has significant implications both for the welfare of Mexican labor-sending communities that have come to depend upon wage remittances and the health of California's reintensified agricultural industry that depends heavily upon the availability of Mexican migrant workers.

Immigrant Farm Workers

Until recently, few Mexican migrant farm workers risked abandoning their circular migration practices to settle near the California farm employment sites. After trekking from crop to crop throughout the state, most farm workers returned to their home communities and families in Mexico. The low rate of farm-worker settlement in rural California was undoubtedly the result of an industry that could not provide stable employment or the wage income needed for their families to live in California while withstanding long seasons of unemployment. Those who did venture to immigrate, moreover, did not remain long in farm employment or in the rural environment but quickly moved on to non-farm jobs available in California's rapidly growing cities. While they remained in agriculture, settlers were dispersed among isolated ranches and farms as year-round, live-in workers or formed small, marginalized, and segregated *colonias,* occupying neighborhoods, barrios, and old labor camps within or near larger communities mostly peopled by farmers as well as businessmen and merchants who serviced the agricultural industry (Galarza, 1978:14).

Nonetheless, agriculture served as the gateway for Mexican immigration to California. Growing numbers of immigrant settlers used entry-level farm jobs as stepping stones to better and more secure manufacturing and service jobs in California's developing cities, which, moreover, offered the improved housing and robust urban infrastructure (including schools) usually lacking or altogether absent in the rural *colonias.* As a result, agricultural employers perpetually sought to satisfy their labor needs by recruiting new settlers to replace the old ones. This practice, the "revolving door syndrome" that attracts immigrants to agriculture and quickly ushers them out to other branches of the economy, has prevailed until recently. When IRCA's amnesty provisions were enacted in 1986, they included a SAW program to regularize undocumented workers and a RAW program to replace those SAW workers who were expected to abandon farm employment soon after becoming legalized (Rosenberg, 1988).

It has not been business as usual for some time in rural California, however. Once the process of reintensification of agriculture overtook the state's farms in the late 1970s and early 1980s, an increasing number of migrant farm workers began to settle permanently into the agricultural landscape, boosting rural population growth and transforming rural communities. The combination of several factors is responsible for this novel development. First and foremost, an increase in jobs and extended employment seasons have created improved opportunities for employment and wages for farm workers. Second, since 1977, eligibility for state unemployment insurance programs has been extended to farm workers, decreasing somewhat the uncertainty and hardship of the unemployment seasons (Palerm, 1991:14). Third, immigrant families have been able to place multiple workers in the job market and, by pooling wages, to generate a combined income that offsets generally low wages and intermittent and seasonal employment.

These changes, moreover, were taking place at a time when the rural-to-urban movement of California's immigrant population was slowing and becoming more difficult. By the early 1980s entry-level non-farm jobs had lost much of their luster in terms of wages, benefits, and stability, and metropolitan cities no longer offered the comparative advantages that they had once held over rural towns. The decreasing value of minimum-wage jobs and rapidly deteriorating urban conditions (overcrowding, crime, drugs, and violence) made agricultural employment and rural life into an acceptable, and even attractive, proposition for many immigrant families. In increasing numbers, they began to settle permanently in the countryside. Opportunities to make the rural-to-urban transition began to wane as urban employers eschewed the supply of farm workers and became direct importers of labor from Mexico and Central America. Immigrant farm workers with aspirations to move out of agriculture found they were competing with new immigrants for entry-level jobs that were not much better than the farm jobs they already held.

Finally, IRCA exerted considerable influence in further boosting the settlement of migrant farm workers and their families throughout agricultural California. Special amnesty provisions for farm workers in IRCA's SAW program made it possible to legalize a large portion of a migrant and immigrant work force that had been mostly undocumented. Many SAWs, as a result, opted to remain permanently in California, bringing their spouses, children, and parents to join them either as new undocumented immigrants or by using family reunification programs.

The combined effect of rural settlement, diminished rural-to-urban transition, and increased representation of young families among the immigrant population

Table 2. Farm-Worker Settlements in California, 1980-1990

Community	County	1980			1990			Change 1980-1990	1990	1990
		Total Pop.	Latino Pop.	Percent Latino	Total Pop.	Latino Pop.	Percent Latino	Latino Percent	Per Capita Income	Latino Per Capita Income
CITIES WITH POPULATION FROM 1,000–20,000										
Arvin	Kern	6,863	3,974	57.9	9,286	6,960	75.0	75.1	$7,252	$6,641
Avenal	Kings	4,137	1,862	45.0	9,770	5,224	53.5	180.6	6,461	6,124
Avocado Heights	Calaveras	11,721	6,599	56.3	14,232	9,596	67.4	45.4	12,374	10,001
Brawley	Imperial	14,946	8,684	58.1	18,923	13,076	69.1	50.6	9,408	6,396
Calexico	Imperial	14,412	13,562	94.1	18,633	17,806	95.6	31.3	6,595	6,194
Calipatria	Imperial	2,636	1,761	66.8	2,690	1,995	74.2	13.3	6,952	5,386
Calwa	Fresno	6,640	4,309	64.9						
Castroville	Monterey	4,396	3,240	73.7	5,272	4,185	79.4	29.2	8,032	6,841
Coachella	Riverside	9,129	8,152	89.3	16,896	16,107	95.3	97.6	5,760	5,367
Corcoran	Kings	6,454	3,337	51.7	13,364	6,919	51.8	107.3	8,270	5,898
Cutler	Tulare	3,149	2,800	88.9	4,450	4,234	95.2	51.2	4,334	4,195
Del Rey	Fresno	1,126	1,036	92.0	1,150	1,089	94.7	5.1	4,368	4,137
Delano	Kern	16,491	9,466	57.4	22,762	14,214	62.5	50.2	7,491	5,975
Dinuba	Tulare	9,907	4,815	48.6	12,743	7,693	60.4	59.8	8,354	5,915
Earlimart	Tulare	4,578	3,324	72.6	5,881	4,804	81.7	44.5	4,909	4,604
El Rio	Ventura	5,674	3,246	57.2	6,419	4,116	64.1	26.8	10,708	8,156
Fillmore	Ventura	9,602	4,599	47.9	11,992	7,111	59.3	54.6	10,674	7,883
Firebaugh	Fresno	3,740	2,607	69.7	4,429	3,573	80.7	37.1	6,836	5,842
Fowler	Fresno	2,496	1,206	48.3	3,208	1,874	58.4	55.4	9,585	6,252

Gonzales	Monterey	2,891	1,969	68.1	4,660	3,828	82.2	94.4	7,834	6,566
Goshen	Tulare	1,809	1,089	60.2	7,464	5,763	77.2	107.3	7,710	6,571
Greenfield	Monterey	4,181	2,780	66.5	5,479	4,546	83.0	67.7	6,663	5,493
Guadalupe	Santa Barbara	3,629	2,711	74.7	1,811	1,351	74.6	63.6	8,364	6,551
Hamilton	Glenn	1,337	826	61.8						
Hollister	San Benito	11,488	6,307	54.9	19,212	10,786	56.1	-71.0	11,415	8,217
Holtville	Imperial	4,399	2,094	47.6	4,820	3,011	62.5	43.8	9,631	5,147
Huron	**Fresno**	**2,768**	**2,527**	**91.3**	**4,766**	**4,597**	**96.5**	**81.9**	**5,501**	**5,393**
Kettleman City	Kings	1,051	881	83.8	1,411	1,342	95.1	52.3	5,129	4,431
King City	Monterey	5,495	2,671	48.6	7,634	5,091	66.7	90.6	11,642	7,474
Lamont	Kern	9,616	5,577	58.0	11,517	8,826	76.6	58.3	5,964	5,297
Livingston	Merced	5,326	3,254	61.1	7,317	5,354	73.2	64.5	6,834	6,229
London	Tulare	1,257	686	54.6	1,638	1,331	81.3	94.0	3,246	2,683
McFarland	Kern	5,151	3,905	75.8	7,005	5,809	82.9	48.8	6,056	5,211
Mecca	Riverside	1,698	1,498	88.2	1,966	1,869	95.1	24.8	5,271	4,996
Mendota	**Fresno**	**5,038**	**4,267**	**84.7**	**6,821**	**6,405**	**93.9**	**50.1**	**4,920**	**4,735**
Orange Cove	**Fresno**	**4,026**	**2,907**	**72.2**	**5,604**	**4,820**	**86.0**	**65.8**	**4,385**	**3,735**
Orosi	Tulare	4,076	2,486	61.0	5,486	3,964	72.3	59.5	6,662	5,142
Pajaro	Monterey	1,426	1,206	84.6	3,332	3,113	93.4	158.1	6,555	5,734
Parlier	**Fresno**	**2,902**	**2,641**	**91.0**	**7,938**	**7,707**	**97.1**	**191.8**	**4,784**	**4,586**
Parlier, West	Fresno	2,811	2,760	98.2						
Patterson	Stanislaus	3,908	2,052	52.5	8,626	4,156	48.2	102.5	11,504	7,108
Piru	Ventura	1,284	944	73.5	1,157	872	75.4	-7.6	8,386	7,405
Planada	Merced	2,406	1,942	80.7	3,531	3,104	87.9	59.8	5,197	4,655
Richgrove	Tulare	1,398	1,156	82.7	1,899	1,607	84.6	39.0	4,053	3,776
San Joaquin	**Fresno**	**1,930**	**1,162**	**60.2**	**2,311**	**1,743**	**75.4**	**50.0**	**5,356**	**3,813**
San Juan Bautista	San Benito	1,276	587	46.0	1,570	714	45.5	21.6	12,137	9,181
Sanger	Fresno	12,542	8,253	65.8	16,839	12,269	72.9	48.7	8,461	6,455
Seeley	Imperial	1,058	491	46.4	1,228	847	69.0	72.5	8,846	6,411
Selma	Fresno	10,942	5,416	49.5	14,757	9,043	61.3	67.0	8,175	5,830
Soledad	Monterey	5,928	4,908	82.8	7,146	6,394	89.5	30.3	6,889	6,142

City	County									
Terra Bella	Tulare	1,807	1,026	56.8	2,740	1,940	70.8	89.1	5,204	3,698
Walnut Park	Los Angeles	11,811	8,965	75.9	14,722	13,566	92.2	51.3	7,891	7,409
Wasco	Kern	9,613	4,614	48.0	12,412	7,858	63.3	70.3	7,097	5,176
Weedpatch	Kern	1,553	1,027	66.1	1,892	1,619	85.6	57.6	4,081	3,849
Westmorland	Imperial	1,590	1,051	66.1	1,380	997	72.3	-5.1	7,342	5,544
Woodlake	Tulare	4,343	2,810	64.7	5,678	4,238	74.6	50.8	6,241	5,103
Woodville	Tulare	1,507	808	53.6	1,557	1,163	74.7	43.9	5,396	4,266

Cities with Population from 20,000–50,000

City	County									
El Centro	Imperial	23,996	11,974	49.9	31,384	20,301	64.7	69.5	9,898	6,357
Gilroy	Santa Clara	21,641	9,760	45.1	31,487	14,762	46.9	51.3	14,241	8,805
Hanford	Kings	20,958	5,050	24.1	30,765	8,803	28.6	74.3	11,283	7,288
Indio	Riverside	21,611	12,145	56.2	36,793	24,880	67.6	104.8	9,244	6,411
Madera	Madera	21,732	9,040	41.6	29,305	15,685	53.5	73.5	8,883	5,648
Merced	Merced	36,499	10,292	28.2	56,216	16,228	28.9	57.7	10,237	6,644
Santa Maria	Santa Barbara	39,685	13,294	33.5	61,284	27,909	45.5	109.9	12,118	7,155
Santa Paula	Ventura	20,552	10,379	50.5	25,062	14,701	58.7	41.6	11,650	8,229
Tulare	Tulare	22,526	6,285	27.9	33,249	11,244	33.8	78.9	9,878	6,403
Visalia	Tulare	49,729	9,547	19.2	75,636	18,121	24.0	89.8	12,994	6,582
Watsonville	Monterey	23,543	11,324	48.1	31,099	18,551	59.7	63.8	10,422	6,544
Woodland	Yolo	30,235	6,863	22.7	39,802	10,314	25.9	50.3	13,854	9,389

has caused a rural population explosion driven by immigration and increased fertility. The rural growth rates are comparable to those observed for urban Latinos over the past two decades. The rural population explosion is especially evident in small towns, cities, and communities located within the state's principal farming regions where agricultural reintensification has taken place—that is, the San Joaquin, Imperial, and Central Coast valleys. The city of Guadalupe, located in a Central Coast valley, illustrates the rural population explosion as well as the resulting transformation of rural communities. Before the reintensification of farming took hold—in Santa Barbara County, this was evident in the expansion of fruit and vegetable crops—Guadalupe had a small, diminishing, and aging population of 3,225 of which 600 (18%) were Hispanics, mostly Mexican-immigrant farm workers. By 1990, once strawberries and broccoli came to dominate the county's agricultural output, the town's population had nearly doubled to 5,479 and the number of Hispanics had increased eightfold to 4,546 or 83% (Palerm, 1991:21 and 1994:3). Recent estimates that place the current population at 6,333 indicate that the process of growth continues. Equally drama-tic is the transformation of Guadalupe from a sleepy and aging farm community into a vibrant place populated by young immigrant families with high fertility rates.

The larger city of Santa Maria, an important hub of agro-industrial activity also located in Santa Barbara County, has experienced a delayed but similar demo-graphic transformation. According to the latest census reports, Santa Maria grew from 39,600 to 61,200 inhabitants—by 54%—during the 1980–1990 inter-census period. At the same time, Santa Maria's Hispanic population grew from 13,200 to 28,000, or by 109%. Indeed, three-fourths of the city's population growth between 1980 and 1990 is Hispanic, the result of young immigrant families from Mexico settling permanently near agricultural and agro-industrial employment sites.

Many other rural California towns and cities have experienced growth similar to that of Guadalupe and Santa Maria. More than 150 communities with a population of less than 20,000 have been seen to mirror the Guadalupe experience and account for more than 500,000 new settlers, while more than a dozen small cities with a population of from 20,000 to 50,000 follow the Santa Maria exper-ience and add at least another 200,000 settlers. Table 2 lists the most important farm-worker settlements and provides data regarding population growth and income. Other larger cities located near agricultural production sites—among them Fresno, Stockton, Oxnard, and Salinas—also contain growing numbers of farm workers who regularly commute from urban neighborhoods to the fields (*The Challenge*, 1989: 144–47). We estimate that nearly one million people, mostly immigrant farm-worker families, have settled into all of these communities over the course of the past two decades.

These new communities, reshaped by immigration and agricultural prosperity, are peopled by young, eager, hard-working individuals who are determined to shed nomadic practices, reunite their disjointed and dispersed families, and build new lives in the places where they have chosen to settle. Work participation is extraordinarily high and apparently limited only by the availability of farm jobs and the seasonality of employment. It is common, for example, for a typical family of six to have at least two members striving to work full-time and another two who work part-time and intermittently; the workers include a large number of adult women and teenaged dependents (Palerm, 1991:87). Family members work closely together and pool resources with the goal of overcoming the intrinsic difficulties that accompany agricultural jobs (low wages and intermittent employment) and of building an economic base that will permit them to prosper while creating improved opportunities for the next generation. Despite having low income levels and large families, rural immigrant settlers rarely use welfare services and other forms of state and federal public assistance (Garcia, 1992). Many have become home-owners, have opened small businesses, and are actively engaged in local schools, government, and community affairs. Some even have become independent producers and have established small family and large commercial farms (Figueroa, n.d.). They are clearly not living transitionally in rural towns while working temporarily in agriculture, but rather are truly home-steading into the new agricultural landscape.

Despite the vigor of their inhabitants, the new California rural communities are troubled. First and foremost, because they are mostly populated by poor immigrant families, they are places of concentrated and persistent poverty. Table 2, which lists the major immigrant farm-worker settlements in rural California, also reveals that many of these communities have a per capita income that is less than one-half the state's average of $16,409. In effect, five of the top ten poorest incorporated cities in California are on this list: Huron, Mendota, Orange Cove, Parlier, and San Joaquin; all are in Fresno County, the most agriculturally productive county in the state, and probably in all the nation. Although many immigrant farm workers' households with multiple workers pool their income, most remain at or below poverty levels as defined by the federal government (Palerm, 1991:87; Villarejo and Runsten, 1993:23).

To be sure, these communities are overpopulated and overcrowded; housing is not only insufficient and inadequate, but the physical and service infrastructure also has been severely overtaken by growing demand. Farm-worker settlements often hold up to three times the population of twenty years ago, with hardly any additions or improvements. Making matters worse, the concentration of poor low-income families is in part responsible for a rapidly eroding tax base, which further impedes the communities' ability to satisfy increased demand for basic public services and, moreover, to expand or repair an already inadequate and aging infrastructure. Also contributing to the erosion of the local tax base has been the out-migration of local businesses, businessmen, and other members of the "traditional" farm community, along with decreasing property values. Many of the new farm-worker communities are on the brink of bankruptcy, and most are certainly under great fiscal stress.

The immigrant community has many unmet needs that the traditional community cannot provide. Among these requirements are special educational and health services. In the city of Guadalupe, for example, local schools serve a large and growing student population that is 97% minority (Latino), with high levels of limited English proficiency—63% in the elementary grades and 44% in the middle school. Few of the immigrant parents, moreover, have attained more than an elementary-level formal education, and most are not fluent in English. Regarding health, it is important to note that only rarely do agricultural employers provide health insurance to their employees and their dependents; therefore, most farm workers and their families remain unprotected and without proper health care. This situation is particularly pertinent when considered in the context of the overall living and working conditions of the farm-worker community and the generally young profile of the population.

Finally, despite the population they hold and the critical part they play in the state's agricultural economy, there is little awareness of the existence of the new farm-worker communities and even less understanding of their problems and needs. These communities are truly invisible. Although the 150 rural places in California where immigrant farm workers have settled contain as many as 500,000 new poor people, the United States Department of Agriculture (USDA) has not included a single California location in its list of rural places with persistently high poverty levels (Beale, 1993).

A New Perspective on Mexican-Origin Immigration

The two types of communities discussed above—the "peasant" sending communities in Mexico that provide seasonal migrant labor to California farms and the new "farm worker" receiving communities in rural California where immigrants have settled—are integral to the state's modern and productive agricultural industry. This relationship challenges a number of well-established paradigms and mindsets regarding the course of modern agriculture and rural society. California's new farm-worker communities, for example, defy a view about American rural communities that we have come to accept: their inevitable demise as they become socially and economically irrelevant. Today, as we have documented, rural communities in California are demographically alive and economically relevant, if not indispensable. A revision, or at least a substantial review, of existing rural community paradigms is therefore in order. Moreover, the interdependent symbiotic relationship between traditional peasant communities in Mexico and the world's most modern and advanced agricultural economy in California also demands explanation, because conventional paradigms regarding agricultural modernization and the development of capitalist agriculture typically preclude this outcome. Also, the simple fact that California farms have become more, rather than less, attached to manual labor counters the common conviction that machines will ultimately replace farm workers.

The observable reality in rural California not only belies much of our assumed understanding about agriculture and rural society, but it also evidences our woeful inability to correctly anticipate events and plan intelligently for them. Much of what has transpired in rural California over the past two decades was not only unexpected, but even diametrically opposed to what was predicted with much fanfare and certainty.

Addressing the issues raised above is well beyond the plan and scope of this essay. But it is fitting to conclude that these peasant-worker communities in Mexico and California—the people who live in them, and their circumstances— are very much the product of the way that California agriculture has evolved. Conversely, without access to such communities, the successful development and operation of the state's cutting-edge and prosperous agricultural industry would not have occurred. With this in mind, it is possible and timely to return to the questions that prompted this essay in the first place. Do Mexican immigrants add to or subtract from the national and state economies? What is the cost/benefit ratio and can it be measured accurately? And do immigrants come to California to use and abuse generous public services and welfare benefits, or do they come to work?

With regard to California agriculture, an industry that operates almost exclusively with Mexican-origin laborers, it is clear that immigrant and migrant workers are a net asset; without them, California agriculture would not exist as it is and the state would be, to say the least, deprived of its $24.5 billion farm-gate value while U.S. consumers would be deprived of affordable and wholesome fruits and vegetables. Admittedly, the growing immigrant population that has settled into California's rural towns (including the families and other dependents of immigrant farm workers) creates new needs for vital and costly community infrastructure and health and education services necessary to ensure an appropriate standard of living, but in reality many of these basic needs remain unmet. Most immigrant farm workers live with substandard wages and in substandard conditions, with little or no access to public assistance programs. The cost/benefit ratio is unquestionably in favor of the California economy and the U.S. taxpayers, who reap the benefits of Mexican immigrant and migrant labor with little burden except, perhaps, the shame of witnessing the existence of impoverished farm communities in the midst of the richest and most productive agricultural enterprise in the world.

Immigrant and migrant farm workers endure, as they always have, hard work for poor pay. But today they are further plagued by the anti-immigrant and anti-Mexican fervor that is fanned for political purposes, and they have become the principal and most vulnerable targets of recent immigration and welfare reforms. Sojourning migrants now are burdened with increased border control, violence, and other risks. Modifications to immigration laws will obstruct and prevent family reunification and, in effect, will cause painful family divisions as the undocumented dependents of legal immigrants are forced to return to their Mexican home communities with little hope of earning legal entry to the United States in the near future. Welfare reform will deny basic health services such as prenatal care to unauthorized immigrants and will, moreover, considerably diminish legal immigrants' access to the services that other taxpayers receive. If all of the provisions of California's Proposition 187 were to be upheld by the courts and enforced, the schools of rural California would be emptied and the children of many immigrant farm workers would be deprived of education as well.

It is clear to this author that California's reluctance to accept the true nature of the convenient and profitable articulation established between its agriculture and Mexican peasant-worker communities, and the government's refusal to manage that relationship properly, have resulted in the development of legislation and the mobilization of people toward ends that are self-defeating and ultimately contrary to the economic interests of the state and the nation, not to mention exploitative of the rights of immigrant workers. The welfare of agricultural industry is jeopardized. As a result, we are condemned to visit these issues in future legislation. They will not be resolved as long as California agriculture stays on the course that it chose to follow nearly two decades ago. Instead of mean-spirited measures that will satisfy only short-term and short-minded political campaigns, we urgently need appropriate policy to regulate the revitalized labor system in such a manner that it will benefit and protect both farmers and workers. We will be wise to implement policies and programs designed to aid and meet the needs of the new farm-worker communities and to enable them to develop and grow until they fulfill the modest aspirations of the new homesteaders.

The issue is especially pressing because the model of agricultural development adopted by California is being reproduced in other parts of the nation, and Mexican migrants and immigrants are increasingly becoming the mainstay of the nation's agricultural industry. Indeed, without their involvement, many of the farm products that comprise America's huge agricultural industry would not be grown and harvested. This is true in the field-rich southwestern United States as well as in other parts of the nation. Immigrant and migrant farm workers from Mexico, Central America, and the Caribbean are harvesting tobacco in Tennessee, peaches in Georgia and South Carolina, oranges and tomatoes in Florida, mushrooms in Pennsylvania, cucumbers in Michigan, apples in Washington and New York, and hops in Idaho—and in the process they are both forming and transforming rural American communities. Latino farm workers and new Latino settlements are to be found in different states of formation in such disparate locations as Yakima and Granger, Washington; Caldwell, Idaho; Hood River, Oregon; Twin Falls, Utah; Immokalee, Florida; the Delaware-Maryland-Virginia Peninsula; and Kennett Square, Pennsylvania (Griffith and Kissam, 1995; Commission on Agricultural Workers, 1993; Garcia, 1995).

It is incumbent upon the United States, and in the best interests of the nation's agricultural industry, to accommodate the labor system and the new farm-worker communities, made up of both immigrants and migrants, into mainstream America. Punitive measures, including immigration and welfare reform, exclusion, and discrimination, will only drive the labor system and its workers further underground. Clandestine operation of the agricultural labor market makes workers more vulnerable to abuse and prevents attainment of a desirable long-term solution to management of farm labor needs that few people would oppose: the revitalization of rural California by the establishment of healthy and secure communities striving to achieve prosperity in the best tradition of America's history.

REFERENCES

Beale, Calvin L.
1993   "Poverty Is Persistent in Some Rural Areas." Agricultural Outlook. September.
California Agricultural Statistics, 1980–1994.
                California Agricultural Statistics Review, 1980–1989. Sacramento: California
                Department of Food and Agriculture.
Campos, Peter V., and Suzanne Kotkin-Jaszi
1987   "California Farmworkers Enumeration Report." Sacramento: Department of
                Health and Human Services.
The Challenge: Latinos in a Changing California.
1989   Riverside: University of California Institute for Mexico and the United States.
Commission on Agricultural Workers
1993   Appendix I. Case Studies and Research Reports Prepared for the Commission
                on Agricultural Workers, 1989–1993. Washington, D.C.: U.S. Government
                Printing Office.
Employment Development Department. Report 882A. Agricultural Employment, 1987–1993.
                Sacramento: Labor Market Information Division.
Figueroa Sanchez, Teresa
n.d.   "Against All Odds: Mexican Family Farms in California." Unfinished Ph.D.
                dissertation, University of California, Santa Barbara.
Fisher, Lloyd H.
1953   The Harvest Labor Market in California. Cambridge, Mass.: Harvard
                University Press.
Fuller, Varden
1940   The Supply of Agricultural Labor as a Factor in the Evolution of Farm
                Organization in California. Hearings Before a Subcommittee of the Committee
                of Education and Labor, United States Senate. Washington, D.C.: U.S.
                Government Printing Office.
Galarza, Ernesto
1978   Merchants of Labor: An Account of the Managed Migration of Mexican Farm
                Workers in California, 1942–1960. Santa Barbara: McNally and Loftin, West.
Garcia, Victor
1992   "Surviving Farmwork: Economic Strategies of Chicano/Mexican Households
                in a Rural California Community." Ph.D. dissertation, University of California,
                Santa Barbara.
1995   Finding and Enumerating Migrants in Mexican Enclaves of the U.S. Northeast:
                The Case of Southern Chester County, Pennsylvania. Washington, D.C.: Center
                for Survey Methods Research, Bureau of the Census, Department of Commerce.

Griffith, David, and Ed Kissam
    1995   Working Poor: Farmworkers in the United States. Philadelphia: Temple
            University Press.
Haley, Brian
    1989   "Aspects and Social Impacts of Size and Organization in the Recently
            Developed Wine Industry of Santa Barbara County, California." Santa
            Barbara: Center for Chicano Studies, University of California.
López Castro, Gustavo
    1986   La casa dividida: Un estudio de caso sobre la migración a Estados Unidos en
            un pueblo michoacano. Zamora: El Colegio de Michoacán y Asociación
            Mexicana de Población.
Los Angeles Times
    1997   "Many Find Labor Office Slow to Act." January 13.
    1997   "Officials Crow About State's Farm Economy." July 17.
Mamer, John W., and Varden Fuller
    1978   "Employment of California Farms." In Technological Change, Farm
            Mechanization, and Agricultural Employment, ed. John Mamer and Varden
            Fuller. Berkeley: Division of Agricultural Sciences, University of California.
Martin, Philip L.
    1984   "Labor in California Agriculture." In Migrant Labor in Agriculture: An
            International Comparison, ed. Philip L. Martin. Berkeley: Giannini Foundation
            of Agricultural Economics, University of California.
Martin, Philip L., Wallace Huffman, Robert Emerson, J. Edward Taylor, and Refugio I. Rochin
    1995   Immigration Reform and U.S. Agriculture. University of California, Division
            of Agriculture and Natural Resources.
Massey, Douglas, Rafael Alarcón, Jorge Durand, and Humberto González
    1987   Return to Aztlán: The Social Process of International Migration from Western
            Mexico. Berkeley: University of California Press.
McWilliams, Cary
    1939   Factories in the Field. Boston: Little, Brown and Co.
Mines, Richard
    1981   Developing a Community Tradition of Migration: A Field Study in Rural
            Zacatecas, Mexico, and California Settlement Areas. Center for United States-
            Mexican Studies. San Diego: University of California.
Palerm, Juan Vicente
    1991   Farm Labor Needs and Farmworkers in California, 1970–1989. Sacramento:
            Employment Development Department.
    1994   Immigrant and Migrant Farm Workers in the Santa Maria Valley, California.
            Washington, D.C.: Center for Survey Methods Research, Bureau of the
            Census.
Palerm, Juan Vicente, and José Ignacio Urquiola
    1993   "A Binational System of Agricultural Production: The Case of the Mexican
            Bajio and California." In Mexico and the United States: Neighbors in Crisis,
            ed. Daniel G. Aldrich, Jr., and Lorenzo Meyer. San Bernardino, CA: Borgo
            Press.
Rosenberg, Howard R.
    1988   Emerging Outcomes in California Agriculture from the Immigration Reform
            and Control Act of 1986. Agricultural Issues Center, UC AIC Issues Paper
            No. 88–3. Davis: University of California.
Runsten, David
    1981   Mechanization and Mexican Labor in California Agriculture. San Diego:
            Center for U.S.-Mexican Studies, University of California.
Runsten, David, and Michael Kearney
    1994   A Survey of Oaxacan Village Networks in California Agriculture. Davis:
            California Institute for Rural Studies.

Sosnick, Stephen H.
    1978   Hired Hands: Seasonal Farm Workers in the United States. Santa Barbara:
                 McNally and Loftin.
Villarejo, Don, and Dave Runsten
    1993   California's Agricultural Dilemma: Higher Production and Lower Wages.
                 Davis: California Institute for Rural Studies.
Wall Street Journal
    1997   "Loss of Farmland Masks Switch to Pricier Crops." May 14.
Wells, Miriam J.
    1996   Strawberry Fields: Politics, Class, and Work in California Agriculture. Ithaca:
                 Cornell University Press.
Zabin, Carol, Michael Kearney, Anna Garcia, David Runsten, and Carole Nagengast
    1993   Mixtec Migrants in California Agriculture: A New Cycle of Poverty. Davis:
                 California Institute for Rural Studies.

Gender and International Labor Migration: A Networks Approach

Linda Miller Matthei

EMALES HAVE OUTNUMBERED MALES IN LEGAL IMMIGRATION TO THE UNITED States since the 1930s (Houston, Kramer, and Barrett, 1984), yet until recently issues of gender have received relatively scant attention in the cumulative body of research on migration. Migration researchers have largely overlooked the female component of migrant streams under the assumption that women migrate as dependents of male breadwinners and are thus only passive participants in the process (Pessar, 1986; Simon and Corona DeLey, 1986). The androcentric assumptions that characterize international labor migration scholarship thus (unwittingly) convey the message that when it comes to migration "women [do] little worth writing about" (Pedraza, 1991: 304).[1]

Though labor migration may once have been the relatively exclusive domain of men, it is no longer. Even in Latin America, where migration streams have long been dominated by males, there is a clear trend toward greater female participation in labor flows to the United States (Fernandez-Kelly and Garcia, 1988; Donato, 1994). Perhaps the best indicator of women's increasing role as labor migrants in their own right is their willingness to assume the risks associated with undocumented migration. Despite long-held and oft-repeated contentions that undocumented migration flows to the United States "are composed overwhelmingly of adult men" (Portes and Bach, 1985: 69, see also Massey et al., 1987: 124), 43% of amnesty applications under the Immigration Reform and Control Act of 1986 were made by females (Immigration and Naturalization Service, 1990: *xxiv*).[2] Recent world-system analyses indicate, furthermore, that secondary sector employers in the U.S. increasingly target immigrant women rather than men as a source of low-wage labor (Sassen, 1988; Fernandez-Kelly, 1994). Given these findings, we must begin to consider the broader implications of a trend in which women migrate and men are increasingly the ones "left behind."

In this article I briefly examine the contributions of world-system analyses in bringing to light the significant economic role that female labor migrants play in the U.S. economy. However, I argue that such macro-economic analyses have failed to cast much light on women as *actors* in the migration process. I also

LINDA MILLER MATTHEI is an Associate Professor of Sociology and Anthropology, East Texas State University, Commerce, TX 75429–3011.

69

question the adequacy of approaches that focus on the household as the appropriate unit of analysis in migration research. Though "household strategies" approaches seem to hold promise for bringing human agency back into the migration process, I point out that abstract theoretical models that purport to explain household economic behavior often obscure the role that women play in migration.

I argue instead that an analytical approach that focuses on migration as a gendered process of transnational network-building can help us to move toward a more socially and culturally grounded conception of a modern world-system in which men *and* women respond to the macro-economic forces that shape and constrain their daily lives. Although the social networks approach has a long history in migration research, and has generated many studies that document the role played by transnational networks in generating and sustaining migrant flows, little attention has been given to women's participation in the building and maintenance of the ties that link migration sending and receiving communities.

A large body of cross-cultural research illustrates that "women-centered" networks serve as significant conduits for the exchange of material goods, services, and employment information in developing societies. I argue that, expanded transnationally, women's networks play a similar role in international migration, linking women who remain in sending communities to remittances and women who seek to migrate to employment opportunities and childcare, and, in some cases, paving the way for a potential return to their communities of origin.

World-System Approaches to Migration

The historical-structural approach developed in world-system analyses provides a powerful conceptual framework for the analysis of global processes that give rise to and structure international labor migration. Unlike "modernization" approaches that explain migration flows as the cumulative responses of individuals to "push" factors (e.g., overpopulation and unemployment) in their places of origin and unrelated "pull" factors (e.g., high labor demands) at potential migration destinations, world-system approaches focus explicitly on the structural inequalities that link societies in a single system, the capitalist world-economy (Portes and Walton, 1981; Sassen-Koob, 1981). Migration, from the world-system perspective, is generated by the penetration and expansion of capitalism and acts as a mechanism for the allocation of labor in the global economy (Sassen-Koob, 1981).

Since the 1980s, historical-structural research has documented an increased demand for female immigrant labor in U.S. cities as a consequence of global restructuring of the production process (e.g., Sassen-Koob, 1984; Morokvasic, 1983). In short, the large-scale relocation of manufacturing to nations in the periphery where wages and operating costs are lower has resulted in the loss of blue-collar manufacturing jobs in the core. Thus, the kinds of jobs once sought by male immigrants have largely disappeared, while at the same time female migrants are sought out for employment in the burgeoning low-wage service sector and the garment and microelectronics industries (Sassen-Koob, 1981, 1984; Fernandez-Kelly and Garcia, 1988). As a number of studies illustrate, employers view immigrant women as an ideal source of labor, citing their presumed docility and willingness to accept tedious, and often temporary, low-wage jobs (Hossfeld, 1994; Fernandez-Kelly, 1994).

The documentation of immigrant women's growing economic role in the U.S. labor market represents a significant contribution to migration research. However, feminist scholars argue that the narrow economic approach used in most world-system analyses presents an impoverished view of women in international migration and in the world-system in general (e.g., Ward, 1993; Grasmuck and Pessar, 1991; Pedraza, 1991). In such analyses gender distinctions in labor migration are often deemed significant only in that women represent more, and men less, exploitable sources of labor. Missing in most of these studies is any sense of women's agency in the migration process. As Mirjana Morokvasic (1983: 18) pointedly notes, "the woman remains silent and invisible, present as a variable, absent as a person."

The Household as Unit of Analysis

Efforts to reintroduce human actors who strategize and respond to political and economic pressures have led some migration researchers to adopt a "house-hold strategies" approach to migration (Wolf, 1992). In these studies, households are typically conceptualized as bounded units of production and consumption that pool and control resources (including labor) and make joint decisions regarding their allocation (Wood, 1981; Smith, Wallerstein, and Dieter-Evers, 1984; Schmink, 1984). Migration is thus viewed as a collective strategy intended to ensure the economic viability of the domestic unit through the strategic allocation of labor.

Although the concept of household strategies *suggests* human agency in the migration process, too often the household is treated as a monolithic, altruistic unit in which individual members subsume their own interests and desires for the good of the collectivity. As a result, the household itself is transformed into a social actor that marshals resources and strategizes to send selected members off into the migration circuit, while the conflicts and negotiations characteristic of real domestic relationships are left unexamined.

Feminist scholars have been particularly critical of the household model's lack of attention to the unequal gender distribution of resources and women's lack of access to power within the household (e.g., Beneria and Roldan, 1987; Blumberg, 1991; Wolf, 1992). The household approach, they argue, overlooks the conflicts inherent in domestic relationships, and as a result women are portrayed as nurturers and nest-builders — the ultimate altruists — who selflessly forego their own needs and desires for the sake of the family. Consequently, any woman "who seeks a paying job, earns a wage, or migrates is interpreted as doing so as part of a household strategy" (Wolf, 1992: 12).

The inadequacies of a generic household model have become increasingly apparent as researchers try to apply theoretical assumptions to "real-life" situations. Cross-cultural studies of migration sending communities illustrate that households (and household members) simply do not always behave like the model assumes they should. Although the household model posits discrete, independent units, ethnographic research indicates that household members often exercise rights and are subject to obligations that extend beyond the household (Guyer, 1981; Whitehead, 1978; Stack, 1974). In addition, sometimes relationships with extra-domestic kin are stronger and more enduring than the marital ties that link men and women in households (Guyer, 1981; Kerns, 1983). Moreover, numerous studies indicate that informal networks of social support play an especially critical role among women in less-developed societies. The arbitrary selection of the household as the locus of migration decision-making and organization, therefore, may obscure rather than cast light on women's agency in the migration process.

Migration as a Process of Network-Building

The role that social networks play in fostering migration is well documented (for a brief summary of the research, see Massey et al., 1987: 5). However, to date there has been relatively little attention to women's participation in migration networks — presumably because researchers still tend to assume that women who migrate are either "sent" by their parents or "brought" by their mates.

When women migrate, the standard argument goes, they do so as dependents of males or they tap into already established male networks. A study of Mexican migration by Massey et al. (1987), for example, is representative of this position. The authors dismiss the notion that females might play any active role in their own migration, especially if it involves surreptitious entry:

> ...most men are reluctant to allow their wives and daughters to undertake
> the hazardous crossing of the border without documents, and women are
> usually afraid to try. When women do go to the United States, it is usually
> only after a male relative has gone before her to arrange legal documen-
> tation or, at least, safe passage across the border.

Ethnographic studies that focus explicitly on gender, however, indicate that despite the concerns and protests of husbands and parents, Mexican women do engage in undocumented migration, often arranging passage on their own or through female relatives and friends (Hondagneu-Sotelo, 1994; Curry-Rodriguez, 1988, cited in Hondagneu-Sotelo; Simon and DeLey, 1986). Other studies based on research in the Dominican Republic (Georges, 1990), Malaysia (Stivens, 1984), Portugal (Brettell, 1996), Turkey (Davis and Heyl, 1986), and the English-speaking Caribbean (Foner, 1986) provide further evidence that women play an active role in organizing their own migration. Cross-cultural research also reveals that women often use migration as an avenue of escape from unhappy marital relationships (e.g., Chavez, 1992; Grasmuck and Pessar, 1991; Foner, 1986). Foner (1986: 139), for example, notes that it is common for married Jamaican women to migrate before their husbands do, and some use the opportunity to "bring about or formalize a separation." For these women the decision to migrate is certainly conditioned more by their ability to marshal support and assistance through transnational networks of kin and friends than it is in consultation with and the aid of household members.

Employment Access Through Social Networks

The role that social networks play in linking male migrants to jobs is well documented in the existing migration literature, but there has been little research on the job-seeking strategies of immigrant women. The research that does exist, however, suggests that women, like men, rely on same-sex kin and friends to find work once they arrive in the United States. In my own research with Garifuna immigrants in Los Angeles, for example, I found that women tend to find initial employment through female kin and friends, most often in some sort of domestic service. Caces (1987) reports similar findings among Filipino women in Hawaii and points out that women who already have some work experience sometimes provide informal training to new arrivals or provide them with contacts at private employment agencies. Several studies also note that women are sometimes able to arrange live-in domestic jobs through kin and friends prior to their arrival in the United States (Hondagneu-Sotelo, 1994: 92–93; Miller, 1993: 150–151; Chavez, 1992; Foner, 1986).

Although migrant women's social networks are clearly effective in linking them to jobs upon arrival in the United States, dependence on same-sex ties may also have a downside. Studies among U.S.-born women indicate that "when women gain jobs through female contacts, these jobs are likely to be sex segregated, female, and low paying since women's networks tend to lack the heterogeneity of those of males" (Smith-Lovin and McPherson, 1993). Thus, although unskilled and inexperienced immigrant women who would otherwise find it difficult to get jobs clearly benefit from the use of ties to other women, for skilled and professional women same-sex networks may not be so beneficial. Women who pursued careers as secretaries and teachers in their home communities often find that their networks in the U.S. link them only to low-wage service jobs as domestics and nurse's aides (Colen, 1986: 48; Miller, 1993; Hondagneu-Sotelo, 1994). Again, research in this area is nearly nonexistent, but it would be interesting to see if immigrant women who do tap into male networks or use formal methods of employment acquisition find a wider array of opportunities available to them.

Settlement and the Persistence of Transnational Ties

In general, migration researchers argue that as migrants accumulate time in receiving societies, they begin to put down social and economic roots. As they buy homes, make friends, and raise children in the U.S., the argument goes, they begin to view themselves as "settlers" rather than "sojourners," and their ties to their communities of origin gradually weaken. These arguments are consistent with more general findings in social networks research, which indicate that geographic distance and infrequent contact increase the difficulty of maintaining strong ties (Granovetter, 1974; Wellman and Wortley, 1989).

Recent research — mostly by anthropologists — suggests, however, that social and economic ties between migrants and the folks back home often persist over extended periods of time. Contrary to the notion that the orientation of migrants changes from home to host society as time goes by, Basch et al. (1994) provide substantial evidence that even immigrants who have spent decades in the U.S. often have deep commitments and substantial involvement in the cultural, political, and economic spheres of their nations of origin.

Why do some migrants continue to nurture these transnational ties long after they have seemingly settled in the United States? Despite the strong demand for immigrant labor, for many migrants — especially undocumented ones — life in the U.S. is fraught with uncertainty. Their status as "foreigners," which is often coupled with racism, social isolation, and persistent fears of deportation, makes them reluctant to burn their bridges to their homelands. Thus, they "keep their options open" by maintaining social and economic safety nets in their countries of origin (Glick Schiller et al., 1992: 11).

Gender and Social Networks

Though critical of theoretical approaches that fail to give adequate attention to issues of gender, feminist scholars themselves are sometimes guilty of perpetuating a one-dimensional image of women as "passive victims" of patriarchal domination (Beneria and Roldan, 1987; Wolf, 1992). In focusing almost exclusively on the negative *consequences* women experience as a result of capitalist penetration of developing economies, feminist efforts to "bring gender in" to migration research have often produced analyses that emphasize women's economic dependence on males (e.g., Ward, 1985). According to this "woman as victim" approach, women lose power and resources because their access to the social and economic support of kin back home is cut off when they migrate (see Ward, 1985; Boyd, 1986). Yet can we assume that the ties that link women to their kin are really that brittle?

There is a large body of cross-cultural research that indicates that "women-centered" networks play a critical role in facilitating the flow of goods, services, and information in industrialized *and* developing societies. "Gynocentricity,...the tendency for females to be more emotionally involved and active in kinship interaction than males" (Poggie and Pelto, 1976: 249, quoted in Yanagisako, 1977: 216), has been described in a variety of research settings. Yanagisako, in her study of women-centered networks among Japanese-Americans, observes that women, as "kin keepers," maintain closer communication with kin than males do. According to Yanagisako, women "know the details of kin ties and facilitate communication among households and other groupings of kin" (1977: 211). Stivens argues similarly that among middle-class women in Australia, kinship is "women's business." She adds, moreover, that even when men are the family's financial managers, women often have "considerable say" in the flow of economic aid between families (1984: 189). In her classic study of kinship networks, Elizabeth Bott (1957) also describes a "matrilateral stress" in some of the kinship networks of working and middle-class Londoners and suggests that women's efforts to ensure some measure of economic security may motivate them to foster kin ties. As Bott puts it: "Husbands and fathers might die or desert, but women could use their maternal kin as an informal insurance policy for themselves and their children" (1957: 138).

A substantial body of cross-cultural research suggests that extra-domestic networks play a particularly critical role in the economic survival of families in less-developed societies. In her study of the exchange networks of Mexican shantytown residents, Lomnitz points out that most families "have literally nothing. Their only resources are of a social nature: kinship and friendship ties that generate social solidarity" (1977: 3). According to Lomnitz, women are key actors in the networks that facilitate the flow of goods and services between households:

> The shantytown woman is rugged and accustomed to hardship. She knows her role is essential in the social fabric, especially in the networks of reciprocal exchange on which her economic security depends.... The woman, through her role in centralizing networks of reciprocal exchange, is often the key to survival.

Neuhouser reports similar findings among urban immigrants in Brazil, where sporadic access to employment and income prompts families to engage in exchanges of gifts, loans, and childcare. Like Lomnitz, Neuhouser argues that women are usually the anchors of such networks, "and men often become involved only as a function of their relationships to women members" (1989: 698–699).

Female-led networks are not unique to Latin America; ethnographic studies from less-developed societies throughout Africa, Asia, and the Caribbean document similar patterns of network-building by women seeking to assure an adequate flow of resources into their households in economically unstable environments (e.g., Stivens, 1984; Guyer, 1981; Wong, 1984; Barrow, 1986).

Given these findings, can we assume that the pressures motivating women to build support networks disappear when they migrate? Do migrant women turn over responsibility for the maintenance of transnational ties to their husbands and brothers? What of nonmigrant women — do they limit themselves to local sources of support when members of their networks migrate? Despite the lack of explicit attention to gender in migration networks, there is evidence to suggest that both migrant and nonmigrant women play strategic roles in maintaining transnational networks.

Building and Maintaining Transnational Networks

To date, there has been little research done on nonmigrant women. In those studies that have focused on their experiences, moreover, they are typically portrayed not as actors in the process, but as victims of it — they are merely the "women who wait" or "the women left behind." Women do, of course, experience social and economic hardships as a result of extensive male out-migration, but there is increasing evidence that they do not simply sit back and suffer in silence. In a recently published study, Pierette Hondagneu-Sotelo says, for example, that Mexican wives left behind by their migrant mates often use their ties to other women to subvert their husband's authority and initiate their own migration to the United States:

> Return migrant women and sisters and friends in the U.S. encouraged women to go north and helped write letters imploring their husbands for permission to migrate; when this strategy didn't yield results, they lent money for travel costs and *coyote* assistance, sometimes unbeknownst to the men. In some cases...husbands, much to their chagrin, did not learn of their wives' and children's migration until after the fact (1994: 72).

Of course, not all women migrate, but many still assiduously cultivate their ties to migrant kin in the United States in order to establish a flow of remittances. Since income-generating opportunities for women are usually limited in migration-sending societies, they often ensure a regular flow of money and goods by offering to care for the children of daughters and sisters who have left to find work or join their mates in the United States (Soto, 1987; Miller, 1993). Although this practice of "child fostering" is most often associated with the English-speaking Caribbean and various African societies, it is also a generalized strategy among Puerto Rican and Dominican migrants (Soto, 1987; Georges, 1990). It appears that child fostering is becoming increasingly common in Mexico also as women join their male counterparts in international labor migration. Chavez (1992: 122), for example, notes that "most" single mothers leave their children with their mothers, sisters, or other relatives for varying lengths of time while they work in the United States.

Child fostering provides nonmigrant women with a relatively stable source of remittances from migrant kin, but it provides other potential benefits as well. In addition to the money she receives, a woman who fosters the children of migrants builds a reservoir of social capital that she can draw upon to launch her own migration or that of her children. Moreover, since she plays a vital role in maintaining the ties that link potential migrants to kin in the U.S., she ultimately holds a good deal of power in determining which members of her household will be selected for migration (Miller, 1993).

The advantages of building and maintaining strong transnational ties are perhaps clearest for nonmigrant women. However, migrant women often face extraordinary social and economic pressures in the United States that make them equally eager to nurture close relationships with the folks back home. Concentrated in inner-city areas where crime rates, the drug trade, and gang activity have become facts of life, immigrant parents are increasingly reluctant to raise children in the United States (Basch et al., 1994; Gmelch, 1992; Miller, 1993). As a result, child fostering arrangements, initially devised as temporary mechanisms to free women from childcare responsibilities during their initial settlement in the United States, have become more permanent. Since women bear the primary responsibility for childcare, they typically set up child fostering arrangements with their own kin back home; they also make regular visits and phone calls to ensure that their children's needs are being met in their absence (Brydon and Chant, 1989; see also Chavez, 1992; Basch et al., 1994). As a result of their responsibilities as mothers, then, women are positioned to maintain closer contact with their home communities than are their male counterparts (Soto, 1987).

Although childcare needs clearly induce women to nurture ties to nonmigrant kin, economic pressures in the U.S. also make women unwilling to burn their bridges. For migrant women, employment in the U.S. only rarely offers financial security and upward mobility. Unlike immigrant males, who are found in a fairly wide variety of occupations in the U.S., about half of females are concentrated in two occupational categories — operatives and services (Sassen, 1988: 77). Often lacking educational credentials and employment skills, female immigrants are drawn into dead-end jobs in garment factories and electronic assembly plants where employers often view them as supplemental wage earners and pay them accordingly (Hossfeld, 1994; Fernandez-Kelly, 1994). Such plants are rarely unionized and, as a result, workers often have few benefits and little job security.[3]

Although the garment and electronics industries have become significant sources of employment for immigrant women, many still spend their working lives in the U.S. as housekeepers, aides to the elderly, and nannies in private homes. There are, of course, certain advantages associated with domestic employment. Jobs are widely available even during periods of economic depression, and they are relatively easy to find through women's personal networks (Foner, 1986; Miller, 1993). In addition, prospective employers typically do not ask for legal documents. Indeed, working in a private home may be the "safest" employment option for women seeking to avoid detection by immigration officials (Simon and DeLey, 1986).

Moreover, women who "live-in" needn't assume the expense of establishing their own households and can begin to send remittances home almost immediately. The advantages of domestic work may be apparent to men as well. For example, a man I interviewed in Belize offered the following assessment of live-in work:

> It's a very profitable job — very profitable, I say, because that woman has a salary she receives, then she do not pay rent, she do not pay food, she do not pay utilities, etc., etc., — and that make it very profitable. So your income is an income. That's the way I see it. But it's not so with men, you know.

Despite the immediate advantages of domestic work, however, there are also significant risks. Because their employers are often aware of their undocumented status, domestic workers are vulnerable to a variety of abuses including sexual harassment, prolonged work days, sub-poverty level salaries, and, in some cases, complete lack of payment for their services (Foner, 1986; Chavez, 1992; Colen, 1986). The long-term risks involved in domestic work are most significant, however. With few (if any) formal benefits such as health insurance or retirement pensions, women who have spent decades working in the U.S. must often look to informal sources of support to offset the economic risks posed by extended illnesses, deportation, and periodic unemployment. Rather than depositing their meager earnings in savings accounts, some women invest in houses and small businesses back home where they can live more cheaply than in the United States and perhaps produce a small income as well (Miller, 1993; Basch et al., 1994). Others send regular remittances to kin in order to ensure that they will be welcomed back should circumstances force them to leave the United States. Shellee Colen (1986: 62) states, for example, that all of the domestic and childcare workers she interviewed in New York sent regular remittances to friends and family back home. She estimates, moreover, that remittances of money and gifts may account for 20 to 75% of domestic workers' incomes.

No matter what kind of work they do in the United States, we might expect undocumented women to be particularly diligent about sending remittances home since apprehension by immigration officials might result in deportation. Simon and DeLey's (1986: 129) findings suggest that this is indeed the case. In their sample of Mexican women immigrants, 40% of undocumented women sent remittances, while only 23% of documented women did.[4] Additional research is needed to more fully uncover the extent of women's transnational remittances and the role they play in offsetting the economic uncertainty they experience in the United States. However, the limited evidence that is currently available certainly suggests that women actively nurture transnational ties.

Some Avenues for Future Research

In this article, I have pulled together research from a variety of mostly ethnographic sources to shed some light on the roles that migrant *and* nonmigrant women play as agents in international labor migration. Contrary to long-held assumptions in migration research that males are the primary actors in international labor migration, I have argued that there is substantial, though somewhat fragmentary, evidence that both migrant and nonmigrant women are actively involved and play a central role in building and maintaining the transnational networks that link migration sending and receiving societies.

There is, of course, still much work to be done before we can develop an adequate understanding of the role that gender plays in shaping the migration process. Research on the role that immigrant women's networks play in linking them to jobs in the United States is one area that clearly needs greater attention. We also need to learn more about the extent of women's remittances to their communities of origin and the various ways that money earned in the United States is used to build social and economic safety nets back home and pave the way for potential return.

Recently, interest in the broader implications of migrants' international networks has prompted a small group of researchers to examine the role that international social ties play in the development of "transnational enterprises" (Basch et al., 1994; Portes, 1995). The theoretical implications for world-system analyses are most clearly developed in a recent paper by Alejandro Portes. Briefly, Portes (1995: 11–13) states that migrants are drawn to the U.S. by the demand for low-wage labor, but soon become aware that they are unlikely to achieve the "American Dream" given the restricted employment opportunities and low wages they face in the United States. To circumvent these restrictions, migrants have begun to tap into the resources available through their transnational networks in order to invest the resources they have accumulated in the U.S. in a variety of economic enterprises in the communities from which they migrated. Through periodic trips back and forth between their sending communities and the U.S., these transnational entrepreneurs not only sell their wares, but also recruit new immigrant investors. "What makes these enterprises transnational," says Portes, "is not only that they are created by former immigrants, but that they depend for their existence on continuing ties to the United States" (p. 13).

As Portes makes clear, the viability of these enterprises is dependent on the information and resources that can be marshaled through transnational networks. To date, the research on these transnational enterprises has focused only on immigrants undifferentiated by gender. Yet there is certainly reason to suspect, I think, that women may play a critical role if not so much as entrepreneurs themselves, then as "information brokers" linking individuals to opportunities. There is certainly fertile ground for further research here.

NOTES

1.   Perhaps not surprisingly, most studies that have begun to examine migration as a gendered process are done by female scholars (e.g., Sassen-Koob, 1981, 1988; Morokvasic, 1982; Fernandez-Kelly, 1981; Grasmuck and Pessar, 1991).

2.   Though women's applications for amnesty nearly equaled those of males, far fewer women than men actually legalized their status under the IRCA provisions. Perhaps this is because women, who are more likely to have been employed in the informal sector as housekeepers and nannies, were unable to provide the documentation required for legalization.

3.   The proportion of women who head households may, in fact, be substantial. Karen Hossfeld (1994: 74) reports that 80% of the immigrant women she interviewed in the Silicon Valley semiconductor industry were "the main income earners in their families." Simon and DeLey (1986: 128) also report that the undocumented Mexican women in their study were likely "to be on their own economically."

4.   Though remittances provide a measure of security for migrant women, they can also become a substantial burden as the following interview excerpt with a Haitian woman illustrates:

> Since I was a young girl, I supported my whole family, you hear? Now that I've come to N.Y., it's worse. I have bills here and there to pay.... If I quit my job now, what would I do for the bills here and in Haiti? Because once the month starts, in 15 days, they start watching the mail to see when I am sending the money. Well, I can tell you, if I leave my job, my whole family would die, because I'm the one who keeps them afloat (Kerner, 1991: 4, quoted in Basch et al., 1994).

REFERENCES

Barrow, Christine
1986   "Finding the Support: A Study of Strategies for Survival." Social and
                  Economic Studies 35,2: 131–175.
Basch, Linda, Nina Glick Schiller, and Cristina Szanton Blanc
1994   Nations Unbound: Transnational Projects, Postcolonial Predicaments, and
                  Deterritorialized Nation-States. United States: Gordon and Breach Publishers.
Beneria, Lourdes and Martha Roldan
1987   The Crossroads of Class and Gender: Industrial Housework, Subcontracting,
                  and Household Dynamics in Mexico City. Chicago: University of Chicago
                  Press.
Blumberg, Rae Lesser
1991   "Introduction: The Triple Overlap of Gender Stratification, Economy, and the
                  Family." Gender, Family, and Economy: The Triple Overlap. Newbury Park:
                  Sage Publications: 7–32.
Bott, Elizabeth
1957   Family and Social Network: Roles, Norms, and External Relationships in
                  Ordinary Urban Families. London: Tavistock.
Boyd, Monica
1986   "Immigrant Women in Canada." Rita J. Simon and Caroline B. Brettell (eds.),
                  International Migration: The Female Experience. Totowa, New Jersey:
                  Rowman and Allanheld: 45–61.
Brettell, Caroline B.
1996   "Women Are Migrants Too: A Portuguese Perspective." George Gmelch and
                  Walter P. Zenner (eds.), Urban Life. Prospect Heights, Illinois: Waveland
                  Press: 245–258.

Brydon, Lynn and Sylvia Chant
    1989   Women in the Third World: Gender Issues in Rural and Urban Areas.
                 Aldershot, England: Edgar Elgar Publishing, Ltd.

Chaney, Elsa
    1982   "Women Who Go, and the Women Who Stay Behind." Migration Today
                 10,3–4: 8–13.

Chavez, Leo R.
    1992   Shadowed Lives: Undocumented Immigrants in American Society. Fort
                 Worth: Harcourt Brace Jovanovich.

Colen, Shellee
    1986   "With Respect and Feelings: Voices of West Indian Child Care and Domestic
                 Workers in New York City." Johnetta B. Cole (ed.), All American Women.
                 New York: The Free Press: 46–70.

Curry-Rodriguez, Julia E.
    1988   "Labor Migration and Familial Responsibilities: Experiences of Mexican
                 Women." Margarita B. Melville (ed.), Mexicanas at Work in the United States.
                 Boulder: Westview Press: 47–63.

Davis, F. James and Barbara Sherman Heyl
    1986   "Turkish Women and Guestworker Migration to West Germany." Rita J.
                 Simon and Caroline B. Brettel (eds.), International Migration: The Female
                 Experience. Totowa, New Jersey: Rowman and Allanheld: 178–196.

Donato, Katharine M.
    1994   "U.S. Policy and Mexican Migration to the United States, 1942–1992." Social
                 Science Quarterly 75,4: 705–729.

Fernandez-Kelly, M. Patricia
    1994   "Broadening the Scope: Gender and International Development." A. Douglas
                 Kincaid and Alejandro Portes (eds.), Comparative National Development.
                 Chapel Hill: The University of North Carolina Press: 143–168.

Fernandez-Kelly, M. Patricia and Anna M. Garcia
    1988   "Invisible Amidst the Glitter: Hispanic Women in the Southern California
                 Electronics Industry." Anne Statham, Eleanor M. Miller, and Hans O.
                 Mauksch (eds.), The Worth of Women's Work: A Qualitative Synthesis.
                 Albany: State University of New York: 265–290.

Foner, Nancy
    1986   "Sex Roles and Sensibilities: Jamaican Women in New York and London."
                 Rita J. Simon and Caroline B. Brettell (eds.), International Migration: The
                 Female Experience. Totowa, New Jersey: Rowman and Allanheld: 133–151.

Georges, Eugenia
    1990   The Making of a Transnational Community: Migration, Development, and
                 Cultural Change in the Dominican Republic. New York: Columbia University
                 Press.

Glick Schiller, Nina, Linda Basch, and Cristina Szanton Blanc
    1992   Towards a Transnational Perspective on Migration. New York: New York
                 Academy of Sciences.

Gmelch, George
    1992   Double Passage: The Lives of Caribbean Migrants Abroad and Back Home.
                 Ann Arbor: The University of Michigan Press.

Granovetter, Mark
    1974   Getting a Job: A Study of Contacts and Careers. Cambridge: Harvard
                 University Press.

Grasmuck, Sherri and Patricia R. Pessar
    1991   Between Two Islands: Dominican International Migration. Berkeley:
                 University of California Press.

Guyer, Jane
    1981   "Household and Community in African Studies." African Studies Review
                 24,2–3: 87–137.

Hondagneu-Sotelo, Pierrette
    1994   Gendered Transitions: Mexican Experiences of Immigration. Berkeley:
                    University of California Press.
Hossfeld, Karen J.
    1994   "Hiring Immigrant Women: Silicon Valley's Simple Formula." Maxine Baca
                    Zinn and Bonnie Thornton Dill (eds.), Women of Color in U.S. Society.
                    Philadelphia: Temple University Press: 65–94.
Houston, Marion F., Roger G. Kramer, and Joan Mackin Barrett
    1984   "Female Predominance in Immigration to the United States Since 1930: A
                    First Look." International Migration Review 18,4: 908–961.
Immigration and Naturalization Service
    1990   Statistical Yearbook of the Immigration and Naturalization Service.
Kerns, Virginia
    1983   Women and the Ancestors: Black Carib Kinship and Ritual. Urbana:
                    University of Illinois Press.
Lomnitz, Larissa
    1977   Networks and Marginality: Life in a Mexican Shantytown. New York:
                    Academic Press.
Massey, Douglas S., Rafael Alarcon, Jorge Durand, and Humberto Gonzalez
    1987   Return to Aztlan. Berkeley: University of California Press.
Miller [Matthei], Linda R.
    1993   Bridges: Garifuna Migration to Los Angeles. Unpublished Ph.D. dissertation,
                    University of California, Irvine.
Morokvasic, Mirjana
    1983   "Women in Migration: Beyond the Reductionist Outlook." Annie Phizacklea
                    (ed.), One Way Ticket: Migration and Female Labour. London: Routledge and
                    Kegan Paul: 13–31.
Neuhouser, Kevin
    1989   "Sources of Women's Power and Status Among the Urban Poor in Contempo-
                    rary Brazil." Signs 14: 685–702.
Pedraza, Silvia
    1991   "Women and Migration: The Social Consequences of Gender." Annual
                    Review of Sociology 17: 303–325.
Pessar, Patricia
    1986   "The Role of Gender in Dominican Settlement in the United States." June
                    Nash and Helen Safa (eds.), Women and Change in Latin America. Massachu-
                    setts: Bergin and Garvey Publishers, Inc.: 273–294.
Piore, Michael J.
    1979   Birds of Passage: Migrant Labor and Industrial Societies. London: Cambridge
                    University Press.
Poggie, John J. and Pertti J. Pelto
    1976   "Matrilateral Asymmetry in the American Kinship System." John J. Poggie et al.
                    (eds.), The Evolution of Human Adaptations. New York: Macmillan: 247–258.
Portes, Alejandro
    1995   "Transnational Communities: Their Emergence and Significance in the
                    Contemporary World System." Keynote address delivered at the 19th Annual
                    Conference on the Political Economy of the World-System.
Portes, Alejandro and Robert L. Bach
    1985   Latin Journey: Cuban and Mexican Immigrants in the United States. Berkeley:
                    University of California Press.
Portes, Alejandro and John Walton
    1981   Labor, Class, and the International System. Orlando: Academic Press.
Rubenstein, Hymie
    1987   Coping with Poverty: Adaptive Strategies in a Caribbean Village. Boulder:
                    Westview Press.

Sassen, Saskia
1988   The Mobility of Labor and Capital: A Study in International Investment and
            Labor Flow. Cambridge: Cambridge University Press.
Sassen-Koob, Saskia
1984   "Notes on the Incorporation of Third World Women into Wage-Labor
            Through Immigration and Off-Shore Production." International Migration
            Review 18,2: 1144–1167.
1981   "Labor Migration and the New Industrial Division of Labor." June Nash and
            M. Patricia Fernandez Kelly (eds.), Women, Men, and the International
            Division of Labor. Albany: Sate University of New York: 175–204.
Schmink, Marianne
1984   "Household Economic Strategies." Latin American Research Review 19: 87–
            100.
Simon, Rita J. and Margo Corona DeLey
1986   "Undocumented Mexican Women: Their Work and Personal Experiences."
            Rita J. Simon and Caroline B. Brettell (eds.), International Migration: The
            Female Experience. Totowa, New Jersey: Rowman and Allanheld: 113–132.
Smith, Joan, Immanuel Wallerstein, and Hans Dieter Evers
1984   Households and the World-Economy. Beverly Hills: Sage Publications.
Smith-Lovin, Lynn and J. Miller McPherson
1993   "You Are Who You Know: A Network Approach to Gender." Paula England
            (ed.), Theory on Gender/Feminism on Theory. New York: Aldine De Gruyter:
            223–251.
Soto, Isa Maria
1987   "West Indian Child Fostering: Its Role in Migrant Exchanges." Constance R.
            Sutton and Elsa M. Chaney (eds.), Caribbean Life in New York City. New
            York: Center for Migration Studies, Inc.
Stack, Carol
1974   All Our Kin: Strategies for Survival in a Black Community. New York:
            Harper and Row.
Stivens, Maila
1984   "Women, Kinship, and Capitalist Development." Kate Young, Carol
            Wolkowitz, and Roslynn McCullogh (eds.), Of Marriage and the Market.
            London: Routledge and Kegan Paul: 179–192.
Thadani, Veena N. and Michael P. Todaro
1984   "Female Migration: A Conceptual Framework." James T. Fawcett, Siew-Ean
            Khoo, and Peter C. Smith (eds.), Women in the Cities of Asia: Migration and
            Urban Adaptation. Boulder: Westview Press: 36–59.
Ward, Kathryn
1993   "Reconceptualizing World System Theory to Include Women." Paula England
            (ed.), Theory on Gender/Feminism on Theory. New York: Aldine De Gruyter:
            43–68.
1985   "Women and Urbanization in the World-System." Michael Timberlake (ed.),
            Urbanization in the World-Economy. New York: Academic Press: 305–
            323.
Wellman, Barry and Scott Wortley
1989   "Different Strokes from Different Folks: Which Type of Ties Provide What
            Kind of Social Support?" Research Paper No. 174. Centre for Urban and
            Community Studies, University of Toronto.
Whitehead, Tony L.
1978   "Residence, Kinship, and Mating as Survival Strategies: A West Indian
            Example." Journal of Marriage and the Family 40,4: 817–828.
Wolf, Diane L.
1992   Factory Daughters: Gender, Household Dynamics, and Rural Industrialization
            in Java. Berkeley: University of California Press.

Wong, Diana
    1984   "The Limits of Using the Household as a Unit of Analysis." Joan Smith, Immanuel Wallerstein, and Hans Dieter-Evers (eds.), Households and the World Economy. Beverly Hills, Cal.: Sage Publications.

Wood, Charles
    1981   "Equilibrium and Historical-Structural Perspectives on Migration." International Migration Review 16: 298–319.

Yanagisako, Sylvia J.
    1977   "Women-Centered Kin Networks in Urban Bilateral Kinship." American Ethnologist 3: 207–226.

Are Immigration Controls Ethical?

John Isbister

A MERICANS TYPICALLY EXPRESS THEIR OPINIONS ABOUT IMMIGRATION WITH certainty and moral outrage. This article argues that many of us are in an ethically fraught position with respect to immigration, however. We have deeply held convictions about the equality of all people. At the same time, though, we use immigration policy to perpetuate a privileged lifestyle at the expense of foreigners. We are not prepared to abandon either this use of immigration policy or the ideology of equality. At the very least, therefore, our moral stance should be one of humility, not outrage.[1]

The moral muddle in which we find ourselves arises in part because of a tendency to confuse our interests with ethics; we persuade ourselves that what is best for us is best, period. It is not.

Most of the current debate about immigration has to do with the national interest or with the interests of various groups inside the U.S. Elsewhere I have explored the interests of Americans with respect to immigration (Isbister, 1996). Briefly, I think that from an economic point of view, some Americans are helped and others are hurt by immigration. On the whole, the former tend to be at the top of the income ladder, the latter at the bottom. Economics is not everything, however, Bill Clinton's 1992 presidential campaign to the contrary notwithstanding. Immigration is transforming the social structure of the U.S., changing it from a white country with several minority groups into a genuinely multicultural country in which no ethnic group will prevail, all ethnic groups will be able to meet each other on a basis of relative equality, and the possibilities for mutual enrichment rather than suspicion, exploitation, and racism will be enhanced. Since this social transformation is so important to the U.S., I think that the interest of the country lies in welcoming relatively large numbers of immigrants. The numbers cannot be unlimited, however, since the maintenance of one of the world's highest standards of living requires some restrictions on the inflow of newcomers.

Interests of Americans are central; the national political system responds, it can be argued, to nothing else. Interests are not synonymous with morality, however. By definition, the national interest excludes the interests of foreigners.

JOHN ISBISTER is a Professor of Economics and Provost of Merrill College at the University of California, Santa Cruz, CA 95064. This article is based on material in *The Immigration Debate: Remaking America* (1996, Kumarian Press). The author would like to thank Peter Isbister, Susanne Jonas, Sherri Paris, and Roz Spafford for their suggestions.

It would be a curious ethical system that denied moral standing to some people simply because of the accident of their nationality. The ethics of immigration controls require investigation, therefore, separate from the interests that Americans have in immigration. In the end, of course, interests will count more than ethics in the formulation of national immigration policy. We would do well, however, to keep in mind the conflict between the two perspectives.

Equal Moral Worth

The equal moral worth of all people is the principle on which the ethical arguments in this article are grounded. Philosophers have made many attempts to demonstrate equal worth.[2] For the most part, however, those of us who believe in equality treat it as an assumption, an axiom, not something to be proven. The axiom of equal worth is at the core of the two most important statements of political philosophy in U.S. history, the Declaration of Independence and the Gettysburg Address.

In the Declaration of Independence, Thomas Jefferson wrote, "We hold these Truths to be self-evident, that all Men are created equal." He did not argue the point; it was "self-evident." The importance of equality was that equal rights accrue to all people: "They are endowed by their Creator with certain unalienable Rights, that among these are Life, Liberty, and the Pursuit of Happiness."

Neither Jefferson nor his Virginian compatriots conducted their lives in accordance with these "Truths," for they were slave holders. Similarly today, most people do not base their actions on a commitment to the equality of all people. Nevertheless, many of us believe in equality, not because we have reasoned it out and considered the arguments pro and con, but because it is "self-evident."

The radical equality of the Declaration of Independence was restricted sharply by the more conservative Constitution of 1789, a document that among other things protected slavery. As Gary Wills has argued, however, Abraham Lincoln's Gettysburg Address of 1863 had the effect of subverting the Constitution by restoring equality as the central American value (Wills, 1992). It began, in words now as familiar to Americans as those of the Declaration, and more familiar than any in the Constitution, "Fourscore and seven years ago, our fathers brought forth upon this continent a new nation, conceived in liberty and dedicated to the proposition that all men are created equal."

Neither document says "all Americans are created equal." Jefferson and Lincoln may or may not have implied "people" by their use of the word "men," but in our current reading, we do. These most formative of American documents assume the equality of all human beings.

People are equally valuable and therefore have equal rights. It does not follow from this that they have unlimited rights. Rights often conflict one with another; when they do, the liberal state (that is, the state based on the presumption of equal worth) is justified in restricting some rights, in order to protect others. Whenever it restricts rights, however, the state must be able to give morally justifiable why it has done so — else it forfeits its claim to liberalism and descend despotism.

An Argument for Open Borders

Immigration controls restrict free movement by establishing groups that have unequal rights. Among the people who wish to live in the U.S., some favored ones are allowed to, while others are not. Can one successfully argue that, while immigration controls infringe on some people's liberties, they are justified because they protect more important rights and liberties? Or does their allocation of unequal rights to people who are of equal worth make them morally impermissible?

Freedom of movement is a facet of the "Liberty" that the Declaration of Independence takes to be an inherent right of equal human beings. Countries that systematically restrict the movement of their people are rightly criticized. In recent years, the clearest example of the morally unjustified restriction of internal movement was in South Africa, which enforced its apartheid system with pass laws.

As a mental exercise, one could ask how a law passed by the residents of the city of New York, restricting the permanent entry of Americans who were not city residents, would be judged. Leaving aside the fact that it would be unconstitutional, would it be morally justified? The people of New York could offer some good reasons for the law. New York is already crowded and cannot tolerate further population growth, they might argue. The sanitation system is close to breaking down, the schools are crowded, the welfare system is bankrupt, the homeless shelters are inadequate, and the unemployment rate is rising.

These sorts of arguments would not prove convincing to most Americans, who would find the restriction on personal freedom too onerous. Every day, people migrate into (and out of) New York for compelling reasons. They move in order to accept a job or to look for a job or because their job has been relocated to New York. They could not have the same job in Boston or Chicago because New York is unique (as also Boston and Chicago are). They move to New York to be with their family or to care for a friend or for one of any number of other reasons. The decision to migrate to New York is seldom taken lightly; people have good reasons. The interests that New Yorkers may have in restricting entry, while perhaps meritorious, are not of sufficient weight to permit such massive violations of the rights and interests of outsiders. Morally, New York could not justify an immigration policy of its own.

If this argument is accepted, how can one accept immigration restrictions in the U.S.? What makes the U.S. fundamentally different from New York? Nothing much, except sovereign power.

Reasoning by analogy, it is difficult to find an ethical justification for the United States to restrict entry across its borders. In fact, it is more difficult, since the people of the U.S. are privileged, *vis-à-vis* the rest of the world, in a way that the residents of New York are not, in comparison to other Americans. New Yorkers could argue plausibly that among U.S. cities, their city is not so special, that people denied entry into it could find comparable amenities in other cities. The U.S. occupies a unique position in the world, however, or at least the long lines of potential immigrants would so indicate. The great majority of immigrants and potential immigrants hope to enjoy a significantly higher standard of living in the U.S. than they experienced in their home countries. Immigration controls on the U.S. border therefore restrict access to privilege.

It is the protection of privilege that is so damaging, ethically, to the country's immigration laws. It makes U.S. border controls even less justifiable than New York's would be. The purpose and effect of U.S. immigration controls are to maintain a state of inequality in the world between the haves (the Americans) and the have-nots (the foreigners, especially the potential immigrants). Americans maintain immigration laws because they fear that unrestricted entry would lead to a major influx of people, that the newcomers would compete for scarce resources and jobs in the U.S. and that they would drive down the standard of living of residents. No doubt it is in the interest of the privileged to protect their privileges, but it cannot be ethical if that protection has the effect of further disadvantaging the unprivileged.

The ethical case against immigration controls is based, therefore, not just on the fact that they convey unequal rights to morally equal people, but that they do so in a particularly damaging way, so as to protect advantage and deepen disadvantage. To understand the importance of this, one can consider the argument that some types of unequal treatment are morally justified. For example, a system of preferential hiring in which race is taken into account treats different groups of people unequally, but it may be fair if it is designed to benefit people who have been exploited or to dismantle a system of racial injustice (Wasserstrom, 1986). Unequal treatment is clearly unjust, however, when it is used to perpetuate rather than break down a system of privilege and disadvantage. This is just what U.S. immigration controls do. They violate the equal worth and equal rights of people in an egregious way, by sheltering already advantaged Americans at the expense of relatively disadvantaged potential immigrants.

Arguments for Immigration Controls

This section considers six ethical arguments that are made in favor of immigration controls, in ascending order of persuasiveness. They are not the only arguments made in the academic literature and the political discourse, but they seem to me to be the strongest.[3] In the end, I find that the first five are rationalizations used to perpetuate a structure of advantage and disadvantage in the world while allowing Americans to avoid this truth, and that their moral logic fails. The sixth argument, however, has merit and leaves us with a conflict of rights.

1. *"Immigration is theft."* It is argued that the U.S., with all its wealth, is the property of Americans, to treat as they wish. Immigrants want to share in the country's wealth, but they have no right to it unless Americans willingly offer it to them. People have the legal and moral right to protect their property against theft. They are under no obligation to give it away.

Is the country the private property of Americans? Can one say that Americans own the U.S., just as an individual owns a house? Or would a better analogy be to a public beach? Whoever arrives first on a secluded beach would perhaps like to claim title and keep others from access to it, but the first-comer has no right to do so, because the beach is common property. International law gives Americans the legal right to treat the country as their private house, but I think that morally the U.S. has more of the characteristics of a public beach.

The U.S. is both a land area and the society that has been built on it. As to the land itself, Americans are in a weak position to claim exclusive ownership of it, since they are such recent arrivals themselves. Most Americans are only a few generations removed from immigration. If they were to take seriously the claim of prior ownership, they would have to return the land to the descendants of the Native Americans, whom their forbears pushed aside and slaughtered. They are not prepared to do this. They cannot successfully claim, therefore, that a new wave of entrants has fewer rights of access to the land than their immigrant predecessors did.

The U.S. is more than the land, however; it is the improvements as well. Today the U.S. is far different from the place the settlers wrested from the Natives. It is now a rich country — and it is because of its standard of living, not its land mass, that it is a Mecca for immigrants. Can Americans claim that they created the wealth they enjoy and that they therefore have the sole right to decide whether and which foreigners have access to it? I think not.

For the most part, Americans now living did not create the wealth; they inherited it. At the time they were born, the U.S. was already one of the world's richest countries and its wealth was growing rapidly. If anything, the collective actions of Americans over the last quarter century have diminished their inheritance. By living beyond their means, both personally and publicly, Americans have actually lowered the standard of living of a good many people. They are living off their inheritance.

In other words, Americans now living found a lovely beach; they did not build or buy a new house. Since they are not responsible for their good fortune, they do not have the moral right to deny other people the opportunity to share in it.

Not so, Americans might reply. We have a right to our inheritance. Our ancestors built this country not just for their own pleasure, but for the well-being of their children. If one could ask them who has a claim to the riches they built up, they would reply that it is we, their descendants.

This argument is not silly, but it is not transparently valid either. Inheritance presents ethical difficulties. Ordinary, small inheritances are certainly morally justifiable, since they represent a simple expression of family love. Just as a mother cares for her baby, so does she want to pass some of her gains on to her children after her death. To want to do so is not wrong; indeed, to fail to do so would be thought by most people to mark a lack of parental love. It is when inheritance is so substantial that it perpetuates a system of privilege and disadvantage that it lacks moral justification, since it violates the norms of equal access, equal opportunity, and equal treatment, the norms that follow from the axiom of equal worth. Americans would reject as immoral the rigid class system of medieval Europe or the caste system of India, in which one's prospects in life were completely determined by the accident of birth. That sort of inheritance is immoral. It is just the sort of inheritance that Americans as a whole have received from their ancestors, an inheritance that gives them enormously greater privilege than most of the rest of humankind. It does not give them the right to exclude others from their country.

One cannot, therefore, defend immigration restrictions as protection against theft. Immigrants are not burglars.

2. *"Open immigration would destroy important American values."* The second argument for border controls is that unrestricted immigration might destroy institutions or values in the U.S. that are of transcendent importance. Open immigration might destroy something that is vital not only to Americans, but also to foreigners and potential immigrants.

    What might such institutions or values be? Political scientist Frederick Whelan argues that liberal values — equal moral worth, democracy, equal access, etc. — are scarce and precious in the world and need protection. It is a mistake to use liberal principles to argue for open access if open access would diminish liberal values and institutions in the world (Whelan, 1988).

    The concern is one of absorptive capacity and the assimilative powers of the U.S. A massive influx of foreigners who were unfamiliar with and uncommitted to American political values might use the democratic procedures of the country to destroy the institutions that support those procedures. This might happen before they had the opportunity to adopt as their own the principles of freedom and self-government. Under such circumstances, Whelan and others have argued that the state is morally justified in restricting immigration.

    A closely related argument is that members of a community have the right to protect their values and culture by excluding outsiders if necessary (Walzer, 1983).

This argument perhaps has theoretical merit. However, no evidence exists that it relates to a real danger in the U.S. Native groups have often opposed the political positions taken by immigrants, regarding them as inimical to their interests, but this is simply evidence that the immigrants have adapted to the political norms of the country and have used the political process to their own benefit. Disagreement over political goals is not the same as rejection of basic political philosophy. During the entire period before the 20th century, when the U.S. maintained open borders, the principal threat to a liberal political system came not from recent immigrants, but from the slave holders who were descendants of the first white settlers.

3. *"We have better ways of helping the world's disadvantaged."* The third argument in favor of immigration controls is that while Americans may be morally obliged to redress the imbalance of privilege in the world, they can do so more effectively through policies to improve standards of living in poor countries than they can by allowing a few residents of those countries to immigrate. Immigration focuses the benefits of U.S. resources upon just a few people. Better to take action to improve the entire economies of poor countries, actions that will affect far more people. The policy tools available to the U.S. government are innumerable, including foreign aid, loans and technical assistance, and trade, investment, and fiscal and monetary policies designed to benefit poor countries. In addition, individuals can contribute best to world justice by making personal charitable contributions.[4]

An effective rejoinder to this argument is that while rich countries and their citizens may have a duty to assist in the economic development of poor countries, fulfillment of this duty does not relieve them of the obligation to allow immigration. The two policies are not alternatives; they can be thought of rather as complements with different sorts of effects. Foreign economic aid, while never enough and often ineffective, is normally designed to effect small improvements in the lives of large numbers of people. Immigration enables a relatively small number of people, the immigrants, to make a radical change in their living situation. One would like to find a policy that combines the merits of both, that in a short period of time lifts the economic disadvantage of a large fraction of the world's people. No such policy exists. In its absence, therefore, the residents of the world's richer countries have a duty to do what they can on all fronts. The case for open borders is not refuted just because other ways exist for Americans to redress injustice.

4. *"Americans have a special obligation to their fellow citizens."* The fourth argument for immigration controls is that Americans have greater obligations to their fellow citizens than to foreigners. If there is a reasonable possibility that immigration may hurt some U.S. citizens, therefore, Americans are justified in restricting entry, even though restrictions may violate the rights of foreigners.[5]

Consider a parallel case that is clearer. A middle-class couple has enough savings to provide either a basic education for a poor orphan or supplementary educational enrichment for their own child. The orphan has the greater disadvantage and the greater need, but few would criticize the parents for deciding that their priority was to provide the best possible education for their own child. Can Americans not make a similar case relating to their fellow citizens?

Perhaps they can. Perhaps one can posit a series of widening circles, outside each of which our obligations diminish. Our greatest obligation is to our family, then perhaps to our friends, then to our neighbors, then perhaps to our ethnic group, then to our fellow citizens, and finally to all people. No doubt a great many people think this way. To test oneself, one might think back to the spring and summer of 1994 when hundreds of thousands of innocent Rwandans were murdered and ask whether that event occasioned as much moral anger in oneself as did a smaller, more local violation of rights, such as the burglary of one's home. Most Americans had some sympathy for the Rwandans, but not as much as they would have, had they been neighbors.

People think this way, but that does not mean that this kind of thinking is morally justified. Before accepting this view as the proper basis for national immigration policy, one should understand how devastating it is to the proposition with which this inquiry began: that all people are morally equal and as a consequence have equal rights. The fourth argument denies this "Truth" of the Declaration of Independence. If the argument is accepted, Americans have greater moral standing than foreigners and more rights, at least as seen through the eyes of Americans.

I think we must concede that kin have greater standing than nonrelatives in the moral considerations of most people and that this is natural and good. In all likelihood, it is an evolutionary necessity. Further departures from the norm of equal moral worth seem to me, however, to be unjustified. The failure to recognize the full humanity of people who are different from oneself — people who have different ethnic backgrounds, languages, religions, citizenships, and so forth — is at the root of much of the warfare and suffering in the world today. We may feel a more natural connection to people who are like us in some ways, but if we act on that feeling, we are in danger of creating terribly unjust situations as, for example, in Rwanda and Bosnia.

I do not mean to disparage patriotism. Love of one's country can be an affirming, healthy sentiment. Yet an ethical patriot recognizes that his or her patriotism does not diminish the rights of others. It is critical that patriotism and other kinds of group identity be grounded in the understanding that everyone else has equal rights and that one's own group is not justified in reducing the rights of other groups in any way.

Although it is tempting, therefore, the fourth argument for immigration controls fails. If we develop public policy on the presumption of unequal worth, we are heading down a path toward conflict and selfishness, not moral clarity.

5.   *Americans are not obliged to be heroic.* The fifth argument for immigration controls is that although people may have an obligation to

come to the aid of other people in distress, that obligation holds only if it can be done without undue sacrifice. The idea is sometimes called the "the principle of mutual aid" or "the cutoff for heroism." To incur or risk great sacrifice on behalf of someone else is commendable because it is heroic, but because it is heroic it is not required. Ordinary people have an obligation to take ordinary care for their fellow humans, but not to be saints (Wolf, 1982). Andrew Shacknove describes the principle this way:

"In its classic form, the principle of mutual aid envisions a passerby who encounters a drowning child. If the passer-by can easily save the child, she is morally obligated to do so, even if the child is a complete stranger. Failure to save the child under such conditions would be universally condemned as callousness. If, to the contrary, the passer-by could hope to rescue the child only at great personal risk, no one would chastise her for not acting. The passer-by is not expected to sacrifice life or limb because of a chance encounter with a stranger. Doing so is heroic, but heroism by its nature is voluntary; it exceeds the limits of obligation" (Shacknove, 1988).

The analogy to immigration policy is obvious. If the cutoff for heroism is a valid principle and if it takes precedence over other moral principles, if we are required to help our fellow human beings only when doing so is not very difficult or dangerous, then we may be rescued from the obligation to open our borders to all comers. For in the long run at least, open borders would probably entail a real sacrifice for many Americans. Immigrants come to the U.S. partly because of its high standard of living; they would likely continue to come until they had driven down wages and driven up unemployment to such an extent that immigration was no longer so attractive.[6]

Perhaps we can say, then, that morality does not require such a heroic sacrifice. Americans are obliged to do what they can to alleviate suffering in the world, as long as they do not have to pay a significant price.

The argument is respectable, but it is too comforting to the rich and privileged to stand unmodified. It is a justification for continued injustice. If it is applicable to Americans, why is it not equally applicable to anyone in a position of privilege? Could it not be used by any reactionary to justify keeping his status and income: by the King of France before the Revolution, by southern slave holders before the Civil War, by South African whites before the transfer of power? Any readjustment of a privilege-disadvantage relationship calls for sacrifice on the part of the privileged. If the principle of the cutoff for heroism is dominant, if it holds greater weight than the principle of the equal moral worth of all people, then the privileged are morally justified in maintaining their privilege.

Attractive though the fifth objection is, therefore, it fails as an ethical justification for immigration controls. The cutoff for heroism may be a valid principle when a passer-by is considering saving a drowning child, because in that case the two people are not connected by a relationship of privilege and subordination. When it is used as an argument for protecting privilege, however, it does not have greater moral weight than the principle of equal worth or even the Golden Rule.

6.   *"Immigration controls protect the disadvantaged."* The sixth and strongest argument against open borders is that immigration controls may not protect the privileged at all, but rather the unprivileged. The discussion so far has tacitly assumed that all Americans are the same, but they are not. Some are privileged while some are severely disadvantaged: the poor, the unskilled, and many members of non-Anglo ethnic groups.

It must be conceded that the research conducted so far on the impact of immigration on the prospects of disadvantaged Americans is not definitive.[7] Nevertheless, it is likely that an increased and unending supply of low-wage labor from Third World countries would keep the earnings of unskilled workers low and profits high, thereby increasing the gap between the poor and the rich in the U.S. If so, it is argued, immigration should be curtailed.

Sometimes this argument is mixed with either the fourth or the fifth argument. It should not be, because those arguments can be refuted, as we have seen. The sixth argument should not depend on the assertion that Americans are more worthy than foreigners; they are not. Neither should it depend on the assertion that immigration should require no sacrifice from Americans; sacrifice may be morally required.

Can the sixth argument be refuted successfully? One way of attempting to do so would be to say that immigration policy need not bear the burden of reducing the inequities among Americans. Many other policy tools are available, one might argue, among them welfare, education, social insurance programs, the minimum wage, job training, etc. In the conservative political atmosphere of the mid-1990s, these policies are being de-emphasized — but if the country had a commitment to reducing poverty, it could reverse those trends. If it did, it could promote social justice at home while still allowing increased immigration. Put differently, the obligation to rectify the imbalances of privilege in the world rests on the shoulders of the privileged in the rich countries, not on everyone in those countries. Morality requires them to transfer resources to their less fortunate brethren at home *and* to allow immigrants from the Third World to enter their country.

This refutation is valid, but only up to a point. Certainly rich and middle-class Americans cannot ethically argue that the welfare of their poor fellow citizens requires them to discriminate against poor foreigners when they are actually reducing their help to their own people. Still, it is likely that, even if the U.S. made a massive good-faith effort to reduce domestic poverty, it could never be successful if completely open immigration were permitted. Whatever advances were made in the welfare of the U.S. poor would just be swallowed up by new immigrants from poor countries who were seeking to take advantage of American generosity.

A second possible refutation is to assert that the needs of foreigners are more pressing than the needs of even disadvantaged Americans. The relative gap between the rich and the poor in the U.S. is substantial and shameful, but it is far from the largest in the world; the gap in many Third World countries, including the largest senders of immigrants to the U.S., is greater. The standard of living of most poor Americans is higher than the *average* standard of living in most poor countries and certainly higher than the standard of living of most immigrants. Many Mexicans, for example, enter the U.S. to earn wages that, while low by American standards, are several multiples of what they could earn at home. In the hierarchy of advantage, therefore, poor Americans occupy an intermediate position, much worse off than other Americans, but still better off than many immigrants. Therefore, one might maintain, it is morally permissible to harm poor Americans, if this is the price that must be paid to improve the lot of poor immigrants.

This refutation is not persuasive. Poor Americans are genuinely needy and unfairly impoverished. It simply cannot be right to take conscious, public action to worsen their plight. Morality obliges us to protect the welfare not just of the most disadvantaged people in the world, but of all who suffer disadvantage.

The sixth argument in favor of border controls is therefore valid. So, however, is the argument in the previous section for open borders. We are left with an ethical conflict. Disadvantaged foreigners have a moral right to enter the world's most privileged country, in an attempt to improve their position. On the other hand, poor Americans have the right of protection against so much competition from low-income newcomers that their own circumstances deteriorate. The conflict cannot be resolved completely; in the end, the best solution may be a compromise.

Although the conflict of rights cannot be resolved completely, it can be resolved partially. Recall the point made above that as long as the U.S. is a rich country, with a majority of its people very well off or at least comfortable, it is not ethical to depend upon immigration restrictions alone to improve the position of poor Americans. Such a policy would put the burden of sacrifice on even poorer foreigners, rather than where it rightfully belongs: on comfortable Americans, the truly privileged among equally worthy human beings.

The sixth argument is therefore a valid justification for immigration restrictions only (1) if the restrictions are accompanied by a major national commitment to improve the quality of life of the U.S. poor and (2) if, in the absence of

s, the flow of immigrants would be too great to allow that program to be
.

Conclusion

An ethically defensible immigration policy, based on the principle of equal moral worth, would be just one component of an integrated program in which rich and middle-class Americans fulfilled their obligations to those less fortunate. The policy would harm no one who was in an already disadvantaged position, would help as many disadvantaged people as possible, and would require sacrifice on the part of the privileged.

The program would consist of at least the following elements. First, privileged Americans (the majority in the U.S.) would greatly increase their commitment to improving the well-being of the American poor, by transferring such a significant portion of their resources to them that they bore a real sacrifice. Second, the U.S. would increase its commitment to foreign aid and other ways of improving the standard of living in poor countries.

Third, the U.S. would raise the flow of immigrants, in order to increase the number of foreigners who had a chance of participating in the advantages of American life. Two reasons exist for thinking that immigration could be increased substantially without hurting the domestic poor: (1) the fact that empirical research can detect little effect of current immigration upon the welfare of the U.S. poor and (2) the increased commitment to the poor postulated in the previous paragraph.

Fourth, the U.S. would maintain some quantitative limit on immigration, or at least the stand-by authority to impose a limit if the flow of immigration became too great to be absorbed without sacrifice by the U.S. poor.

Fifth, if the U.S. had to restrict the number of immigrants, and therefore had to choose among applicants, it would give first priority to the neediest, the refugees who are increasing in number around the world and who have no secure place to live, even if this meant cutting back on immigrants who were admitted for reasons of employment or family reunification.

In the end, the case for completely open borders can probably not be sustained; some limits on immigration may be required. Note, however, how different this argument is from the usual discourse. The usual view is that American immigration policy should maximize the interests of American residents. The argument I am making is that privileged Americans have a moral obligation to redress the balance of privilege in the world, through immigration policies and other policies. How exactly to do this is complex, because the structure of privilege and disadvantage in the world is not straightforward. Any adjustment of that relationship in the direction of greater equity, however, will require sacrifice by those who currently have the advantage, not the enhancement of their own self-interest.

This conclusion is troubling because it is so completely at variance not only with U.S. immigration policy, but also with every country's policy and with the opinions of almost every American. Faced with such overwhelming rejection of one's reasoning, a prudent person should consider the possibility of being in error. Of course, I may be. I think, however, that what has been uncovered is a fundamental dilemma. Americans are not about to admit so many immigrants that they bear a significant cost. For those who are comfortable simply with the pursuit of self-interest, this will not cause any sleepless nights. Those Americans who are genuinely altruistic, however, those who try to think out their positions from an ethical perspective and who believe in the equal worth of all people, those most admirable of Americans need to come to terms with the fact that they are among the world's privileged (their differential location on that scale in the U.S. notwithstanding), that immigration controls protect their privilege, and that they are not going to abandon that protection.

It is a dilemma familiar to thoughtful people, if not necessarily in the context of immigration. Who has not, at least momentarily, compared his or her life to Mother Teresa's and concluded that it is wanting in courage and ethics? Can those of us who are not willing to abandon our worldly goods and devote our lives completely to the service of the poor claim to live moral lives?

This investigation into the ethics of immigration policy has concluded that, if completely open borders are not required, Americans should still welcome immigrants to their country in such large numbers that they sacrifice and that their position of privilege in the world is reduced. We can be certain that this conclusion is not going to be translated into policy. Almost no American would stand for it. We are up against the uncomfortable realization, therefore, that our actions to maintain our standard of living through our immigration policy are inherently immoral. If this understanding does not change our behavior, it may at least clarify where we stand.

NOTES

1. In thinking about the ethics of immigration, I have been influenced by the stimulating collection of papers in Gibney (1988). For a comprehensive discussion of philosophical reasoning about immigration, see Weiner (1995: Chapter 8).

2. See especially the interesting attempt by Carens (1987) to base the case for open borders upon three philosophical traditions, those of Rawls and of Nozick, and of utilitarianism. These explorations are expanded in several other pieces (Carens, 1988; 1991; 1992).

3. They are not necessarily the most widespread or popular arguments. Peter Brimelow (1995) has received a great deal of national attention, for example, for a book that argues against immigration primarily on the grounds that today's immigrants are not European and that his blond, blue-eyed son may have to grow up surrounded by people of somewhat darker hues. I have not thought this sort of argument to be worth refuting in this article.

4. For an argument outlining the obligation of individuals in rich countries to contribute charitably to the world's poor, see Singer (1993: Chapter 8).

5. Something like this appears to be Brimelow's (1995) argument in his Chapter 13 on ethics.

6. I assert this point here rather than argue it. For the argument, see Isbister, *The Immigration Debate*.

7. The research on the economic impact of immigration is reviewed in *The Immigration Debate*. See also Borjas (1994).

REFERENCES

Borjas, George J.
    1994   "The Economics of Immigration." Journal of Economic Literature (December): 1667–1717.
Brimelow, Peter
    1995   Alien Nation, Common Sense About America's Immigration Disaster. New York: Random House.
Carens, Joseph H.
    1992   "Migration and Morality: A Liberal Egalitarian Perspective." Brian Barry and Robert E. Goodin (eds.), Free Movement: Ethical Issues in the Transnational Migration of People and Money. London: Harvester Wheatsheaf: 25–47.
    1991   "States and Refugees: A Normative Analysis." Howard Adelman (ed.), Refugee Policy: Canada and the United States. Toronto: York Lanes Press: 18–29.
    1988   "Immigration and the Welfare State." Amy Gutmann (ed.), Democracy and the Welfare State. Princeton: Princeton University Press: 207–230.
    1987   "Aliens and Citizens: The Case for Open Borders." The Review of Politics 49: 251–273.
Gibney, Mark (ed.)
    1988   Open Borders? Closed Societies? The Ethical and Political Issues. Westport, Conn.: Greenwood Press.
Isbister, John
    1996   The Immigration Debate: Remaking America. West Hartford, Conn.: Kumarian Press.
Shacknove, Andrew E.
    1988   "American Duties to Refugees, Their Scope and Limits." Mark Gibney (ed.), Open Borders? Closed Societies? The Ethical and Political Issues. Westport, Conn.: Greenwood Press: 131–149.
Singer, Peter
    1993   Practical Ethics, Second Edition. New York: Cambridge University Press.
Walzer, Michael
    1983   Spheres of Justice: A Defense of Pluralism and Equality. New York: Basic Books.
Wasserstrom, Richard
    1986   "One Way to Understand and Defend Programs of Preferential Treatment." Robert K. Fullinwider and Claudia Mills (eds.), The Moral Foundations of Civil Rights. Totowa, New Jersey: Rowman and Littlefield: 46–55.
Weiner, Myron
    1995   The Global Migration Crisis: Challenge to States and to Human Rights. New York: HarperCollins.
Whelan, Frederick G.
    1988   "Citizenship and Freedom of Movement, An Open Admission Policy?" Mark Gibney (ed.), Open Borders? Closed Societies? The Ethical and Political Issues. Westport, Conn.: Greenwood Press.
Wills, Gary
    1992   Lincoln at Gettysburg: The Words That Remade America. New York: Simon and Schuster.
Wolf, Susan
    1982   "Moral Saints." Journal of Philosophy: 419–439.

Rethinking Immigration Policy and Citizenship in the Americas: A Regional Framework

Susanne Jonas

T HE CURRENT DEBATES OVER IMMIGRATION POLICY, TAKING PLACE FROM THE HALLS of Congress to inner-city communities nationwide, raise some of the most profound issues of race, class, and politics facing the United States today. No less than the civil rights issues of the 1960s, these debates are ultimately about the nation's soul: What kind of country will we be in the 21st century? Yet today it makes sense to take the question beyond our national boundaries, locating the U.S. within an increasingly integrated Western Hemisphere. This article addresses the multiple cross-border realities affecting U.S. immigration policies, as well as their political consequences throughout the Americas. To put it another way, there are regional dimensions of the domestic debate; at stake is what kind of region the Americas will be in the 21st century.

From this perspective, I shall offer a critique of existing U.S. policies and an alternative framework, based on the following arguments: Current U.S. policies deal with Latin American immigrants as if they constituted a major threat to U.S. "national security." This strictly (and narrowly) "U.S. interest"-driven approach retains some aspects of Cold War thinking even in this post-Cold War era. Quite apart from its questionable effectiveness in a transnational environment, it has multiple negative (antidemocratic and destabilizing) political repercussions throughout the region, as well as for the immigrants affected. Critics of this approach have yet to develop a comprehensive alternative, but have begun rethinking the bases for policy. The alternative framework suggested here is rooted in very different conceptions of citizenship and democracy; additionally, it views immigration within the context of enhancing integral socioeconomic development throughout the region, and it proposes to build upon the transnational

SUSANNE JONAS teaches in Latin American and Latino Studies, University of California — Santa Cruz, Santa Cruz, CA 95064. The research upon which this article is based was funded by the North-South Center at the University of Miami, as well as the Chicano/Latino Research Center (CLRC) of the University of California, Santa Cruz. Thanks to Suzie Dod Thomas, Max Castro, Manuel Angel Castillo, Gisela Gellert, Mario Lungo, Sonia Baires, Elizabeth Martínez, Néstor Rodríguez, Nora Hamilton, Frank Bonilla, Richard Falk, John Isbister, and colleagues at CLRC and the *Social Justice* Editorial Board for feedback on earlier drafts.

practices and networks being developed by the immigrants themselves. Aside from being more humane, I shall argue, a policy starting from these premises would also be more rational for the U.S. over the medium and long range, and far more appropriate in this era of hemispheric integration.

The Need for a Regional Framework

Underlying these observations is a broadly structural view that the Western Hemisphere is becoming increasingly integrated. There is already an extensive literature within a general world-systems framework (e.g., Wallerstein, Portes, Fernández Kelly, Bach, Sassen, Ong, Bonacich) on the complementarity of capital and labor flows, particularly within economic systems characterized by relations of unequal exchange. This has received wide discussion, most recently in relation to NAFTA — the linkages it creates and the disruptive and displacing effects of economic integration for some sectors of the population on each side of the border. In this process, cross-border flows of capital and goods are being actively promoted by state policies and interstate agreements (e.g., NAFTA and its projected extension to other Latin American countries).

Coming on the heels of the devastating economic crises of the 1980s throughout Latin America, the economic integration of the 1990s has stimulated new cross-border flows of people — not only because integration on a neoliberal basis leaves many families and communities without adequate economic prospects in their home countries, but also more importantly, because even at a time of economic recession and restructuring in the U.S. (accompanied by an anti-immigrant backlash), the demand for low-waged immigrant labor in the U.S. remains high. As Portes (1996) puts it, immigration is "not an optional process, but one driven by the structural requirements of advanced capitalist accumulation."

In some cases, the linkages are also political. Direct U.S. involvement in situations of political upheaval in Central America and the Caribbean since the 1960s, for example, has been a key factor in generating the exodus of hundreds of thousands of refugees from their home countries to the U.S. Other political linkages have been forged by opponents of U.S. policy (sanctuary cities, church activists, asylum lawyers, and human rights groups). Moreover, today the degree of progress toward resolving such situations of political upheaval affects people's living conditions in the home countries and, hence, their migration decisions. (See Jonas, forthcoming, and Hamilton and Chinchilla, 1996.)

Finally, at the social level, the movement of people has itself become a structural factor of integration: prior migrations from various countries have created "bridges" (based on kinship, household, and community networks) that new migrants are crossing today. These prior relationships and interactive networks have created an increasingly integrated social region in the Americas, through which people move north *and return*. These movements and circuits of migration have created binational or transnational communities and networks — social, economic, and cultural — between Latin American immigrants in the U.S. and their home communities or countries. (A concrete indicator of these networks is that the economies of several Latin American countries are dependent on remittance flows from immigrants living in the U.S.)

To address these realities, this article adopts a multidisciplinary conceptual framework, drawing on structural arguments from a general world-systems perspective as well as political, sociological, and ethnographic approaches. Immigration lends itself to interdisciplinary study because it is a crossing-point where several different disciplines and concerns come together, as well as a point of intersection between domestic and foreign policy concerns. Various authors have referred to its "theoretical centrality" (Portes and Walton, 1981), its "potential (in the international as well as domestic spheres) to open windows into key mechanisms of social change" directly related to the life-experiences of many individuals (Mitchell, 1989). As we shall see, it calls for redefinitions even at the epistemological level.

Focusing more specifically on Latin American immigration to the U.S., current realities require a regional approach. As a consequence of growing integration at various levels, events in one country have ever-greater repercussions in other parts of the region. A regional or cross-border perspective on immigration policies, I suggest, will prove useful for understanding why U.S. immigration policies significantly affect not only Latin American immigrants, but also the prospects for democracy and stable, viable development in their home countries — and less directly, even in the U.S. itself. This kind of perspective can also illuminate why many of the policies that seem "rational" in the immigration debate within the U.S. are seriously problematic and unwise if we consider their long-range repercussions throughout the hemisphere.

A regional approach takes into account the past and present conditions in the countries of origin, which are crucial factors shaping decisions about cross-border migrations and movements in both directions. At the same time, I suggest, the policies adopted toward immigrants (and in some cases refugees) who are already in the U.S. will have significant effects upon the prospects for stable development in the home countries. In this sense, our research, like their migrations, reaches across the borders between Latin America and the U.S., and aims to reflect the interactive realities throughout the region. A regional perspective also focuses on the close linkages between U.S. immigration policy and U.S. foreign policy (see Mitchell, 1989). However, there are radically different kinds of regional perspectives. I shall distinguish between perspectives that take U.S. "national security" as their starting point and alternative policies that could be based on a very different conception of citizenship and democracy, and informed by a concern for integral socioeconomic development in the region.

U.S. "National Security" as a Basis for Immigration Policy

At the broadest level, national security-based policies start from a strictly interest-driven conception of "policy." Hence, they define immigration policies only in relation to the various domestic and foreign policy interests *of the U.S.* and treat immigration as a function of U.S. "national security," however that is being defined at the moment. Since the end of World War II, such policies have been rooted in the entire complex of foreign and domestic policies adopted by bipartisan policymakers to fight the Cold War; as will be seen, elements of this approach have persisted in the post-Cold War era, although with new content. Weiner (1995: 131*ff*) characterizes a "security/stability" approach as revolving around "governments' concerns to protect their territory and population against threats to the stability of the regime, to social well-being, or to the important societal values of the country." This kind of approach gives significant emphasis to state decision-making; in practice, as Bach (1992: 268) points out, it is characterized by an "overall strategic use of migration policies," i.e., their subordination to geopolitical or domestic concerns of the receiving country.

Throughout the Cold War era, U.S. immigration policies were subordinated in large measure to geopolitical (anticommunist) foreign policy priorities, although they were also influenced by independent domestic concerns.[1] In the Western Hemisphere, during the Alliance for Progress years following the Cuban Revolution, migration was used "as an essential tool in the defense of the inter-American system" as defined by the U.S. (Bach, 1992: 267). The most obvious example of "national security" as the basis for immigration policy has been the foreign-policy-based refugee policy, as opposed to equal application of human rights standards (see Zolberg et al., 1989; Zolberg, 1995) — hence the enticement of Cuban exiles as contrasted with the exclusion of Haitians and others. Increasingly after the middle to late 1970s, Latin American immigration itself came to be more explicitly defined as a "national security problem,"[2] as geopolitics coincided with economic crises and restructuring in Latin America, with the latter stimulating new waves of labor migration during the 1980s and 1990s.

To take one example of the interaction among these factors, Central Americans became the focus of attention with a particularly geopolitical twist during the "New Cold War" of the 1980s (i.e., the Reagan administration's response to the Sandinista victory in Nicaragua and the civil wars in El Salvador and Guatemala). Like the rest of Latin America, these countries suffered a devastating economic crisis during the 1980s, which stimulated labor migrations to the U.S. However, in this case the additional factor of U.S. involvement in the civil wars of El Salvador and Guatemala, through support for their counterinsurgent armies and governments, contributed to the massive exodus of refugees from those countries. Yet that very U.S. policy led to systematic denial of asylum petitions for Salvadoran and Guatemalan refugees on the grounds that they were antigovernment "subversives" (in the clinical language, "opponents of friendly regimes") — in stark contrast to a more mixed reception for refugees from the "Communist" regime of Sandinista Nicaragua.[3] The subordination of refugee policy to U.S. foreign policy — in open violation of both international law (the U.N. Refugee Convention) and the U.S. 1980 Refugee Act accepting international standards — was so systematic that it was eventually found to be illegal: the 1990 settlement of the ABC class action lawsuit (*American Baptist Church* v. *Thornburgh*) forced the INS to rehear the cases of several hundred thousand Guatemalans and Salvadorans who had suffered "wrongful discrimination."[4]

The current version of the national security approach since the late 1980s has reshuffled the equation somewhat (in response to both the winding down of the Cold War and the persistence of economic crises in the hemisphere), but maintains the essential link of treating Latin American immigrants and refugees as if they constituted a threat. The redefinition of U.S. national security doctrine, as laid out in various 1994 and 1995 documents (see also Teitelbaum and Weiner, 1995), actually includes immigrant and refugee flows as a top priority concern, along with drug trafficking and terrorism. According to one highly informed observer, the current approach to immigration closely parallels the "drug wars" and "antiterrorist" wars of the late 1980s and early 1990s: as in the earlier cases, anti-immigrant policy begins as discourse or rhetoric catering to domestic political constituencies, but is subsequently written into policy legislation. Meanwhile, the militarization of immigration policy moves from metaphor to "self-fulfilling mandate."[5]

In fact, the redefinition of "national security" in the 1990s is even more exclusionary toward migrants, as it incorporates domestic political concerns and perceived threats — in Keely's (1995: 223) terms, "soft security issues," which also include "culture, social stability, environmental degradation, population growth." In the conception of another analyst (Zimmerman, 1995: 90–91), security means freedom not only from danger, but also "from fear or anxiety" (on the part of U.S. citizens), and hence is threatened by perceived "economic and/or cultural damage." This much broader definition of security expands the reasons to exclude immigrants and refugees.

All of this, of course, corresponds to real economic changes affecting the U.S. In an era of economic recession and restructuring and radical corporate downsizing, many communities in the U.S. have valid concerns about job loss, declining wages, and service cutbacks. These changes are aggravated by economic integration in the neoliberal NAFTA mode, which exports many jobs to take advantage of low-wage labor in Mexico. Additionally, as seen above, there has been a real increase in Latin American immigration to the U.S. It is indeed a contradictory panorama, in which national security-based immigration *policy* is in part a response to the *politics* of economic *insecurity*. Such politics take the form of blaming immigrants for the loss of jobs and services to native-born Americans, the social construction of undocumented immigrants in the mass media as "illegal aliens" (as foreign invaders from another planet, like Communists during the 1950s), and of the border as our "protection" from that alien invasion. (See Rodríguez, 1996.)

However — quite apart from the questionable effectiveness of border control (see Espenshade, 1994, and Kossoudji, 1992) — the national security approach to immigration policy does not really address the root causes of the widespread economic insecurity within the U.S. In the public debate, facts about those causes, most of which are independent of immigration, have been obscured or overshadowed by xenophobic fears, particularly toward Mexican migrants. These fears have been shaped into a widespread notion that undocumented immigrants are "illegal" by definition and therefore have no rights — even when they have been actively recruited by employers in the U.S. (Hence the contradictory situation that immigrant-bashing coincides with proposals for a new Bracero Program.) Going far beyond the issue of undocumented immigrants, recent congressional bills have proposed significant reductions in legal migration, while denying public services to all immigrants (both legal and undocumented). Meanwhile, refugee/asylum legislation faces drastic restrictive "reforms" in Congress (narrowing the definition of "persecution," expediting exclusion and deportation, et cetera).[6]

Antidemocratic and Destabilizing Effects of National Security-Based Immigration Policies

As seen above, the hemisphere is in the process of being increasingly integrated, but what kind of region will it be politically? I suggest that U.S. immigration policies directed against Latin Americans, i.e., increased deportations, drastic tightening of refugee laws, and "keeping out" new migrants at the border — or, more realistically, forcing them to enter under conditions of increasing vulnerability and with virtually no rights — have very negative regional consequences. Beyond the dehumanizing effects for the individual migrants, treating them as if they constituted a "national security threat" for the U.S. promotes *exclusionary politics* in various forms throughout the region. Furthermore, anti-immigrant policies are likely to have *destabilizing* consequences that are counterproductive to lasting peace and development in the home countries — a stated U.S. goal, if for no other reason than to prevent future *mass* migrations from those countries. (Independent of U.S. policies, migrant flows can be expected to continue at more modest levels in any case.)

The case of El Salvador provides several examples. During the 1980s, the U.S. invested six billion dollars in an attempt to defeat the FMLN insurgency. By 1991, Washington was finally forced to support a genuine peace process, which in fact constituted the best hope for El Salvador's future. Today, however, there are disturbing signs that some of the new policies toward Salvadorans living in the U.S. could undermine what was finally achieved and sow the seeds of new problems in El Salvador. A visible example is deportation from Los Angeles and other U.S. cities of Salvadoran gang members (*Los Salvatruchos*) who ended up in jail. This has contributed to an extremely dangerous situation in postwar El Salvador — not only because of the reformation of the gangs there and the spread of common crime, but also because it has become an excuse (one among many) for the reformation of countervailing armed vigilante groups such as the *Sombra Negra* (reborn death squads). The number of deportees in this case is not large, but under these conditions, even a small number has had a very destabilizing effect, creating new foci of conflict in a situation already plagued by other forms of social discontent. Of course, U.S. immigration policies are only one element in that situation (others are nonfulfillment or even sabotage of the Peace Accords, neoliberal economic policies, declining resources for social programs, and so on). In short, El Salvador, which seemed to have real prospects as a success story in peacemaking and reconciliation, today has degenerated into a very volatile and uncertain peace, and U.S. immigration policies are increasing that uncertainty.

Another element in the Salvadoran situation stems from the legal limbo in which hundreds of thousands of Salvadoran asylum seekers of the 1980s now find themselves in the U.S. It seems unlikely that they will be massively deported, given the huge backlog of Salvadorans who were granted Temporary Protected Status (TPS) in the early 1990s or who are awaiting a rehearing of their cases because of the outcome of the 1990 *American Baptist Church* v. *Thornburgh* lawsuit. However, to the extent that the U.S. attempts to send back as many Salvadorans as possible, with the end of TPS in 1995, and to the extent that asylum laws will deny protection to new applicants, the result will be very negative for El Salvador and counterproductive to long-range U.S. goals of "stabilizing" the situation there.

For one thing, even a steady stream of returnees (which is more likely than a massive deluge) would create difficulties for an already overburdened labor market. At a more macroeconomic level, remittances from Salvadorans working in the U.S. have become the pillar of the Salvadoran economy (at least one billion dollars a year, far higher than coffee export earnings). At both the community and national levels, these remittances are a safety valve for the economy. Reducing or cutting off these remittances by targeting Salvadoran immigrants in the U.S. is likely to have devastating effects; certainly it will not contribute to the consolidation of conditions for people to realize their raised expectations *in El Salvador*, rationalize the flow of new migrants, or permit Salvadorans in the U.S. to return voluntarily, with the expectation of decent work opportunities and stability at home. (On all of the above, see Hamilton and Chinchilla, 1996.)[7]

This set of examples suggests the short-sightedness of current U.S. policies. To the extent that such policies at every level (including U.S. immigration policies) fail to contribute to genuine, long-range, and viable development in El Salvador, these failures will affect the migration decisions of people in both sites, maintaining the incentive to leave the home country and/or not to return home from the U.S.

Turning now to the U.S., I suggest that anti-immigrant policies will have indirect, negative (exclusionary) effects for American society. To begin with, militarization of the border with Mexico and lack of respect for even the most basic due process rights for undocumented migrants at the border have reached such major proportions as to render the U.S. a human rights violator. Incidents such as the videotaped Riverside beatings of undocumented immigrants in the spring of 1996 were shocking; in reality, however, these incidents were a rather logical extension of the dehumanization and criminalization of undocumented immigrants, as well as their treatment as people with no rights. Second, the idea of restrictive changes in refugee laws has become so commonly accepted as to pave the way for the attachment to the (totally unrelated) 1996 Anti-Terrorism Bill of provisions drastically curtailing asylum rights for those arriving or having arrived without documentation. Beyond the obvious damage to immigrants, both of these developments are harmful to the historical self-conception of the U.S. as an "open society."

Third, we are seeing a "spread effect" from policies designed to exclude undocumented immigrants to campaigns denying services to and targeting legalized Latino immigrants as well. If unchecked, this dynamic could ultimately affect Latino citizens, for example, by rolling back anti-discrimination and other protective legislation affecting Latinos and other communities of color. INS raids in Latino communities, homes, and workplaces, designed to seek out the undocumented, often result in violating the civil rights of permanent legal residents and even citizens. Within this climate, it scarcely seems surprising that anti-Latino hate crimes are on the rise, with daily incidents reported in the Spanish-language media.

Finally, the anti-immigrant climate is becoming a threat to basic principles of "American democracy." Serious discussion is now being given to extremist proposals *to repeal the 14th Amendment of the Constitution and/or to eliminate its basic guarantees, so as to deny citizenship to U.S.-born children born of undocumented parents.* Provisions to deny public school education to children of undocumented parents are also being considered in Congress, despite being in open violation of existing Supreme Court rulings. In addition, we are witnessing the creation of a two-tiered system of citizens/noncitizens and voters/non-voters — a kind of "electoral apartheid" that denies Latino immigrants any form of political participation.[8] The result of immigration policies and practices that treat a significant sector of the population as having *no rights* — as was actually stated by the authors of Proposition 187 in California — could be a "de-democratizing" trend within the U.S. itself, to borrow a phrase from Castañeda (1993). (See also Cornelius, 1996.)

Alternatives: "Citizenship" Redefined and Integral Regional Development

The alternative regional approach proposed below also looks at events affecting immigrants in all the different sites of the Americas and makes connections between U.S. foreign policies and immigration policies. However, it lays the basis for a very different set of policies than those stemming from the national security approach. It is based on very different conceptual and epistemological foundations and principles in regard to state and society, as well as practical policy priorities. As will be developed below, it differs from state-defined national security doctrines by incorporating the notion of *people's rights*; theoretically, it involves a reconceptualization of democracy to address new transnational realities and the *accountability of states* to civil society, both within and across borders.

On the dimension of immigration-related foreign policy (which is intertwined with, but distinct from, immigration policy), this approach proposes an alternative to neoliberalism: it includes considerations of social equity as part of any equation for integral socioeconomic development. More generally, this approach is founded on a comprehensive notion of "policy" that goes beyond state-defined "interests" to include *taking responsibility for the effects* on individuals and communities affected by those state policies. Put another way, a social policy approach includes effects on the quality of people's lives — a concept more generally accepted in Europe than in the U.S. Beyond that, it implies policies that maximize well-being or the "common good" across borders. In an age of hemispheric integration, this is especially relevant to a discussion of immigration policies.

Before proceeding, my emphasis on alternatives that differ so radically from existing policies, rather than focusing on (equally necessary) incremental reforms, deserves explanation. First, the actual situation within the hemisphere (economic crisis, restructuring, and integration on a neoliberal basis) is radically transforming the prospects for millions of workers in the U.S.; new initiatives by capital require a rethinking of old categories and premises. Put another way, the real ability of the state to control cross-border movements of people has been somewhat relativized as a consequence of the lifting of restrictions on cross-border capital and commodity flows, since the two dynamics tend to be closely associated with each other (see Sassen, 1992). Second, the debate has already been polarized by restrictionist "immigration reform" advocates, as demonstrated by current proposals within the U.S. Congress. Under these conditions, more immediate pro-immigrant struggles (e.g., naturalization campaigns, defense of legal immigrants' rights) remain essential but insufficient. It also makes sense to address the issues facing both undocumented immigrants and permanent legal residents (hence the discussion of "citizenship") because in the current political climate, attacks on the former are having a "spill-over" effect on the latter and even on Chicano and Latino citizens.

To elaborate more specifically, I suggest the following concepts as bases for alternative immigration and immigration-related foreign policies:

(1) At the most basic level, the alternative starting point presented here is a conception of citizenship that is not strictly defined or limited by the legal status assigned by nation-states. ("Citizenship" is the point of reference because we are dealing with people who live in more than one nation and, for the purposes of our discussion of U.S. policy, because so many of those affected are legally noncitizens or undocumented.) Rather than granting the *absolute* rights of states in determining and delimiting citizenship, it starts from a concept of citizenship that also includes the rights and entitlements that accrue to all human beings (Dagnino, 1993). As laid out by Richard Falk (1993: 39), a pioneer in writing about the emergence of global civil society:

> Citizenship in general expresses membership and the quality of partici-
> pation in a political community. Its conditions can be specified by law,
> but its reality is a matter of politics and the rigors of experience. Thus,
> citizenship can be understood both formally as a status and, more
> adequately, existentially as a shifting set of attitudes, relationships, and
> expectations with no necessary territorial delimitation.

From this perspective, undocumented immigrants are not simply noncitizens with no rights, but are socially de facto citizens of more than one state. The definition of immigrant and refugee rights has only begun to be addressed in some U.N. documents (e.g., the Universal Declaration of Human Rights, the Refugee Convention and Protocol, and the 1990 U.N. International Convention on the Protection of the Rights of All Migrant Workers and Members of Their Families) and at the regional level in the 1984 Declaration of Cartagena. However, many of these foundations are vague, nonbinding, and/or unrealized in practice — i.e., they lack even the expectation of enforcement beyond what sovereign states are willing to concede. As of 1996, moreover, existing refugee protections are actually being weakened rather than strengthened around the world, even as violent conflicts generating refugees are increasing. Beyond refugees, the norm of legal protections for labor migrants has virtually no acceptance in most receiving countries — precisely at a time when such protective agreements have taken on increasing importance given the great upsurge in immigration around the world.

Beyond international law, actual experience suggests the increasing centrality of immigrants in the Americas (see Massey, 1995). In a sense, immigrants stand to become the universal transnational citizens of the 21st century, not only because of their growing numbers and their necessary labor, but also because their lives have already been transnationalized and they are already acting simultaneously in more than one site of the region. As Basch et al. (1994: 15) put it, "by living their lives straddling several nation-states, they are affected by, pose special challenges to, and contribute to hegemonic processes in several separate states." Bonilla (1994: 6) makes a similar point:

> The increasing need for millions around the globe to anchor their existence in more than one social formation for generations at a time is transforming the very idea of citizenship, human rights, and the role of cultural expressions and identities in sustaining sociability.... What we are now stretching for, more urgently than ever, are new standards of international responsibility and solidarity.

Moreover, from a political stance, precisely because the present world order makes migrants the most vulnerable to human rights and civil rights violations, provisions for their rights and protection are central to struggles for full democratization. The "democratic promise" that has inspired revolutions since the 18th century cannot be fully realized unless it is inclusionary in the broadest sense — in stark contrast to the exclusionary politics that prevail today. The struggles of immigrants and refugees will have to be at the heart of civil rights and other progressive movements within the core countries, as those movements demand "universal fulfillment of the old liberal [democratic] ideology," as Wallerstein (1992) put it.[9]

(2) Linked to the above-mentioned challenge to the absolute primacy of nation-states *vis-à-vis* migrants is a notion of the *accountability of states across borders*. Although this may sound like a radical questioning of state sovereignty, it is already the case in relation to transnational capital (markets). I am suggesting that new realities also make this concept more relevant in relation to civil societies, including transnational citizens who move across borders. In practice, states have already conceded that their sovereignty has been considerably relativized with regard to capital and commodity flows, but they have resisted acknowledging new realities with regard to cross-border movements of people. Accountability *across* borders — and minimally, *at* borders — will require further elaboration in international law, e.g., to include human rights standards for the treatment of immigrants at those borders and within transit countries such as Mexico. In short, to the extent that states will always insist on their right to regulate entry at their borders (and hence will not adopt open border policies), they should also be held accountable to regulations about their treatment of people crossing those borders.[10]

To push for these legal codifications, however, we must begin to incorporate cross-border accountability into our discussions of democracy itself. More broadly, at the theoretical level, this suggests the need for a 21st century cross-border reconceptualization of democracy, which includes but also goes far beyond the nation-bound, strictly formal/institutional conceptions of electoral democracy. Indeed, by themselves the latter today often become justifications for exclusionary politics in practice. (Is it not the ultimate irony, for example, that the electoral system is being used in the U.S. to propose revoking 14th Amendment guarantees for the U.S.-born children of undocumented immigrants, hitherto legal citizens?) In addition to cross-border accountability, a 21st century reformulation could include the participatory dimension of democracy, opening up space for autonomous cross-border/transnational activism at the grass-roots level, as well as direct participation by immigrant and refugee communities in discussions of immigration policy.

(3) Immigration policies of nation-states can and should build upon the autonomous transnational practices already being developed by networks between immigrants and their home communities or countries "from the ground up." As has been seen in numerous studies, such linkages have stabilizing effects. A clear example is the central role of remittances from immigrants in stabilizing the economies of the home countries.[11] Equally important, although less visible, are the experiential and cultural bonds between sending and receiving countries, constructed by migrants in their cross-border movements and contacts. Recognizing the positive contribution of these transnational practices and linkages would be more practical and more humane than restrictionist anti-immigrant policies.

(4) With regard to foreign (economic) policy, there is a need for regional and international agreements concerning the rights of migrant workers (as well as the ratification and implementation of such protections as do exist on paper). For example, regional and international free trade agreements must deal with the issue of labor mobility (free movement of people and capital) and, more specifically, with the rights of workers who move across borders. Even from a strictly practical longer-range perspective, given that we are dealing with a region currently plagued by multiple social crises, state policies should recognize and reflect the fact that migration frequently serves as a safety valve or stabilizing factor in addressing those crises. Certainly, that approach is more realistic than policies that attempt (with only relative success) to restrict immigration, and that meanwhile penalize individual migrants for crossing borders.

(5) Rational (as opposed to massive) migration flows can be enhanced by international and regional free trade agreements designed to maximize *social* well-being throughout the region. Current neoliberal policies (as expressed in NAFTA and in U.S. relations with Latin America generally) proclaim that the internationalization of capital will automatically "democratize" these regions. To the contrary, I suggest, free trade agreements can be compatible with a more integral notion of democracy (including its social dimension) only if they set limits on the degree of exploitation of Latin American and other Third World workers within the U.S and in their home countries. Hence, in contrast to neoliberal approaches, such as that enshrined in NAFTA, or those that are "developmentalist" in the 1960s or Alliance for Progress sense, a hemispheric social policy would adopt an explicitly progressive orientation, i.e., upward harmonization of wage,

environmental, and political standards, rather than downward harmonization. It would also include human rights standards, as reflected in the American Convention on Human Rights (which the U.S., unlike most governments in the hemisphere, has not signed).

A further element of a coherent regional policy would be to prioritize the resolution of social problems *at their roots* in the home countries (e.g., maximizing job creation). Very immediately, this means a policy that takes responsibility for the conditions *in which* Latin Americans live and *to which* some immigrants return in their home country—e.g., assistance specifically directed toward reincorporation and employment for those who do return. In the medium or long run, a comprehensive regional social policy is more likely than are existing policies to rationalize immigrant flows.

The above ideas may sound visionary, but they also represent practical adaptations to a changing world. They are grounded in an integral understanding of current social crises within the U.S. (i.e., immigrants as being caught up in, rather than being the primary cause of those crises). In addition, I suggest, they will go much farther than do current U.S. policies toward addressing hemispheric realities for the 21st century.

Toward a Rational Cross-Border Policy

Finally, let us try to visualize what could be the positive consequences of an alternative policy, rooted in the principles suggested above and building on transnational practices of the immigrants themselves. Beyond being more humane, I suggest, they are also more appropriate to 21st century hemispheric realities.[12] In the face of the attack on immigrants from their countries, Latin American governments have begun to recognize the anachronistic and counterproductive character of U.S. immigration policies (even as they enthusiastically embrace neoliberal, socially regressive policies at home). Prompted in large measure by Proposition 187 and other attacks on Latino immigrants, various proposals are currently emerging from Mexico and other Latin American countries regarding dual nationality and/or dual citizenship.[13]

Apart from their home governments, however, Latin American immigrants themselves, even those who are legally disenfranchised, are in some respects far ahead of U.S. immigration policies in addressing the transnational realities of this region. They are constituting themselves collectively as new social actors in the region, through binational family/household and community networks. At the practical level, they are taking initiatives that (through remittances) contribute significantly toward economic survival and reconstruction "back home," at the household, community, and national levels. A more constructive U.S. immigration policy would recognize and build upon the contribution these families and communities in the U.S. make to stabilizing the home countries, and would actively encourage binational development strategies.[14] Such a stance toward immigrants who are already here could rationalize the immigrant flows of the future, and would at least avoid *massive* outflows resulting from further deterioration of conditions in the home countries.

On another level, some of these immigrants/refugees (including undocumented) are becoming actors in struggles for democratization in various ways throughout the region and are engaging in "transnational grassroots political practices," as some have called them (Smith, 1994).[15] Yet they will need solid support from progressive movements in the U.S. This suggests the need to build a new civil rights movement with an internationalist orientation and a regional, Americas-wide political consciousness to combat rapidly rising xenophobia. To be truly effective, such a movement must go beyond defensive focuses (against restrictionist legislation), to initiate campaigns for the rights of Latino and other Third World immigrants (including their rights as workers, as part of the U.S. organized labor movement), and to build cross-border coalitions and alliances.

Let us return to the question of what kind of region the Americas will be in the 21st century. Building upon these initiatives and adopting a regional social (versus "national security") approach as the basis for alternative U.S. foreign and immigration policies would enhance the now-uncertain prospects for stable development and democracy in Latin America over the long run. As noted, current U.S. immigration policies that start from a national security perspective are contributing to that uncertainty. The underlying question is whether the conditions of economic crisis (and in some cases, political upheaval) that generated the great wave of Latin American migration to the U.S. during the 1980s and early 1990s have changed enough to reduce (or rationalize) the flow of immigration. The adoption of a comprehensive regional development policy by the U.S. would be a crucial part of the equation. Herein lies the best hope for reducing the likelihood of further *massive* migrations of the type that occurred from Latin America in the 1980s, while dealing in a rational and humane way with the *continuing*, indeed, by now permanent, flow of migrants across borders in both directions.

NOTES

1.   The "revolving door" syndrome with regard to Mexicans in particular has always had its own specific dynamic, one more responsive to domestic-based economic cycles in the U.S.

2.   CIA Director William Colby (recently deceased) stated as early as 1977 that the flow of migrants across the U.S.-Mexico border constituted a greater security threat to the U.S. than did the Soviet Union.

3.   During the late 1980s, Nicaraguan asylum seekers enjoyed a 26% approval rate, as compared with 2.6% of Salvadorans and 1.8% of Guatemalans. The Reagan State Department openly stated (*Bulletin*, 1983) that only the "expansion of communism to El Salvador and Guatemala" would generate bona fide refugees; Reagan himself and his top adviser, Jeane Kirkpatrick, evoked the specter of a tidal wave of "feet people" from the region to justify the wars against Nicaragua's Sandinistas and the FMLN in El Salvador.

4. *American Baptist Church* v. *Thornburgh* was a class-action suit against the U.S. Justice Department that charged discrimination and unfair treatment through the use of foreign policy criteria rather than the cases' individual merits, to judge applications for political asylum.

5. Besides Pentagon involvement in implementing anti-immigration policy — current proposals vary from direct to "supporting" involvement (*New York Times*, September 10, 1995, and January 13, 1996) — the State Department has set up an Office of Drugs, Terrorism, and Immigration. In a press conference of April 13, 1995, Deputy Attorney General Jamie Gorelick referred to INS "contingency planning." For example, a "mass immigration emergency plan" was used during the summer 1994 Haitian and Cuban crises and is now being "updated" to include land-based immigration from Mexico and Central America. Even more moderate policymakers and advisers are shifting toward restrictionist policies. The 1994 American Assembly report, for example, argued that, in view of public perceptions of immigration as a "threat to domestic well-being," "it is in the domestic and foreign policy interests of the U.S. to demonstrate tangible evidence of a reduction in current and prospective illegal immigration." To take another example, during the 1993 NAFTA debate, both sides resorted to immigration-baiting arguments.

6. Two examples of restrictive applications of asylum law can be cited. First, the distinction between economic and political immigrants is being construed rigidly; hence, for example, it excludes as "economic migrants" refugees from a factory that shut down in the home country in response to union organizing efforts by workers — clearly a mixed situation. Second, as Tom Farer (1995: 266–267) points out, under narrowing interpretations of refugee legislation, persecution must be proven on an individual basis, hence excluding members of groups suffering systematic persecution. Beyond legal measures, the U.S. has acted in a number of situations to prevent potential asylum applicants from reaching U.S. soil (e.g., repatriation of Haitians on the high seas and pressure on the Mexican government to turn back Central Americans at Mexico's southern border).

7. This is a preliminary conclusion of the collaborative study in which I am involved, a survey of 600 Salvadoran and Guatemalans in Los Angeles and San Francisco, that focuses on their plans to remain or return to their home countries, now that the civil wars there are over (almost over, in the Guatemalan case). (See Chinchilla and Hamilton, 1995.) In addition, as Mahler (1995) and others suggest, the culture of migration built up over recent years is an independent factor that will contribute to continuing migration, regardless of U.S. immigration policies.

8. In the November 1994 election, according to the Field Institute analysis of January 1995, although Latinos made up 24% of the adult population in California, they constituted 15% of citizen-eligible voters and a bare nine percent of actual voters. Latinos were the only ethnic group to vote against the anti-immigrant initiative, Proposition 187 (overwhelmingly so, with 73% against). Obviously, the gap would be greatly lessened if all those eligible to vote did so, and if all those eligible to become naturalized did so — as will increasingly be the case in the future. (See Note 12.)

9. In Wallerstein's (1992) eloquent formulation, a "multi-front strategy" of anti-systemic movements

> will have one tactical weapon at its disposal which may be overwhelming for the defenders of the status quo. It is the weapon of taking the old liberal ideology literally and demanding its universal fulfillment. For example, is not the appropriate tactic faced with the situation of mass unauthorized migration from South to North to demand the principle of the unlimited free market — open frontiers for all who wish to come? Faced with such a demand, liberal ideologues can only shed their cant about human rights and acknowledge that they do not mean freedom of emigration since they do not mean freedom of immigration. Similarly, one can push on every front for the increased democratization of decision-making.... What I am talking about here is the tactic of overloading the system by taking its pretensions and its claims more seriously than the dominant forces wish them to be taken.

10. Elsewhere in this volume and in their other writings, Saskia Sassen and Néstor Rodríguez, among others, argue that state sovereignty in regard to immigrants and refugees is already being contested on a number of fronts.

11. The Salvadoran case has been mentioned above. Guarnizo (1993) concludes his study of Dominican return migration with an argument that the Dominican "ethnic economy" in the U.S. and migrant remittances have important stabilizing effects for the economy of the Dominican Republic. A similar point is a major thrust of the argument by Portes (1996).

12. As Bonilla put it in a recent paper (1994: 6–7),

> The present mobility of capital both requires and promotes an equivalent infrastructure for others in the social order.... Over the last several decades, Latinos in the U.S. have emerged as strategic actors in major processes of social transformation.... The perception that Latinos are now positioned to share in bringing about change in the Americas from within the U.S. has increasingly taken hold and has sparked renewed interest and specific initiatives by hemispheric governments to cultivate new forms of relationships with emigrant communities.

13. One proposal for dual nationality under consideration by the Mexican government would permit Mexicans permanently residing in the U.S. (several million, over half in California) to naturalize themselves as U.S. citizens while retaining some of their rights as Mexican nationals. More radical proposals for dual citizenship, from the opposition PRD, would also permit them to vote in Mexico. Any of these would encourage legal Mexican residents in the U.S. to become voting U.S. citizens. Other countries such as El Salvador have already moved to permit double citizenship.

14. Many grass-roots community organizations and nongovernmental organizations are developing binational strategies and projects along these lines. Additionally, their work is being studied within the framework of "hometown associations" and binational or transnational community-building. See the case studies in Hamilton and Chinchilla (1996).

15. To give a few incipient examples: During the 1994 Salvadoran election campaign, progressive candidate Rubén Zamora came to California to establish ties with the large Salvadoran community here (as did Cuauhtémoc Cárdenas from the Mexican PRD); in both cases, the issue of their voting rights "back home," and dual citizenship more broadly, is on the agenda. Meanwhile, a group of Guatemalan "Displaced Persons living in the U.S." gained representation in the multi-sectoral Assembly of Civil Society in Guatemala, which is deeply involved in the peace process and the struggle to democratize Guatemala. In the U.S., the same group has been part of the coalition fighting to gain TPS status for Guatemalan refugees.

REFERENCES

American Assembly
1994   "World Migration and U.S. Policy." International Migration Review (Winter).
Bach, Robert
1992   "Hemispheric Migration in the 1990s." Jonathan Hartlyn, Lars Schoultz, and
                Augusto Varas (eds.), The United States and Latin America in the 1990s:
                Beyond the Cold War. Chapel Hill: University of North Carolina Press.
Basch, Linda, Nina Glick Schiller, and Cristina Szanton Blanc
1994   Nations Unbound: Transnational Projects, Postcolonial Predicaments, and
                Deterritorialized Nation-States. Langhorne, Penn.: Gordon and Breach.
Bonilla, Frank
1994   "The Global Society and the Latino Community: Changing the Americas from
                Within the U.S." (manuscript).
1992   "Circuits and Cycles: A Century of Puerto Rican Migration." Connecticut
                Humanities Council.

Castañeda, Jorge
1993   "Mexico and California: The Paradox of Tolerance and De-democratization."
               Abraham Lowenthal and Katrina Burgess (eds.), The California-Mexico
               Connection. Stanford: Stanford University Press.
Chávez, Leo, Estevan Flores, and Marta López-Garza
1990   "Here Today, Gone Tomorrow? Undocumented Settlers and Immigration
               Reform." Human Organization 49,3.
Chinchilla, Norma and Nora Hamilton
1995   "Sojourners, Settlers, or Returnees? Factors in Decisions of Central American
               Immigrants to Remain or Return." Presented at Latin American Studies
               Association conference.
Cornelius, Wayne
1996   "The Latin American Presence in the U.S.: Can Scholarship Catch Up with the
               Immigration Backlash?" LASA Forum (Winter).
Dagnino, Evelina
1993   "An Alternative World Order and the Meaning of Democracy." Jeremy
               Brecher, John Brown Childs, and Jill Cutler (eds.), Global Visions: Beyond
               the New World Order. Boston: South End Press.
Department of State
1983   Bulletin.
Espenshade, Thomas
1994   "Does the Threat of Border Apprehension Deter Undocumented U.S.
               Immigration?" Population and Development Review (December): 871–892.
Falk, Richard
1993   "The Making of Global Citizenship." Jeremy Brecher et al. (eds.), Global
               Visions: Beyond the New World Order. Boston: South End Press.
Farer, Tom
1995   "How the International System Copes with Involuntary Migration." M.
               Teitelbaum and M. Weiner (eds.), Threatened Peoples, Threatened Borders.
               New York: Norton.
Fernández Kelly, M. Patricia and Alejandro Portes
1992   "Continent on the Move: Immigrants and Refugees in the Americas." Alfred
               Stepan (ed.), Americas: New Interpretive Essays. New York: Oxford
               University Press.
Field Institute
1995   "California Opinion Index: Voting in the 1994 General Election" (January).
Gorelick, Jamie
1995   Justice Department Press Conference (transcript) (April 13).
Guarnizo, Luis
1993   "Going Home: Class, Gender, and Household Transformations Among
               Dominican Returned Migrants." Report prepared for Commission for
               Hemispheric Migration and Refugee Policy, Georgetown University.
Hamilton, Nora and Norma Chinchilla
1991   "Central American Migration: A Framework for Analysis." Latin American
               Research Review 29,1.
Hamilton, Nora and Norma Chinchilla (eds.)
1996   Central Americans in California. Los Angeles: Center for Multiethnic and
               Transnational Studies, University of Southern California.
International Migration Review
1991   Special Issue: "International Convention on the Protection of the Rights of All
               Migrant Workers and Members of Their Families" (Winter).
Jonas, Susanne
1997   "'National Security,' Regional Development and Citizenship in U.S.
               Immigration Policy: Reflections from the Case of Central American
               Immigrants and Refugees." Max Castro (ed.), Transnational Realities and
               Nation States. Miami: North-South Center (forthcoming).

1996   "Transnational Realities and Anti-Immigrant State Policies: Issues Raised by
               the Experiences of Central American Immigrants and Refugees in a
               Trinational Region." Roberto Korzeniewicz and William Smith (eds.), Latin
               America in the World Economy. Westport: Greenwood.
Keely, Charles
1995   "The Effects of International Migration on U.S. Foreign Policy."
               M. Teitelbaum and M. Weiner (eds.), Threatened Peoples, Threatened
               Borders. New York: Norton.
Kossoudji, Sherrie
1992   "Playing Cat and Mouse and the U.S.-Mexican Border." Demography 29,2
               (May): 159–180.
Loescher, Gil and John Scanlan
1986   Calculated Kindness: Refugees and America's Half-Open Door, 1945 to the
               Present. New York: Free Press.
Mahler, Sarah
1995   "Vested in Migration: Salvadorans Challenge Restrictionist Policies"
               (manuscript).
Massey, Douglas
1995   "The New Immigration and Ethnicity in the U.S." Population and Develop-
               ment Review 21,3 (September): 631–652.
Massey, Douglas et al.
1994   "An Evaluation of International Migration Theory: The North American
               Case." Population and Development Review 20,4 (December): 699–751.
Mitchell, Christopher
1989   "International Migration, International Relations, and Foreign Policy."
               International Migration Review 23,3 (Fall): 681–708.
Ong, Paul, Edna Bonacich, and Lucie Cheng
1994   The New Asian Immigration in Los Angeles and Global Restructuring.
               Philadelphia: Temple University Press.
Portes, Alejandro
1996   "Transnational Communities: Their Emergence and Significance in the
               Contemporary World-System." Roberto Korzeniewicz and William Smith
               (eds.), Latin America in the World Economy. Westport: Greenwood.
Portes, Alejandro and John Walton
1981   Labor, Class, and the International System. New York: Academic Press.
Rodríguez, Néstor
1996   "The Social Construction of the U.S.-Mexico Border." Juan Perea (ed.),
               The New Nativism. New York: New York Press.
Sassen, Saskia
1992   "Why Migration?" In NACLA Report on the Americas (July).
1988   The Mobility of Labor and Capital. Cambridge: Cambridge University Press.
Smith, Michael Peter
1994   "Can You Imagine? Transnational Migration and the Globalization of
               Grassroots Politics." Social Text 39 (Summer): 15–33.
Teitelbaum, Michael and Myron Weiner (eds.)
1995   Threatened Peoples, Threatened Borders. New York: Norton.
Wallerstein, Immanuel
1992   "The Collapse of Liberalism." Ralph Miliband and Leo Panitch (eds.),
               Socialist Register 1992. New York: Monthly Review Press.
Weiner, Myron
1995   The Global Migration Crisis. New York: HarperCollins.
White House
1995   "A National Security Strategy of Engagement and Enlargement" (February).
Zimmerman, Warren
1995   "Migrants and Refugees: A Threat to Security?" M. Teitelbaum and M. Weiner
               (eds.), Threatened Peoples, Threatened Borders. New York: Norton.

Zolberg, Aristide
    1995   "From Invitation to Interdiction: U.S. Foreign Policy and Immigration Since 1945." M. Teitelbaum and M. Weiner (eds.), Threatened Peoples, Threatened Borders. New York: Norton.
Zolberg, Aristide, Astri Suhrke, and Sergio Aguayo
    1989   Escape from Violence: Conflict and the Refugee Crisis in the Developing World. New York: Oxford University Press.

Chinese Suburban Immigration and Political Diversity In Monterey Park, California

John Horton

You're from Los Angeles? Isn't that near Monterey Park?

— Heard in Taiwan

W ITH ONLY EIGHT SQUARE MILES AND A POPULATION OF ABOUT 63,000, Monterey Park is one of 84 cities incorporated within the administratively fragmented County of Los Angeles (4,090 square miles, more than nine million people). Not in the standard tourist guide, Monterey Park is nevertheless recognized by Chinese the world over as America's first suburban Chinatown, sometimes disdained as "Mandarin Park" by disgruntled Anglo, Latino, and Asian American old-time residents, and regularly monitored by politicians, reporters, and social scientists as a microcosm of the ethnic, economic, and political changes wrought by immigration.

The ethnic transformation of Monterey Park began slowly with the migration of domestic minorities from the city to the suburbs. In 1960, Monterey Park was an Anglo town (85%) giving way to the suburban aspirations of primarily native-born Latinos (12%) and Asian Americans (3%). By 1970, Monterey Park had become a middle-class home for Mexican Americans from nearby working-class East Los Angeles and for Japanese Americans from enclaves in the east and west sides of L.A. and from regions of forced wartime internment and exile. There was also a migration of Chinese from the old Chinatown located just west of Monterey Park. The migration of Asian and Latino minorities to the suburbs was the combined result of postwar economic mobility and the legal and informal erosion of discrimination in housing.

The second ethnic transformation of Monterey Park, clearly visible by the mid-1970s, was primarily the result of the immigration of Chinese and other Asians

JOHN HORTON is an Emeritus Professor of Sociology at the University of California, Los Angeles, CA 90095–1551. This article is based on his recent book written with the assistance of José Calderon, Mary Pardo, Leland Saito, Linda Shaw, and Yen-Fen Tseng, *The Politics of Diversity: Immigration, Resistance, and Change in Monterey Park, California* (Philadelphia: Temple University Press, 1995). The research, which was conducted between 1988 and 1994, used ethnography, interviews, exit polls, and census data.

rather than the out-migration of native minorities. Their impact on the ethnic balance of Monterey Park was rapid and dramatic. In 1980 the city was almost evenly divided among Anglos (25%), Latinos (39%), and Asians Americans (35%). The small population of African Americans made up just over one percent. By 1990 Asian residents had become the majority, with about 60% of the population, while Anglos declined sharply to 12% and Latinos declined slightly to 31% of the total. The composition of the Asian population also shifted, with the younger Chinese newcomers now decisively replacing older native-born Japanese Americans as the largest Asian group.

Today, Monterey Park is a city completing its transition from a quiet, racially mixed bedroom suburb of aging single-family dwellings and dying commercial streets to a Pacific Rim hub with higher-density housing and a globally oriented financial and service center for a rapidly expanding regional Chinese population. The physical transition has been uneven. The city looks unfinished, caught between a Middle America of tranquil parks, tree-lined streets, and modest houses, and the encroaching restaurants, banks, supermarkets, mini-malls, condominiums, and traffic of a Chinese boom town.

In its size, composition, and pattern of settlement, the Asian immigration into Monterey Park and the surrounding western San Gabriel Valley created a new demographic and economic order, a break with rather than a mere continuation of earlier trends. It was the local manifestation of global restructuring: the movement and increased integration of human labor and capital on a world scale.

The new order brought together in a suburban setting an ethnic mix of primarily middle-class newcomers and established residents. It created unforeseen human problems and opportunities in the areas of ethnic relations and economic development. Newcomers and established residents never intended to be neighbors. Thrown together by forces reflecting decisions made in Washington, D.C., and the capitals of Asia, they found themselves sharing the space of a potential community and confronted with new conditions and the daunting task of forging civic bonds at the points where their lives collide and intersect.

Political Breaks and Transitions

The lives and interests of newcomers and established residents definitely collided in the realm of local politics. The old white power structure was in full decline, weakened by age, size, and the loss of its economic base to new Asian entrepreneurs. Replacing the old-timers were grass-roots rebels, some resisting and others pushing for change: established residents who wanted to turn back the clock; women who thought they could do a better job than men; people of color bent on empowerment; and a multiethnic business elite eager to translate its resources into governmental power.

Together these forces carved out the political options for a multiethnic community transformed by the new Asian immigration. The tradition of white, male business domination of local politics was at stake. Would it be maintained? Would it be ethnically modified, its class and gender base preserved under the rule of Chinese American males? Or would newcomers and established residents bring about a fundamental political transformation in the direction of greater ethnic and gender representation and more control over local economic development?

Also at stake was the relative interethnic harmony that had been achieved under the aegis of Anglos before the new Asian immigration had restructured the old ethnic and economic hierarchies. Would the old forms of white-sponsored accommodation collapse into political conflict based on ethnicity and divisions between newcomers and established residents? Would it be reimposed in a surge of nativism and Americanism? Or would new forms of coalition and cooperation grow from the soil of diversity in a city where Latino and Asian minorities had become the numerical majorities?

The answers lie in the evolving political process and its effects on the structure of power and political relations between immigrant newcomers and the multiethnic population of established residents. During the course of our research, the political process evolved from an initial stage of cooperation between immigrant newcomers and established residents at elite levels, to nativist conflict expressed in slow-growth and "English Only" movements, and, finally, to new points of conflict and accommodation. The last stage was characterized by the changing and situational formation of interethnic alliances (including immigrants and native-born) around issues of development and representation. Each of these stages was associated with a different alignment of class and ethnic forces and different levels of political struggle.

The Politics of Diversity: Immigration, Resistance, and Political Change in Monterey Park traces the evolution of political struggles, in particular, the neutralization of nativist currents and emergence of greater political and cultural diversity. Our electoral data, collected during local elections in 1988 and 1990, revealed two important political outcomes: the rising representation of women and people of color in the city council and the defeat of the most vocal white nativists. Our ethnographic data describe how these changes came about through a complex process of shifting positions and alliances.

One factor behind this transition was the continuing development of Latino, Asian American, and Chinese immigrant politics, the tendency to organize for ethnic representation and against nativist policies and candidates. A second factor was the increased ability of residents to separate slow-growth from nativist struggles, class from ethnic issues. The incentive for change was practical and points to a third factor in the evolution of local politics — the development of interethnic alliances on candidates and issues in a multiethnic city where no single group could determine political outcomes.

The local movement away from the dominance of nativist reactions to immigration and economic change did not, of course, eliminate racial, ethnic, and class problems; they were merely rearticulated into a different pattern with a different potential for conflict. The following ethnographic description of the lineup of forces for and against a proposed gambling parlor is but one example of the new pattern of forming shifting interethnic alliances. In this instance, we find Anglos who had initially led the slow-growth struggle against development with a Chinese face supporting the development of a Chinese-owned gambling facility. On the other side, a coalition of Chinese immigrants, Asian Americans, and Latinos came together to stop the development.

The Politics of Diversity: The Card Club Battle

The setting is the packed and raucous Monterey Park city council meeting of February 22, 1993. Tonight the council members will listen to public opinion and vote on the resolution introduced by Councilman Samuel Kiang, a naturalized citizen, "to take all steps necessary to keep gambling establishments illegal" in Monterey Park. By mobilizing community support and pressuring for compliance on the city council, Kiang and his allies hope to stop BCTC Development, a Taiwan-based company, from going ahead with its plans to build a $30-million card club in Monterey Park.

Approximately 700 people from Monterey Park and areas potentially affected by a card parlor fill the council chamber and flow into adjoining spaces. Some press into an antechamber to watch the fireworks through a long, open sliding-glass door. Others turned the wide entrance hall into a people's forum — a bustling space to watch the televised meeting, pass out no-gambling petitions, and form lively discussion groups with friends and strangers.

Greatly outnumbered and feeling like a besieged minority, the supporters of the card club gathered in angry clutches at the peripheries. Standing in the back of the antechamber at the Coke machine with several other elderly Anglo friends, Irv Gilman (former councilman and leader of the Residents Association of Monterey Park, or RAMP, a slow-growth organization) is conspicuously ignoring the meeting and offering words of warning:

> The crime isn't gambling, but the budget. These people are a moral majority who are against Monterey Park. You want my predictions? [Unless we solve the budget crisis]...the council will cut fire and police and we'll be a million in the hole. You asked, "Does RAMP have a position on the casino?" [He looked puzzled.] This is not a growth issue!

Working the crowd and collecting copy for his xenophobic local newspaper, the *Citizen's Voice*, Frank Arcuri, dismisses the protesters as "a bunch of outsiders and communists."

Irritated by the loud talking, a group of Latinos and Chinese against gambling start shaking their protest signs and strain to hear what is going on in the council chamber. Their orange placards with black letters in English, Spanish, and Chinese send an interethnic message of community empowerment: "Save Our Neighborhood." Other symbols injected a tone of moral condemnation: a "no" sign superimposed over a devil with a pitchfork lurking behind an Ace of Spades, Queen of Hearts, King of Clubs, and 10 of Diamonds — a losing poker hand. To the consternation of the city attorney and several council members, larger versions of the signs had been pasted on the council dais, and the vociferous majority and Councilman Kiang made it clear that they would stay there.

After a half hour of delays and haggling over the agenda, the "oral communications" begin, extending the meeting from seven o'clock to almost midnight. Of the 66 residents who stand at the microphone for their three minutes of free speech, 54 oppose gambling in Monterey Park, six support the card parlor, and six claim neutrality. Given the intimidating opposition, the neutrals look suspiciously like supporters of the card club.

Budget Crises and the Lure of Card Clubs in Los Angeles County

The council meeting of 1993 was a more dramatic and better-attended replay of a 1981 attempt to consider legalizing gambling in Monterey Park. At that time, Councilmen Irv Gilman and Harry Couch, activists in the tax-limitation and slow-growth movements, unsuccessfully floated the idea of capturing needed revenue from legalized gambling. However, city residents had no heart for gambling and developers no heart for slow-growth advocates. A week before the municipal election of 1982, candidates Gilman, Couch, and Sonya Gerlach — their comrade in the no-growth and pro-casino revolt — were proclaimed the "poker-slate" by a developer-financed "hit piece." They lost the election and their casino dream was put on hold for over a decade.

By the 1990s, Southern California cities, their budgets drained by recession, overspending, tax revolts, and the withdrawal of state and federal bailouts, were once again weighing the benefits and social costs of card clubs. This time, in an atmosphere of recession rather than growth, no-tax rebels and quick-profit developers united to sell gambling as a new source of city revenues to residents fearful of crime and big developers.

BCTC developers reasoned that the city was a promising site. Asians were good customers of existing clubs, but they had no facilities conveniently located in Monterey Park, where BCTC had an inside track to development. Their company was doing a good job on local public relations. While the young Chinese owner remained out of sight, his affable Anglo vice president, Mr. J. Richard Myers, was busily charming old-timers. By the time of the gambling controversy, he had become a key member of the local Chamber of Commerce and the president of the politically influential Monterey Park Boys and Girls Club.

However, even the best laid plans can be thwarted by hardball politics. Some residents, objecting to manipulation by developers, became uncharmed with

BCTC. They were put off by the latest scientific methods of persuasion. Preparing the way for a club, the company had hired a public relations firm to survey local opinion and to create opinion by inviting selected residents to attend focus groups on solutions to the city's problems. Their attendance at these promotional meetings was rewarded with a payment of 45 dollars. Myers summarized their findings as support for the card club in the form of an "entertainment center" that could improve the quality of life in Monterey Park, which would otherwise be compromised by the looming budget crisis. Kiang and others disagreed. In the words of one rebel, "This is one battle that you [BCTC and developers generally] are going to lose." The message was resoundingly delivered at the city council meeting held to debate Kiang's resolution against gambling.

"Save Our Neighborhood — Digamos ¡No! a El Casino"

The pro- and anti-gambling forces had very different messages and backgrounds. All 12 of the pro and neutral speakers at the council meeting were from Monterey Park, and the majority were middle-class Anglos. They spoke for themselves, although several were local leaders with their own constituencies.

Defending the card club were former Councilwoman Betty Couch and her mother-in-law, Evelyn Diederich, both fiscally conservative founders of RAMP, which had not taken an official stand on the issue. Some members opposed gambling as a development and quality-of-life issue; others supported it as a pure revenue issue.

The speakers opposed to gambling were more numerous and multiethnic, organized from the grass roots, and equally divided between primarily working-class and middle-class Latinos on the one side, and on the other, middle-class Asian Americans, Chinese immigrants, and a smaller number of left-leaning Anglos. Seventy-two percent were residents of Monterey Park, while the rest came from neighboring East Los Angeles, Alhambra, and Rosemead. The Chinese and Anglos tended to speak out against gambling as individual citizens, although some represented churches and the elderly. The Latinos, in particular, spoke as members of organized groups — churches, neighborhood associations, small businesses, and the elderly. Much in evidence were Latinos from the church-sponsored, Saul Alinsky-inspired, United Neighborhood Organizations (UNO). Their militant presence threatened a widened protest against any card parlor bordering the *barrio* of East Los Angeles.

The opposition testified to the social costs of gambling: crime, big money with power to corrupt public officials, "tarnishing" the image of a middle-class bedroom suburb, and adding to the woes of a working-class corner of Monterey Park where the club would be located. Some of the opposition spoke out of religious conviction. James H.K. Lau, M.D., the chair of the Community Concern Committee and member of the Board of the Chinese Evangelical Free Church, said in a written statement to the council:

To allow for the setting up of a casino means that the City Council encourages greediness and an unethical pastime at the expense of financial necessity. The narrow focus on increase in revenue reflects that the city government is short sighted, pragmatic, and has no concern for the long-term development of our community.

By contrast, the speakers for the card club rejected moral and political appeals and made their case on pragmatic and financial grounds: like it or not, gambling was here to stay. The best citizens make regular treks to casinos in Nevada, card clubs in L.A., and bingo games in local churches and senior centers. The less respectable had no difficulty finding high-stakes gambling in Monterey Park. Given the situation, why not recognize gambling, rely on the reputable BCTC to build a facility, and watch the revenue come in to solve the city's budget crisis and build a stronger police department? This type of argument was forcefully made by Evelyn Diederich, a veteran of RAMP:

People who spoke don't realize the financial crisis. The city will never cut enough to matter. We'll have to pay more taxes.... The paper said that a million dollars is spent for illegal gambling in the San Gabriel Valley. Why won't we let people who want to gamble pay our taxes? If this is a moral issue, why don't they fight to close down bars? People drink all evening and go out and drive, and that's dangerous. The gamblers just go out broke after paying a big lump of taxes.... The casino would be located away from homes in the Southwest part of the city, next to East L.A. in a rough area where no restaurant will go because of bad elements. Let the gambler pay the taxes.

Racial and Class Motives for Opposition and Support

The words of supporters and opponents reflected different perspectives on development and land use based on ethnic divisions between old-timers, minorities, and immigrants, as well as class divisions between a sheltered middle-class zone and the working-class zone where the card club would be located. The opposition tended to see racial and class interests behind the "objective" and "pragmatic" arguments for the gambling facility.

Privately, some Chinese American residents suspected a nativist and anti-Chinese element behind the enthusiasm for a card club. A young male, born in Taiwan, but raised in the United States and a resident of Monterey Park for 25 years, asked: "Who's for gambling? Old residents of European descent. Their children have grown up, they think that they are already paying too many taxes and see the casino as a way of preventing more." A middle-aged, American-born woman agreed: "The old whites are for the project. They only see the Chinese as people who love money, as gamblers and people who cause crime, people who should pay to solve the city's budget crisis."

While middle-class Chinese immigrant and Chinese American opponents of gambling were quick to find racial and nativist motives, Latinos, identifying with the plight of poorer populations who would have to live near the proposed card club, invoked the language of class discrimination: "I'm speaking not just for my parish, but for the little people, the poor. UNO is organized to bring power to the little people, and they will gather together and oppose [the facility]," said the Reverend Arnold Gonzalez from Our Lady of Soledad parish in Los Angeles, a member of UNO.

For their part, Anglo supporters of the card club also read between the lines and saw themselves as victims of discrimination. They resented and feared the "undemocratic, dictatorial" tactics of outside groups, minorities, and radicals. One longtime resident, Norman F. Schoff, stated in a written statement to the city council: "city projects and goals cannot be the right and privilege of an appointed few.... We cannot put the burden of choice on the shoulders of the city council or the backs of a few irrational citizens."

Other Anglo supporters of the card parlor held Kiang responsible for deliberately fomenting racial division. During the council meeting, they were passing among each other copies of a newspaper editorial with a yellow-highlighted passage that accused Kiang of "stirring up emotions in the Chinese and non-Chinese communities."

By contrast, the opponents of gambling claimed that their show of organized, grass-roots protest was, to use the words of Councilwoman Judy Chu, "democracy in action." In this case, democracy meant the direct and self-directed action of historically underrepresented minorities, even those who lacked citizenship or local residency. Given that any decision regarding a card parlor could affect their lives, shouldn't they organize to make their voices heard in a forum ordinarily controlled by a relatively unrepresentative corps of regular voters? Was this "mob rule" or "democracy in action"?

The answer depended on the situation and one's position in a community undergoing ethnic and political change. Old-timers who saw outsiders threatening their status and power wanted the issue of gambling settled democratically in an election that they had a good chance of influencing. Yet the majority of residents of color were outside the electoral process and would find their democracy in direct political action.

A Temporary Victory for the Anti-Gambling Forces

In the end, the "democracy in action" of the more numerous opponents of legalized gambling won out over the "electoral democracy" advocated by the supporters. At least for the moment, the plan for a card club was stopped before it could come up before a special election. Kiang's anti-gambling resolution before the city council was strongly endorsed by Councilwoman Chu. Under fire, the three reluctant members of the council (Rita Valenzuela, Fred Balderrama, and

Marie Purvis) bowed to the army of protest and approved an amended resolution pledging to "take all steps legally permissible to keep gambling establishments illegal" in Monterey Park.

BCTC Development also gave in to "democracy in action." Several weeks after the protest at the city council, the company decided not to push for a card parlor. According to Richard Myers, the vice president, "It was too close a business decision to invest half a million dollars on a campaign." Judging from the electoral response elsewhere, this was a wise decision. By August of 1993, Southland voters in five cities in Orange and Los Angeles Counties had voted against proposed card clubs.

The Political Significance of the Gambling Controversy

The casino tempest was significant in several respects. First, it engendered unusually strong grass-roots participation that culminated in what local observers claimed was the largest protest in the city's history. It was certainly the largest that we had seen. Second, the protest involved an unprecedented level of interethnic, interclass, and immigrant/established resident unity. Power flowed from the convergence of grass-roots organizing and leadership by and among Latinos, Chinese, and Anglos. Particularly noteworthy was the strong presence and cooperation of two previously separated and sometimes antagonistic groups — working-class Latinos (immigrants and U.S.-born) from East Los Angeles and the poorer sections of Monterey Park, and middle-class Chinese (predominately immigrants) and Japanese Americans (predominately U.S.-born) from Monterey Park. Asians were particularly sensitive to the danger of gambling tarnishing the image of America's first majority-Asian city. Latinos were particularly sensitive to the location of the facility in their sector of the city.

The alliance merged different class styles of grass-roots politics. Latinos from East Los Angeles brought a tradition of militant working-class and church-supported collective organizing and a philosophy of empowerment. Middle-class residents from Monterey Park brought the power of their networks, the skills of individuals involved in issue-specific, neighborhood organizing, and the knack for working within the system.

In spite of the differences in class, nativity, ethnic background, and political style, the protesters shared the determination to protect their neighborhoods against the unwanted project of a big developer. Improving the depressed quality of local life had been a constant struggle in working-class neighborhoods, which were often the dumping grounds for projects unacceptable to more affluent and powerful residents in the suburbs. By the 1980s, increasingly urbanized suburbs like Monterey Park were no longer safe havens from unwanted development and became combat centers for maintaining an already high quality of life. The protest against gambling was significant in uniting neighborhoods ordinarily separated by class and parochialism. The protesters recognized that their problems were regional and that, in this instance, they shared the same side in the class struggle over land use.

Finally, the mass involvement of Latinos and Asian Americans in the casino battle signaled both the democratization of the movement for control over development and the continuing salience of ethnic divisions within it. Throughout most of the 1980s, the leaders of the controlled-growth movement were Anglo. In 1993, the leaders of the protest against gambling were multiethnic, a point dramatically brought home when a long-established Chinese American resident said publicly in accented English: "Asians like gambling, particularly Chinese, but not in their backyards." Her statement belied the all too common stereotypes of Chinese narrowly focused on making money and unconcerned about community welfare. One does not have to be white to be a NIMBY (not-in-my-backyard).

The demand for control over one's own backyard came with the territory and the structure of economic and governmental power. At one level, it is a simple class issue dividing property users from property profiteers. However, in Monterey Park, because of the new Chinese immigration, the territory had become more ethnically diverse and the movement for control over development was more representative and more divided. Several prominent leaders of RAMP, as they had in the past, supported the card club. Being located outside their neighborhoods and promising increased revenues without increasing taxes for homeowners, it was for them a good development.

The clash between residents who supported and opposed the gambling facility reminded us that ethnicity and class counted in determining what was and was not a development issue. Ironically, given the history of development issues in Monterey Park, Chinese and Latinos were united against a Chinese developer and his supporters, who included a contingent of Anglo leaders of the slow-growth movement. Was the mantle of leadership in the populist struggle over land use passing from a small group of whites to a multiethnic coalition?

Immigration and the Meaning of Diversity

The major implications of these findings concern the possibility of political diversity and multiculturalism in a society that is becoming global in its economic and demographic structure. In Monterey Park, nativism and ethnic conflict were not the inevitable outcomes of the immigration of Asian people and capital. Under the specific demographic and economic conditions of the region, a level of democracy based on ethnic and cultural diversity was achieved at the grass roots through the formation of interethnic alliances that included immigrants. In electing a candidate, putting on a cultural performance, or just saying "no" to a developer, and "yes" to a safe neighborhood, what counted in the end was not the racist or antiracist beliefs of individuals, but the collective, pragmatic practice of cooperation in civic organizations, neighborhoods, and political arenas.

The case of Monterey Park also clarifies the often contradictory and competing meanings of diversity. Our baptism into local politics taught us that diversity based on ethnicity and immigration favored accommodation when it was connective — that is, associated with the formation of interethnic alliances favoring the empowerment and inclusion of underrepresented populations.

The dilemma of diversity is to legitimate the continual expression and creation of ethnic and other differences while making connections that transcend them. This connective diversity takes place in Monterey Park whenever people from different ethnic and national backgrounds work on common projects. It takes place on an everyday level when residents with very different memories of home and place begin to feel accountable to the place where they now live, and to its people. This pragmatic process of making connections between people in neighborhoods, civic organization, and local politics may be our only hope if diversity is be more than an ornament of the status quo or a polite word for ethnic conflict.

Making interconnections is not an impossible task. Our findings point to the fluidity of American, immigrant, and ethnic identities in Monterey Park. They are continually constructed and reconstructed at the porous borders between residents on the basis of situationally defined political and class interests. These identities are not primordial, nor are they purely voluntary constructions. They count as resources for political organizing. The issue is how they count and how they are constructed as a means of empowerment, whether they facilitate connections, alliances, or set up barriers.

The theoretical and political points about making connections and refusing to essentialize concepts like ethnicity apply also to the concept of immigrant and immigration. In our research, we have refused to enter the debate about the costs and debits of immigration, thereby separating and disconnecting immigrants from the society in which they live. Try as they may, national governments cannot stop people from crossing penetrable borders that have lost their relevance in an interconnected world. Whatever the direction of future policies, immigrants have already changed the ethnic and economic character of border cities like Los Angeles and Miami and become an integral part of economic life. Given the situation, the sensible approach is to take newcomers and established residents as part of the same society, look at their interactions, and learn under what conditions they can cooperate with each other and negotiate their shared problems in a situation of diversity.

From our research, one policy recommendation forcefully emerges. The politics of resistance — singling out for exclusion and control immigrants who have established their lives in a community — will not work. The result in Monterey Park was division and conflict. The only viable alternative is a politics of incorporation and inclusion, encouraging social and political participation, education, and language skills: the tools for citizenship and equality in a society of immigrants.

U.S. Immigration and Intergroup Relations in the Late 20th Century: African Americans and Latinos

Néstor Rodríguez

Introduction

VARIOUS MACRO-STRUCTURAL FORCES ARE TRANSFORMING THE SOCIAL COMPOSItion of large U.S. urban areas in the late 20th century. As in other advanced Western societies, global economic restructuring and international migration are dramatically altering socio-cultural and demographic landscapes in the urban United States. In the short historical span since the 1970s, these processes have produced substantial growth of ethnic/racial populations in large U.S. urban areas, e.g., New York, Los Angeles, and Houston, with strong ties to the global economy. Large-scale immigration from Asia, Latin America, and other world regions has intensified urban change in these settings by creating new culturally distinct communities (Lamphere, 1992). Socially and culturally, and in terms of new patterns of intergroup relations, the large U.S. urban centers of the 1990s are not the same settings of 10 or 20 years ago.

This large-scale social and demographic change has produced new interrelational matrices in U.S. urban areas (Bach, 1993). With the expansion and diversification of Asian, Latino, and other ethnic/racial communities, the poles of urban race relations have been transformed from a mainly binary plane of black-white relations into multidimensional axes of ethnicity, immigrant status, nationality, race, and other social identities. Especially after the social eruptions of African Americans and Latinos in Los Angeles in the spring of 1992, this social recomposition has created concerns among mainstream institutional leaders about the interethnic/racial future of their localities. African American and Latino communities are prominent players in this future, since in many of the largest urban areas they form a collective majority of the population. Among the five largest cities in the country, this is true in New York, Los Angeles, Chicago, and

---

NÉSTOR RODRÍGUEZ is an associate professor in the Department of Sociology at the University of Houston and the director of the university's Center for Immigration, 492 PGH, College of Social Science, University of Houston, TX 77204–3472, (713) 743–3946. The author is grateful to Tatcho Mindiola for comments on an earlier draft of this article.

Houston (U.S. Bureau of the Census, 1994). In the fifth largest city, Philadelphia, African Americans and Latinos compose 45.2% of the population. In the South, Houston is a critical case of emerging intergroup relations between African Americans and Latinos in the context of high immigration levels. The 1990 census found that Houston has more black residents than any other southern city, and has the second largest Latino population in the South (if not the largest by 1995). Over 40% of Houston's 450,000 Latino population consists of first-generation immigrants (U.S. Bureau of the Census, 1993).

In this article, I focus on the arena of intergroup relations between African Americans and Latinos from the perspective of Latino immigration. In the first part of the discussion, I attempt to relate the arena of intergroup relations to larger structural processes with reference to global change and immigration. These processes are important for relations between African Americans and Latinos because they greatly affect the social geographies and related opportunity structures of intergroup interaction.

In the second part of the discussion, using findings from recent intergroup surveys and ongoing ethnographic research in the Houston area, I argue that contrary to some expectations (see Johnson et al., 1995) tensions, conflict, and community instability are not the only resulting relations between African Americans and Latinos in contexts of high immigration. Indeed, I attempt to make the case for varied modes of intergroup reactions in such settings, sometimes varying by social identities other than ethnicity or race, and sometimes forming collaborative relations based precisely on identities of minority status. Using the prominent Houston case, my purpose in this discussion also is to suggest that the highly publicized intergroup patterns of Los Angeles do not necessarily represent the future of the U.S. urban system.

Macro-Structural Contexts of Immigration
And African American-Latino Relations

In the late 20th century, urban intergroup relations have become substantially affected by underlying structural processes whose reach transcends not only specific urban settings, but also the very nation-state. Three such processes — global economic restructuring, transnational community development, and immigrant incorporation — are as significant for the course of black-brown relations in Los Angeles, Houston, and other major U.S. cities as are social-psychological conditions that may predispose intergroup behavior.

Global Economic Change

A number of works have described processes of global economic restructuring that affect areas in core countries and peripheral regions of the world economy (e.g., see Henderson and Castells, 1987). According to Saskia Sassen-Koob (1987), this worldwide economic change involves the recomposition of industrial capital, concentrating managerial and specialized services in major urban areas in core countries and relocating manufacturing in peripheral regions. This restructuring stimulates labor migration among peripheral regions, as well as to new economic centers in core countries. Immigration becomes a major source of labor for the large array of low-wage, service jobs that emerge in the global centers of business management and control in core countries, and in a few semi-peripheral areas as well (*Ibid.*).

Global restructuring significantly affects the intergroup prospects of large urban settings in the United States as shifts in capital and labor arrangements repel certain groups and attract others. For example, Sassen-Koob (*Ibid.*) has demonstrated how the restructured economies of New York City, Los Angeles, and San Francisco have attracted immigrant labor from Latin American and Asia, as middle-income, blue- and white-collar U.S. workers were laid off. Sociologist Rebecca Morales has conducted a detailed study of how the social composition of Los Angeles' automobile industry became increasingly immigrant and Mexican as industry owners and managers restructured production to operate with a lower-paid labor force (Morales, 1982).

Research in Houston has shown that, similar to the recomposition of production, the restructuring of consumption can greatly affect the social landscape and its intergroup relations. According to studies of Houston's vast apartment complex industry, when the world oil economy entered a steep recession in the mid-1980s, apartment real-estate capital in the city's middle-income west side entered a severe crisis as thousands of office workers left the city after losing their jobs in oil- and petrochemical-related industries and in supportive firms (Rodríguez, 1993). Facing the loss of billions of dollars invested in thousands of apartment complexes built mainly for young, single middle-income tenants, apartment owners and managers adopted a temporary strategy of recomposing their shrinking middle-class, and mainly Anglo, tenant populations with newly arriving immigrants from Mexico and Central America. The city's west-side apartment industry underwent a dramatic restructuring as many apartment complexes had their names changed from English to Spanish, hired bilingual rental agents, and reduced rents by half or more to attract immigrant renters. The strategy attracted large numbers of Latino immigrants, mostly low-income undocumented workers, into the predominately white west-side districts of the city. As many apartment complexes in the west side became increasingly identified as new low-cost housing, they also attracted large numbers of African Americans from the wards in the eastern half of the city (*Ibid.*).

To the distress of many middle-income, established residents in the west side, the recomposed tenant populations became heartlands of new communities of color as Mexicans, Central Americans, South Americans, Black Caribs, African Americans, and other groups settled in the apartment complexes. The new apartment communities consisted heavily of working-class families. With the upswing of the area's economy in the late 1980s and 1990s and the expected return of middle-income tenants, apartment owners and managers again restructured their apartment complexes to dramatically reduce the presence of black and brown tenants (*Ibid.*). Living in fewer affordable apartments, African Americans and Latinos in the west side nevertheless remain a major source of black-brown intergroup relations in the Houston area.

Transnational Community Development and Intergroup Relations

Macro-structural recomposition may bring different ethnic and racial groups into the same spatial setting, but it does not necessarily produce extensive intergroup relations initially. The Houston case showed that as large numbers of Latino newcomers settled in the city in the 1970s and 1980s, much of their social interaction was maintained with fellow immigrants in their residences and workplaces. Moreover, much of this in-group interaction was directed to the development of transnational linkages to communities of origin in Mexico, Central America, and other Latin American countries. This led to the creation of transnational communities where family households underwent social reproduction through production and consumption activities both in the United States and in the home country (Rodríguez, 1995).

In the four large, established Mexican *barrios* in Houston's eastern half, the development of transnational communities in the 1970s and 1980s was actually an historical continuation, and dramatic enhancement, of processes started by the city's original Mexican immigrants in the 1910s and 1920s (De Leon, 1987). The inward social development of many new immigrants in the *barrios* initially only reinforced the social and cultural separation between Mexican-origin and African American communities in the city's eastern half. Later, however, as transnational communities prospered and expanded after the city's economic upturn, new Mexican immigrants begin to settle in small numbers in the traditional black wards. While adult African Americans and Latino immigrants mainly interacted separately in the wards, their children came together in nearby predominantly black public schools. In one ward setting, fights between black and brown students brought African American and Mexican American community leaders together to intervene.

Across the city, in the west-side apartment complex areas, new Latino immigrants have also constructed transnational structures linking their family households in Houston with their communities of origin back home (Rodríguez, 1993). Apart from casual encounters, Latino immigrants and African Americans usually live socially and culturally apart in the apartment complexes. Sharing a common settlement space, however, the two groups inevitably cross paths in routine activities of community life. For example, in a large county park in the city's southwest area, Latino and African American residents can be found engaged in recreational activities at the same time, but with African American youth on the basketball court and Latinos on the soccer fields. With the exception of a rugby team that uses a playing field a few times during the week (but which has a 10-year park privilege), the white presence in the park consists mainly of law enforcement officers who occasionally patrol the park grounds. The adjacent Anglo resident population has almost completely stopped using the park.

In addition to participating in public school programs that promote intergroup awareness, some African American and Latino residents in the west side have a chance to learn about each other's cultures and concerns through occasional interethnic festivals organized by churches and other places of worship. In the last few years, social service providers in the city's southwest area have also promoted intergroup encounters through monthly luncheon meetings, where they explain their programs and exchange information. One function in the southwest area that draws large numbers of residents and agency representatives is an annual festival in the county park where Anglos, African Americans, Latinos, and Asians set up booths to represent their organizations and sell different foods to raise funds for a local storefront police station.

The annual fund-raising festival is an exception to the general pattern of separate coexistence among the west side's African Americans and large Latino immigrant populations. Over time, however, transnational communities are sure to lose some of their inward social tendencies for Latinos as the U.S.-born children of immigrants look to the United States, and not their parents' home countries, for social and cultural standards. First-generation Latino immigrants also will look increasingly to the United States for future plans and community growth as they acquire greater social incorporation in this country.

Immigrant Incorporation and Intergroup Relations

Working-class immigrant populations have generally achieved initial incorporation into the U.S. social structure through endogenous institutions, including ethnic places of worship, traditional organizations, and culturally familiar neighborhoods. Actually, in Houston, as in many other immigration settings, many new immigrants achieve initial social, cultural, and spatial incorporation in ethnic communities and economic incorporation in mainstream settings (Rodríguez, 1993). The latter involves service work in a wide variety of workplaces, e.g., restaurants, car washes, supermarkets, office buildings, and so forth, and usually in ethnic crews. Obviously, the levels of incorporation (ethnic versus mainstream, or interethnic) for the different dimensions (social, cultural, etc.) greatly affect the opportunity structure for black-brown intergroup relations.

Native and immigrant Latinos who achieve social and cultural incorporation through ethnic communities will probably have fewer opportunities to develop relations with African Americans, or any other non-Latino group, outside workplaces. In major urban centers with large Latino populations, this may characterize as much as half the Latino residents. For example, if we use Spanish preference as an indicator of ethnic social and cultural incorporation, then in the Houston area 83.9% of foreign-born, and 14.2% of native, Latino adults are characterized by ethnic social and cultural incorporation, according to Mindiola et al. (1996). For this population the workplace becomes a major setting of intergroup relations, often across segmented work crews. Indeed, Mindiola et al. found that most respondents identified their workplaces as the primary settings of their intergroup relations. Yet, Latino incorporation in ethnic communities does not completely restrict interaction with African Americans at the community level, since in a few cases lower-income black residents turn to Latino stores and restaurants in *barrios* for lower-priced goods and services. Here, class similarity overrides cultural differences.

Similar political perspectives also promote intergroup relations between African Americans and Latino immigrants. African Americans, including the Reverend Jesse Jackson, have participated in Latino immigrant marches and demonstrations against Proposition 187 in California and other restrictive measures. For example, African American NAACP leaders and unionists joined Latinos in a San Antonio march against Proposition 187 in the spring of 1995. African American women in Houston have traveled to Mexico as election observers and have responded to a call for collective women's action after a group of armed men assaulted and raped the official U.S. representative of the Zapatista movement in Mexico. These examples indicate that at least the civil rights activist and internationalist sectors in the African American population have supported the political incorporation of Latino immigrants in the United States and abroad.

The macro-structural contexts of global restructuring, transnational community development, and immigrant incorporation set part of the stage for emerging intergroup relations, whether cooperative or conflictive, between African Americans and Latinos. Perhaps more than before, the macro-structural perspective is important for analyzing the evolving relations between these two groups, as interaction and relations between global regions appear to have reached an unprecedented level in the late 20th century.

Houston: Varied Modes of Relations Between African Americans and Latinos

In the Houston area, as I suspect occurs across the country, relations between African Americans and Latinos take on a variety of characteristics. Across different institutional settings, the characteristics range from overt conflict, to peaceful coexistence, to collaboration. Although episodes of conflict get the most media attention, behind-the-scenes collaboration may have as much, or more, significance for the future relations between African Americans and Latinos, including a large immigrant sector, in the city. Research in the 1990s indicates that perceptions of the predominant quality of Houston's black-brown relations vary by the most recent issue, by whether you ask African Americans or Latinos, and, within each group, whether you ask community leaders or ordinary residents

(Romo et al., 1994). Mindiola et al. (1996) found that African American and Latino residents have ambivalent views on the quality of black-brown relations in Houston. In one section of the interview, they respond that relations between the two groups are generally good, while in another section they respond that there is too much conflict between the two groups (*Ibid.*).

Residential Transition and Intergroup Relations

Although the largest numbers of Latino immigrants in Houston in the 1980s have settled in Mexican *barrios* in the city's east side and in new immigrant settlement zones in the west, some newcomers from Mexico and Central America located rental housing adjacent to, and inside, established African American residential communities ("wards") near the city's downtown (Rodríguez, 1993). Similar to developments in Compton, California, described by Johnson et al., this new Latino housing pattern represents at least a partial residential transition in the affected ward areas. The impact of the general residential change for African American-Latino relations has been very evident in public schools, as well as in the politics of the Houston Independent School District (HISD).

Not surprisingly, fights between black and Latino youth are occasionally reported in public schools near areas of residential transition. Yet in many other cases, African American and Latino youth work together in school activities, maintaining at least a peaceful coexistence, if not a harmonious one. In some other cases, African American and Latino youth unite and form black-brown gangs, sometimes with deadly consequences. In the larger teaching work force of HISD, Latino teachers constitute only 13.4% of all teachers (41.2% are black), while Latino students represent 50.0% of all students (Houston Independent School District, 1995). Yet, Latinos have not mounted a sustained effort to pressure the African American superintendent to bring in greater numbers of Latino teachers. (HISD administrators initiated a program to recruit teachers from abroad, but ran into problems validating the credentials of foreign teachers.)

African American-Latino tension and conflict, however, surfaced in the selection of the present African American superintendent of HISD, when the school board selected him from among their own. When the HISD school board announced their decision, several Latino leaders objected to the lack of an open, national search, and especially the absence of any consideration for Hispanic candidates given that Latinos constituted the largest student population in the school district. A group of Latino leaders took the matter to court, but lost when the case was dismissed. Latino interest in the matter eventually died out due to a lack of progress and the absence of a united Latino front, but not before causing a major cleavage between many African American and Latino leaders in the city. A leading African American figure in the city likened the Latino struggle against the appointment of the African American superintendent to a "political lynching." More recently, the African American and Latino school board members have united to maintain a magnet school in an upper-class neighborhood against the wishes of some of the neighborhood residents, who want the school for the neighborhood's children.

The findings of Romo et al. (1994) and Mindiola et al. (1996) demonstrate African American views on how immigrants have affected the Houston area in the 1990s. Using data from a 1992 survey, Romo et al. (1994) found that a majority (53%) of African American respondents indicated that the impact of immigrants had been "good" or "very good," while 40.3% of the African American respondents indicated that the impact had been "bad" or "very bad." The survey, of course, was conducted before the anti-immigrant sentiments generated by Governor Pete Wilson's reelection campaign and the promotion of Proposition 187 in California. (As late as the fall of 1993, 58% of the respondents in a *Time Magazine* poll indicated that immigrants were "basically good, honest people," and only 29% of the respondents favored a fence along the U.S.-Mexico border; see Nelan, 1993.)

Using data from a 1995 survey, Mindiola et al. (1996) found that African Americans in Houston had reversed their perceptions of the immigrant impact in the Houston area. The survey found that 36.3% of the African American respondents judged the immigrant impact to be "good" or "very good," while a majority (53.6%) now viewed the impact to be "bad" or "very bad." Perhaps some of the negative perception concerned worries that immigrants were taking advantage of hard-won affirmative action programs, since at least one African American elected official in Houston recently asked for a study on the issue of immigrant employment through affirmative action.

Intergroup Effects of Asian Entrepreneurship

Similar to highly publicized cases in California, the Houston area has experienced some cases of tension and conflict between African American residents and Asian store owners. In a handful of cases, African Americans have boycotted Asian-owned stores in their neighborhoods to protest what they perceive to be a lack of concern among Asian business owners over the black communities where their businesses are located. In one case, similar to the Latasha Harlins case in California, a young Vietnamese clerk in a convenience store owned by his family shot and killed an African American youth who allegedly had become argumentative and left the store with beer without paying. When the store clerk was not convicted for the death, African Americans boycotted the store and eventually forced the Vietnamese family to sell the business (Inter-Ethnic Forum of Houston, 1995).

To lessen the intergroup tensions generated by this occurrence of African American-Asian conflict, leaders from the two communities met to organize joint community meetings of African Americans and Asians to address their intergroup problems. Of special importance, the meetings involved religious leaders from both communities. Although the intergroup sessions did not reduce class differences between black customers and Asian store owners, it did give both sides an opportunity to address each other in a controlled setting. Perhaps more important, the leaders demonstrated an interest in containing the problem, rather than letting it spread. Also, the intergroup meetings created a model for dealing with future confrontations between black residents and Asian store owners.

To be sure, intergroup leadership collaboration in the Houston area appears to be common in most groups. In a nonrandom mail survey of community leaders, which was conducted along with the 1992 random survey by Romo et al. (1994), the percentages of identified leaders who reported interacting frequently with leaders from other groups were the following: African Americans, 54.8%; Anglos, 43.9%; Asians, 38.5%; and Latinos, 52.5% (*Ibid.*).

The high tension level between Asians and Latinos in the Los Angeles area, described by Johnson et al., is not found in the Houston area. For the most part, the two populations live apart. Asian entrepreneurship has become a significant employment source for Latino immigrants in restaurant businesses. Also, in some cases Asian-Latino partnerships create popular eating places in Latino immigrant neighborhoods. Indeed, such enterprises appear to be creating a new Asian-Latino business form where customers select dishes from bicultural, Chinese-Mexican menus. In one instance, the multicultural restaurant arrangement reached a rather intense level — a group of Korean restaurateurs hired Mexican immigrant cooks to prepare Chinese dishes for mainly African American customers.

Romo et al. (1994) found the following regarding relations among Asians and African Americans and Latinos. Among African American respondents, 41.7% viewed relations between blacks and Asians to be "fair," and 13.3% viewed the relations to be "good" or "very good," while 34.7% viewed the relations between the two groups to be "bad" or "very bad." Among Latino respondents, 44.7% viewed relations between Latinos and Asians to be "fair," and 17.0% viewed relations to be "good" or "very good," while 15.7% viewed the relations between the two groups to be "bad" or "very bad." The responses clearly indicate an absence of polarization between Asians and the two groups of African Americans and Latinos.

Employment and Intergroup Relations

The rise of immigration in Houston over the last two decades produced an abundant labor supply, particularly for the lower echelons of the area's labor market. In some cases, new Latino immigrant workers became highly visible in jobs previously held by African Americans. This employment included domestic workers, hotel workers, and supermarket maintenance workers. Indeed, the rise of immigration created a sort of reserve labor market for immigrant labor, i.e., employment sectors containing only immigrant workers that U.S. workers appeared to avoid because of their immigrant character (Rodríguez, 1995).

The reserve immigrant labor markets functioned as quasi-internal labor markets. As such, recruitment and promotion of immigrant workers in specific work settings were only minimally affected by the labor supply outside the immigrant labor force. In many work settings, immigrant workers' social networks were a major basis for producing work forces, defining the division of labor, and controlling the labor process. A heaven for employers, immigrant reserve and internal labor markets thus provided a self-reproducing and self-regulating work force, and at a bargain price.

Reserve immigrant labor markets reduce direct tension and conflict among U.S. and immigrant workers by reducing contact between the two groups of workers. In many workplaces, immigrants work in crews consisting of only immigrants (see Rodríguez, 1987). Encounters with native workers thus occur mainly through interactions with U.S.-born supervisors. In large workplaces, immigrants may work among native workers, but in separate crews.

Although reserve immigrant labor markets may reduce direct conflict among U.S. and immigrant workers, employment-related tension may develop from the perception that immigrants are taking American jobs. Mindiola et al. (1996), however, found that African Americans in Houston have mixed views on this issue. While a majority (53.7%) of the African American respondents agreed "somewhat" or "strongly" that immigrants take away jobs from black workers, 39.1% disagreed "somewhat" or "strongly" that this is true, and 7.2% had no opinion. Interestingly, about one-fifth (19.8%) of the African American respondents disagreed *strongly* that immigrants take jobs away from blacks. The unemployment rates among the survey respondents were 7.9% for African Americans and U.S.-born Latinos, and 5.2% for foreign-born Latinos.

Language and Intergroup Relations

Language is one of the most sensitive issues in intergroup relations (Bach, 1993). Simply put, in many U.S. areas, Spanish and other non-English languages are being used more frequently and many established residents resent this. The latter perceive "foreign" languages as a threat not only to English, but also to American culture in general. In some cases, language differences may even cause tension among groups from the same world region or the same cultural origin. In Houston, for example, some Vietnamese residents dislike the use of Chinese characters on street signs in predominantly Chinese districts, and some U.S.-born Latinos avoid social settings where interaction is carried on mainly in Spanish.

For African Americans, Spanish may represent an additional barrier to employment or job promotion, especially in business and public workplaces increasingly affected by a growing Latino immigrant presence. The finding in Mindiola et al. (1996), however, indicated that African Americans in Houston have mixed views about the use of the Spanish language. When asked to respond to the statement "It is okay for people to use Spanish in the workplace," about one-half (48.6%) of the African American respondents agreed somewhat or strongly with the statement, and almost a similar proportion (45.4%) disagreed "somewhat" or "strongly" with the statement, while 6.0% had no opinion. When asked what the impact of Spanish usage for the country as a whole was, 46.0% of the African American respondents said it was "somewhat bad" or "very bad," and 42.7% said it was "somewhat good" or "very good" for the country, while 10.7% had no opinion. African Americans in Houston are clearly divided on the issue of Spanish usage.

It is important to understand that the high level of Spanish usage is greatly associated with immigration. In the Houston area, for example, 85.8% of U.S.-born Latinos prefer English over Spanish in public interaction (*Ibid.*). Among Latino immigrants, especially the young, the ability to use English increases with length of residence in the United States. A study of immigrants in Southern California found that 70% of immigrants who had been in the region at ages five to 14 in 1980 had mastered English by 1990 (McDonnell, 1995).

Proposition 187 and Intergroup Relations

As described by Johnson et al. (1995), the black community vote for Proposition 187 affects black-brown relations in two significant ways: the vote has become a source of tension between African Americans and Latinos in Southern California, and the passage of the proposition has prompted Latino immigrants to naturalize and, presumably, to become potential anti-black voters. Apart from the fact that a federal court recently invalidated major portions of the legislation, it is not clear what the long-term consequences of black support for immigration restriction will be from a Houston perspective. Survey results in the Houston area indicate that black concern for immigration restriction is similar to the larger national trend against undocumented immigration and not particularly an anti-Latino sentiment.

The findings of Mindiola et al. (1996) indicate that African American support in Houston for immigration restriction is not generally an anti-Latino position. The study found that a majority (65%) of African Americans favor a national identification card to keep undocumented immigrants from U.S. jobs, but that a majority (58%) of Latinos also favor such a proposal. This finding and the finding mentioned above that over one-third of African American respondents viewed Houston's immigration to be good or very good strongly suggests that African American concerns over immigration restriction are not particularly prone to induce black-brown conflict. Indeed, in HISD, African American administrators can be found hard at work in multicultural programs supporting Latino immigrant children. In the Harris County Commissioner's Court, an African American commissioner (the only minority member in the all-male court) has questioned proposals to investigate the residency status of county hospital users, an effort directed mainly at unauthorized (read undocumented) immigrant patients (Inter-Ethnic Forum of Houston, 1995).

It is also not clear that the record high levels of naturalization by immigrants will produce a Latino voter backlash against African Americans, especially since many Latinos in California also voted for Proposition 187. From the Houston perspective, equating naturalized Latino citizens with Latino voters is still problematic. Mindiola et al. (1996) found that only about 20% of the Latino immigrant respondents were U.S. citizens. Although this proportion will increase, previous research has found mainly a low to moderate electoral interest in Houston's immigrant concentrations. Undoubtedly, the present Latino immigrant interest in U.S. citizenship is significantly motivated by concerns about future restrictions against noncitizens, but how this will affect future electoral politics is not clear.

My attempt in this section has been to suggest that relations between African Americans and Latinos in U.S. settings of high immigration can vary considerably across urban areas. I have specifically attempted to demonstrate that the conflictive and tense character described by some (e.g., Johnson et al., 1996) for African American-Latino relations in the Los Angeles area differs significantly from conditions in the large Houston area. Across U.S. urban settings, social histories, institutional conditions, and political human agency may vary sufficiently to produce at least the potential for different intergroup responses to changes effected by immigration. However, this is not to say that different localities have completely distinct intergroup trajectories. Intergroup relations in major U.S. urban centers may have similar opportunity structures (but not necessarily identical responses) since these areas are affected by common macro-structural processes, e.g., globalization and international migration, which significantly affect the areas' institutional environments.

Conclusion

Black-brown intergroup relations in the United States are evolving from a complicated matrix in the late 20th century that includes global, national, and local levels, as well as varying predisposing social-psychological conditions. Yet, intergroup relations among African Americans and native and foreign-born Latinos are not totally unpredictable. Black Americans are the most economically stressed group in U.S. society, and therefore it seems logical to hypothesize that the most disadvantaged members of this population, such as the unemployed and the working poor, will react against conditions they perceive to be against their interests in an already precarious existence. What happened in Los Angeles in spring 1992, I believe, is a dramatic example of this. As happens in other populations of color, however, not all African Americans react to change from a racial group perspective; some react from a class or political perspective and form linkages with Latino political actors and social movements. It is difficult to predict black-brown relations, therefore, with precision beyond the contours of possible outcomes because so much of these relations is not structurally predetermined, but is the outcome of human agency.

Any attempt to address the course of intergroup relations between African Americans and Latinos in the late 20th century soon runs into the realization that few theoretical apparatuses are available to help channel the discourse. Race and ethnic relations theories of the 1960s and 1970s seem very outdated for explaining black-brown dynamics in globalized urban settings that are dramatically different from their days of two or three decades ago. Anglo-conformity models, for example, are as useless to explain inner-city intra-minority relations, as they are to explain the present-day appropriation of ethnic cultural content and forms by the white dominant group. Indeed, the very concept of the dominant group has become a variable in urban areas like Miami and the Los Angeles suburb of Monterey Park. Macro-structural perspectives of global capitalist development still lend much conceptual power for theorizing about economic relations between groups in advanced Western societies, but appear to need greater sensitivity to the role of noneconomic identities in the development of intergroup relations in the late 20th century.

REFERENCES

Bach, Robert L.
    1993   Changing Relations: Newcomers and Established Residents in U.S. Communities. New York: The Ford Foundation.
De Leon, Arnoldo
    1987   Mexican Americans in a Sunbelt City. Houston: Center for Mexican American Studies, University of Houston.
Henderson, Jeffrey and Manuel Castells (eds.)
    1987   Global Restructuring and Territorial Development. Beverly Hills, California: SAGE Publications.
Houston Independent School District
    1995   District and Schools Profile. Houston, Texas.
Inter-Ethnic Forum of Houston
    1995   "Building Bridges Across Diverse Ethnic and Racial Communities: A Report." Houston: Inter-Ethnic Forum.
Johnson, James H., Walter C. Farrell, and Chandra Guinn
    1995   "Immigration Reform and the Browning of America: Tensions, Conflict, and Community Instability." Paper presented at the Social Science Research Council's Conference on America Becoming/Becoming Americans: International Migration to the United States. Sanibel Island, Florida (January 18–21).
Lamphere, Louise (ed.)
    1992   Structuring Diversity: Ethnographic Perspectives of the New Immigration. Chicago: The University of Chicago Press.
McDonnell, Patrick J.
    1995   "Immigration Study in Southern California Challenges Stereotypes." Houston Chronicle (November 3): A–4.

Mindiola, Tatcho, Jr., Néstor Rodríguez, and Yolanda Flores Niemann
    1996   "Intergroup Relations Between Hispanics and African Americans in Harris
                County." Research report of the Center for Mexican American Studies Center,
                University of Houston.
Morales, Rebecca
    1982   "Transnational Labor: Undocumented Workers in the Los Angeles Automo-
                bile Industry." International Migration Review 17 (Winter): 570–579.
Nelan, Bruce W.
    1993   "Not Quite So Welcomed Anymore." Time 143,21 (Fall): 10–12.
Rodríguez, Néstor P.
    1995   "The Real New World Order: The Globalization of Racial and Ethnic
                Relations in the Late 20th Century." Michael Peter Smith and Joe R. Feagin
                (eds.), The Bubbling Cauldron: Race, Ethnicity, and the Urban Crisis.
                Minneapolis: The University of Minnesota Press: 211–225.
    1993   "Economic Restructuring and Latino Growth in Houston." Joan Moore and
                Raquel Pinderhuges (eds.), The Barrios: Latinos and the Underclass Debate.
                New York: Russell Sage Foundation: 101–117.
    1987   "Undocumented Central Americans in Houston: Diverse Populations."
                International Migration Review (Spring): 4–26.
Romo, Ricardo, Néstor Rodríguez, Luis Plascencia, and Ximena Urrutia-Rojas
    1994   "Houston Evaluation of Community Priorities." Houston: Tomás Rivera
                Center/Department of Sociology, University of Houston.
Sassen-Koob, Saskia
    1987   "Issues of Core and Periphery: Labor Migration and Global Restructuring."
                Jeffrey Henderson and Manuel Castells (eds.), Global Restructuring and
                Territorial Development. Beverly Hills, California: Sage Publications: 61–73.
U.S. Bureau of the Census
    1994   Statistical Abstract of the United States, 1994. 114th Edition. Washington,
                D.C.: U.S. Government Printing Office.
    1993   1990 Census of Population and Housing, Houston-Galveston-Brazoria, TX.
                1990 CPH–3–176C. Washington, D.C.: U.S. Government Printing Office.

Treacherous Waters in Turbulent Times: Navigating the Recent Sea Change in U.S. Immigration Policy and Attitudes

Lowell Sachs

Setting the Stage

AMERICA IS A NATION UNLIKE ANY OTHER. EACH YEAR SCORES OF PEOPLE AROUND the world dream of coming to this country. Some come to be reunited with family, others to find new hope and new opportunity, and still others to escape religious or political persecution. Whatever the details of their particular motivation, inevitably all these people come with the dream of beginning a new life. In truth, except for Native Americans, we all come from somewhere else. We are unique in the world because we are, from our beginnings and at our heart, a nation of immigrants. This historical fact is more than just our tradition; it is the root of our heritage and the secret of our strength.

Arguably, more than any other country in the world, the United States has been a beacon to the peoples of other nations seeking freedom and opportunity. Certainly, at least, that is the image that the United States likes to promote of itself. Through the years, to be sure, the United States has drawn strength from the diversity of its people, richness from the wealth of cultures it contains, and spirit from the continuing infusion of idealism brought by newcomers to its shores.

Today, however, a different attitude is emerging about immigrants. Rather than being welcomed into the melting pot, newcomers to this country are being viewed by some as a liability — a form of charity that we as a nation can no longer afford. Suddenly, there is a rush in the halls of Congress to pull up the welcome mat and shut the door.[1] Politicians claim that they are responding to the will of the American people, but the American people do not seem to be quite so sure.[2] What

LOWELL SACHS is a Government Affairs Representative for Sun Microsystems, Inc., a high-tech computer company, working out of the company's Washington, D.C., public policy office (1300 I Street NW, Suite 420 East, Washington, D.C. 20005). He previously worked as an immigration attorney, and later as a policy associate tracking federal immigration legislation for the National Immigration Forum, a nonprofit membership organization comprised of local, state, and national organizations concerned with immigrant and refugee issues. The opinions stated in this article are solely those of the author, and do not necessarily reflect the views of Sun Microsystems, Inc., or the National Immigration Forum.

does seem to be certain is that there is a growing sense that something somewhere has gone awry. In the ensuing clamor to set things right, anti-immigrant forces have set in motion a campaign of disinformation and fear, hoping to harness the resulting outcry to serve their own ends. For their part, some politicians have come to believe that getting tough on immigrants could help them make some political hay, as if the notion of a politician "getting tough" on something, in and of itself, automatically meant that they were engaged in a worthwhile pursuit. With that belief firmly entrenched, a number of senators and representatives have embarked on a crusade to save America from "the immigrants," not once stopping to consider the irony that, somewhere down the lines of logic and ancestry, they are really attempting to save us from ourselves. It is a goal that could prove very harmful indeed should they succeed.

Currently, Congress is considering major legislation designed expressly to reform this country's immigration system from top to bottom.[3] On top of that there are a slew of provisions in other legislative measures that deal either directly or indirectly with immigrant issues. An example is the sweeping welfare reform bill that emerged from a joint House and Senate Conference Committee complete with measures designed to restrict legal immigrants' access to crucial public benefits. Furthermore, the Clinton administration convened a special commission[4] to look into the matter of immigration and make recommendations on ways to reform current policy. Add to all of this a spate of other bills put forth as measures to combat terrorism,[5] promote English as an official language,[6] and otherwise vilify anything or anyone foreign[7] and you can begin to get a feel for the type of xenophobic mania that is gripping our country's lawmakers.

The Public Mood

Historically, when times are good and the nation's prospects seem bright, immigrants have benefited themselves and the nation through their pursuit of the "American Dream." However, they have just as quickly made for an easy and tempting target against whom to direct anger and frustration during times of political or economic woe. These fluctuations in the national attitude toward immigrants, in other words, tend to have more to do with the prevailing socioeconomic circumstances of the nation at any given moment than they do with the inherent characteristics of the immigrant population itself. Still, there are always those nativists who view immigrants themselves as an anathema because, to them, the immigrants' varied races, religions, cultures, or classes represent a threat to some form of idealized social homogeneity.

Today, America seems to be embarking upon another period of nativist fervor, complete with all of its attendant fear, misunderstanding, and anti-immigrant activism.[8] One of the main factors fueling the public's recently souring attitude on immigration is a slate of widely shared economic concerns. Principal among those concerns are tension caused by a tightening job market, with increased competitiveness among labor, frustration over the costs and value of available housing, anxiety about an increasing tax burden, and anger over the spread of abuse in the welfare system. Although the underlying social dynamics leading to these concerns are myriad and complex — typically having little or nothing to do with immigration trends — the relative political powerlessness of most recent immigrants leaves them a prime target for scapegoating.

Also at work is the public's sense that we as a nation have broken loose from our social moorings — that crime and moral decay are eating away at our social fabric, and that all of these ills can somehow be attributed to the latest wave of newcomers to our shores. There can be no doubt that communities across America are experiencing problems with crime, drugs, and the splintering of the family unit. Moreover, the crime that is being committed, especially in the larger cities, is of an increasingly violent nature. However, attempts to lay the blame for all of these problems on the immigrant community is an exercise in twisted reasoning at best, and vindictive manipulation at worst.

Fanning the Flames; Distorting the Facts

Politicians and anti-immigrant lobbyists have been quick to exploit these fears. They have capitalized on the public's misunderstanding of and lack of knowledge about immigrants to satisfy their need for a scapegoat and a quick-fix solution. It has been a supreme example of baseless, but remarkably effective, finger pointing. Also helping to stir the pot is a carefully concealed, but nonetheless prevalent, appeal to people's racial fears and divisions. Bigoted remarks have replaced rational analysis in the lexicon of anti-immigrant lobbyists. Representatives from anti-immigrant lobbyist groups, such as the Federation for American Immigration Reform (FAIR) and the Center for Immigration Studies, make frequent anecdotal reference to the supposed total absence of "American" cab drivers in Washington, D.C., or the lack of "American" construction workers in Texas. Despite the fact that those racially charged assertions are as patently ridiculous as they are offensive, some influential lawmakers on Capitol Hill who are friendly with the anti-immigrant lobbyists have taken to using those disingenuous claims to bolster their plea for drastic cuts in legal immigration. Though the draconian changes being proposed to our country's current immigration policies could affect every segment of our society, Asians and Latinos may be especially hard hit. Those two ethnic groups have become the implied poster children for the movement against immigrants; in part, the notion that too many of "them" are coming to this country may be spurring on anti-immigrant forces to call for a halt to the current flow of newcomers.[9] The marketing and sale of this political tonic to the public, however, have required a great deal of massaging and spin of the main messages to make them more palatable to the general public.

On Capitol Hill, there is a maxim that "perception is reality." Never has that saying been more true than in the case of the current debate in both houses of

Congress over the issue of immigration reform. The facts relating to immigrants and immigration are distorted, or deliberately and artfully avoided, by politicians who sense that they can gain political mileage by attacking immigrants. For example, while it is political suicide for a politician to say that he or she is in favor of separating mothers and fathers from their children, or children from their parents, as would have occurred if the reforms originally proposed in both the House and Senate bills were enacted into law, it is not nearly so damaging for that politician to say simply that he or she thinks there should be a "breathing space"[10] taken from the current immigration trend to allow those already here time to assimilate. This deliberately salable sentiment would have been more convincing were it not combined in the next sentence with vindictive proposals to make citizenship itself more difficult to obtain for lawful residents, including proposals to deny citizenship outright to the U.S.-born children of undocumented parents.

This need for a positive spin is why, in the debate at issue, immigration has been set up as an evil, while shutting out the immigrants is a supposedly noble cause. Unfortunately, the selection of immigrants as the scapegoats for a nation concerned about its future has far more to do with political expediency than fact. Congressional proponents of curbing or halting the flow of immigration to this country provide a vivid illustration of this point. They speak facilely about the alleged problems of "chain migration," where, supposedly, distant family members such as aunts, uncles, and cousins come pouring across our borders in ever-increasing numbers. This was their battle cry when they were trying to push through drastic cuts to legal immigration because they knew that framing the issue accurately — as one that affects the reunification of parents, children, and siblings — would make it a much thornier subject and would detract from their coveted image as champions of family values. The fact is that aunts, uncles, and cousins cannot and do not come into this country. There simply are no visas for those extended family members. Nonetheless, it makes for good drama, and thus good politics, to distort the facts in this manner.

Another brazen example of the moral duplicity inherent in the current debate over the future of immigration for the U.S. can be found in an amendment to H.R. 2202 promoted by Rep. Elton Gallegly (R.–CA) and offered by Reps. Richard Pombo (R.–CA) and Saxby Chambliss (R.–GA) on the House floor. The amendment, which was soundly defeated in the House, proposed to reestablish an agricultural guestworker program to allow large corporate growers to bring in vast numbers of foreign laborers. The program would have brought into the U.S. several hundred thousand foreign farm workers on a temporary, conditional basis so that the workers would have no ability to protest unfair treatment, wages, or working conditions without the threat of being sacked and deported. For these representatives to vehemently argue for a drastic cut in the number of visas for close family members of U.S. citizens and to sermonize on the supposed negative impact of immigrants (both legal and undocumented) and then to propose the import of virtually hundreds of thousands of foreign workers to appease the desire of the powerful growers' lobby for cheap, easily exploited labor, required a staggering amount of audacity. After all, a primary justification floated by Rep. Gallegly and his crowd for their proposed massive reductions in legal immigration was that foreign workers are taking jobs away from American citizens. Despite the inaccuracy of this charge, its invocation has been used as a powerful tool to push for cuts in legal immigration levels. To then turn around and advocate that temporary foreign workers be deliberately imported, but given no rights or protections such as the ones afforded American workers, is little more than a thinly veiled attempt to create a convenient supply of indentured servants.

Legislative Ins and Outs

The principal immigration reform bill debated in the House of Representatives during 1995 and the first half of 1996 was H.R. 2202, Rep. Lamar Smith's (R.–TX) "Immigration in the National Interest Act of 1996." H.R. 2202 combined the issues of legal and undocumented immigration in its provisions, calling for major reform in both arenas. In the Senate, Sen. Alan Simpson (R.–WY) introduced two companion bills during 1995, which he successfully married together, and was moving forward as one comprehensive bill. The first bill, S. 1664, officially titled the "Immigrant Control and Financial Responsibility Act of 1996," dealt primarily with issues of border security, asylum, exclusion, and deportation law, but also included provisions that would restrict legal immigrants' access to public benefits. Sen. Simpson's companion bill, the "Legal Immigration Reform Act of 1996" (S. 1665), was crafted to institute drastic cuts in the numbers and categories of legal immigrants permitted to enter this country. The joining of these two bills after S. 1665 (then referred to as S. 1394) had been approved by the Senate Immigration Subcommittee left another immigration mega-bill that jibed ominously well with the structure and restrictionist tone of H.R. 2202 in the House.

As the debate on these two bills progressed, however, increasing pressure began to mount for the issues of legal and undocumented immigration to be considered separately. Throughout Congress, but especially within the Republican Party, whose ultimate control over the fate of the bills was unquestioned, the proposed cuts to the legal immigration system became a highly divisive issue. In the Senate, first term Republican Sen. Spencer Abraham (R.–MI) sponsored a bipartisan amendment in the Judiciary Committee that successfully split off the legal immigration provisions from the rest of the recently combined bill, S. 1394. The amendment was passed by a majority of both Republicans and Democrats on the committee despite the enraged, hardball tactics unleashed by Sen. Simpson in opposition to it.[11] That amendment divided the recently combined bill, S. 1394, back into its two original component parts. Those two bills were eventually redesignated as S. 1664 and S. 1665.

This action came auspiciously the week before the full House took up consideration of H.R. 2202 on the floor. At the same time, the House Rules Committee, which sets the parameters for the debate of bills on the House floor, had come out with a very restrictive rule on which amendments would be considered "in order" during the final debate over the bill. Although many pro-immigrant amendments did not make the cut, several key pro-immigrant amendments with strong Republican backing managed to sneak in. Among those was a bipartisan amendment sponsored by Reps. Dick Chrysler (R.–MI), Howard Berman (D.–CA), Sam Brownback (R.–KS), Philip Crane (R.–IL), Calvin Dooley (D.–CA), and Tom Davis (R.–VA) to strike the cuts contained in the bill's family and employment-based immigration categories. The argument in support of the amendment was a simple one — that the issues of legal and undocumented immigration are fundamentally distinct. Each deserves careful, but separate, consideration. The argument was persuasive to a bipartisan majority of the House members and the amendment was passed by a significant margin.

With cuts to the legal immigration system stripped out of the House bill, anti-immigrant forces had to pin their hopes on the Senate bills. Sen. Simpson was well aware, however, that without sufficient political will to back up his vision of a leaner and meaner immigration policy, his legal immigration reform bill, S. 1665, would languish on the back burners of an already packed Senate legislative schedule. Making matters even more precarious for Sen. Simpson was the fact that the cuts in family immigration visa numbers and categories, which he had originally included in his bill, were replaced entirely during the Senate Judiciary Committee's debate with a new, more modest proposal sponsored jointly by Sens. Edward Kennedy (D.–MA) and Spencer Abraham (R.–MI) that, for the most part, left family immigration intact. Furthermore, Sen. Simpson's enforcement bill, S. 1664, was being given first priority on the legislative schedule, while his heretofore legal immigration reform bill, S. 1665, was not yet scheduled for debate at all. The last, best chance for Sen. Simpson and his anti-immigrant cohorts to slash legal immigration levels was to reintroduce those restrictionist proposals back into S. 1664 through an amendment when the bill was being debated on the Senate floor. In the end, even that strategy failed, however, as Sen. Simpson's amendment was defeated by a landslide vote of 80 to 20.

Realizing, nonetheless, that there may be more than one way to skin that cat, anti-immigrant representatives in the House included an income hurdle in their bill that would effectively block the majority of immigrant families from reuniting. Current law instructs that family-sponsored immigrants be admitted only if their sponsor[12] earns an income at least equal to 100% of the poverty level. The House bill, H.R. 2202, changed this provision so that, if it becomes law, the sponsor would be required to earn an income equal to at least 200% of the poverty level for a family unit including the sponsored immigrant. The problem is that nearly 46% of all Americans would fail to meet that income requirement. In effect, then, this requirement would prevent all but the wealthiest half of Americans from petitioning for their spouses, children, or parents to join them. This is one of the issues which the joint House-Senate conference committee[13] is still expected to address.

Strange Bedfellows

In an era of fierce partisan politics, legal immigration was an issue that proved to be the exception to the rule. Drastic cuts in legal immigration proposed by two Republican-authored bills that had strong Republican backing were ultimately derailed not by liberal Democrats — some of whom[14] were actually co-conspirators with anti-immigrant Republicans in a move to slash family immigration — but rather by other ideological Republicans.[15] Conservative think tanks like the Cato Institute and the Alexis de Tocqueville Institution joined together with civil rights and ethnic advocates like the American Civil Liberties Union (ACLU) and National Council of La Raza to fight the bills. Even conservative big business and anti-tax groups, such as the National Association of Manufacturers and Americans for Tax Reform, forged alliances with labor and religious groups, such as the AFL-CIO and the United States Catholic Conference (USCC), in opposition to certain of the bills' provisions. In this sense, the immigration debate has turned the predictable world of Washington, D.C., insider politics on its head.

Political Wedge Issue in the Presidential Race

Surprising alliances notwithstanding, Washington, D.C., will be Washington, D.C., and election-year politics have also played a role in the framing of immigration policy. With concern over undocumented immigration burning hot in California — a state rich in electoral votes — both major parties are jockeying to position themselves as the party that hears the people of California and takes action. Realizing he was weak in California, Senator Bob Dole (R.–KS), the Republican presidential nominee, was planning to concede the state to President Bill Clinton and focus his campaign resources elsewhere in his bid for the Oval Office. His absence from the state, however, would mean that fewer campaign dollars would be channelled there to help with the reelection bid of fellow Republican congressmen. This, in turn, could have had the effect of causing Republicans to lose several key seats in the House. That is, until H.R. 2202 and Speaker Newt Gingrich (R.–GA) came to the Republicans' rescue. The trick was for the Republicans to be able to portray President Clinton as being "soft" on undocumented immigrants. That was not an easy task since the president had already indicated his strong support for passing some form of immigration reform legislation and had successfully made fighting undocumented immigration a priority. The strategy embarked upon by Gingrich and the Republicans to turn the tide takes power politics to new heights of cruelty and callousness.

Rep. Gallegly (R.–CA) offered an amendment to H.R. 2202 during a rare personal appearance on the House floor, which most political observers had expected to meet with certain defeat. Borrowing a chapter from California's Proposition 187 cookbook, the amendment would allow states to deny free public education to undocumented children — basically to kick kids out of school and turn school teachers into deputy INS agents. Speaker Gingrich realized that this issue was so repugnant that it alone could be a deal breaker for President Clinton when the final bill was put on his desk, thus forcing the president to veto the entire immigration reform bill. The problem is that immigration reform, no matter how harsh or cruel, is an absolute must to carry the day in California. With a presidential veto of strongly favored immigration reform legislation as their club, Dole and the Republicans could then enter California swinging. The Republican campaign rhetoric would be crushing — "Good people of California, we heard your cry for help and tried to give you the immigration reform you've been asking for, but the president said 'No.'" Gingrich seized this opportunity and spoke strongly in support of the amendment when it was offered on the House floor, making sure that his fellow Republican members realized that this was an amendment he expected them to pass. And pass it did, by a largely partisan vote of 257 to 163. In the Senate, Dole shied away from getting his fingerprints on this controversial topic directly, and decided not to add a similar measure to S. 1664 when it was on the Senate floor. He opted instead to stay behind the scenes and simply permit the House provision to be adopted in the final version when the two bills were reconciled in conference committee. As a result, President Clinton now finds himself in a political quagmire where he could be pummeled in the electorally critical state of California if he vetoes the bill, but he could infuriate and lose his liberal political base if he does not.

Truth, Lies, and Legislating

The sad truth is that a large number of major factual distortions have come to dominate the immigration debate through sheer repetition, and thus to serve as the *sine qua non* of assumptions surrounding discussions about reform. The first is the assertion made repeatedly by Rep. Smith (R.–TX), champion of H.R. 2202, and by Sen. Simpson (R.–WY), sponsor of S. 1664 and S. 1665, that their bills would actually help to promote the reunification of the nuclear family, and, consequently, should be considered a friend of the largely conservative-driven movement to promote family values. In fact, however, both bills were originally designed specifically to shut out the majority of *immediate relatives* of U.S. citizens and lawful residents — an act that would have left American families permanently fragmented. Another carefully calculated appeal to people's fear, rather than their reasoned judgment, is the cry that immigrants are pouring into this country at unprecedented and uncontrollable levels. This little bit of hyperbole flies squarely in the face of readily ascertainable fact.

A recently published Census Bureau report entitled "The Foreign-Born Population: 1994"[16] revealed that although the percentage of the U.S. population that is foreign-born has increased over the last few decades to a current level of 8.7%, it remains far *lower* than proportions from the entire first half of this century, which reached a high of 14.7% in 1910. How long the recent trend of increasing immigrant numbers will continue is uncertain. It is noteworthy, however, that according to the U.S. Immigration and Naturalization Service (INS), the number of legal immigrants coming to this country just experienced its largest *drop* in 15 years, with current levels of legal immigrants declining a full 9.3% from the previous year. The profile of recent immigrants is also interesting. The Census Bureau report found that a greater percentage of recent immigrants possesses bachelor's or advanced degrees than is the case for either natives or earlier immigrants. Another trend revealed by the report is that the longer immigrants remain in the U.S., the higher their incomes are likely to be.

People are undeniably concerned about the numbers and effect of immigrants entering the country without documentation and there is a pervasive sense that some action should be taken in an effective and responsible manner to help control our nation's borders, as long as the methods employed are careful not to skirt human rights considerations in the process. This concession still leaves a fundamental question unanswered. Why did each of the immigration reform bills try to devote so many of their provisions to the slashing and burning of the current *legal* immigration system? Legal immigration in the U.S. is governed by a tightly regulated system with clear numerical limits and priorities that were crafted to strengthen American values by encouraging family reunification, serve national interests by harnessing the skills and energy of international workers, and stand up for human rights by offering shelter to a manageable share of the world's refugees. Despite the clear distinction between those who play by the rules and wait in line in the legal immigration system, and those who go outside the law and enter the U.S. illegally, it was legal immigrants who found themselves most under attack in those bills. This irony is made even more confounding when one takes into account the favorable profile of today's legal immigrant population as revealed in the Census Bureau report — statistics that have not met with any serious challenge.

The answer reveals the central deceit and strategy of the anti-immigrant movement. The plan to wed the issues of legal and undocumented immigration in the current legislation was adopted as an attempt to ensure that cuts in *legal* immigration, which would surely be acknowledged as unwise and unwarranted if examined by themselves, could get passed on the coattails of the public's concern over undocumented immigrants. Without blurring the issues in this manner, it was unlikely that the public would go along with the type and degree of cuts initially proposed by the anti-immigrant forces and population control groups that were the driving force behind the restrictionist legislation. As it turned out, that strategy proved unsuccessful and the proposed drastic cuts to the legal immigration system were beaten back in both the House and the Senate.

Immigrants have frequently had to travel a rocky road in their quest for acceptance in the United States. Their arrival and assimilation have been going on since this nation was first formed, but at the moment, the road ahead seems fraught with hazards. Will we continue to be a nation of hope and promise, or will we circle the wagons and shut our doors? Will we keep families together and kids in school, or will we separate parents from children, and scapegoat entire communities? Will our elected leaders remember the noble words of Emma Lazarus that are inscribed eloquently on the Statue of Liberty, or the bitter, anti-immigrant diatribe spat out by the likes of Patrick Buchanan and California Governor Pete Wilson? With luck and cool heads, the debate over immigration that is so prominent on the nation's radar screen these days will be decided on the facts rather than the frenzy. Only time will tell.

NOTES

1.   There has been a veritable avalanche of legislation dealing directly or indirectly with immigrant issues during 1995. Immigrant issues have appeared in proposed bills on welfare reform, counterterrorism, and even the repeal of the 14th Amendment, which guarantees U.S. citizenship to all persons born in this country. Recently, bills introduced in both the House of Representatives (H.R. 2202) and the Senate (S. 1664 and S. 1665) proposed the largest cuts in immigration levels and the most sweeping reforms in over 70 years.

2.   In a series of nationwide polls conducted by Republican pollster Vince Breglio of RSM, Inc., that was begun in June 1995 to test public opinion with respect to immigration, legal immigration came in a weak ninth on a list of 10 political issues of concern to Americans. This placed the issue well behind other issues such as crime, education, health care, taxes, welfare reform, and the environment. Furthermore, of the people polled, 83% agreed with the statement: "We have an illegal immigration problem that needs to be dealt with directly and effectively. What we don't have is a problem with legal immigration. It is unfair to penalize those who follow the rules just because others break them and enter the U.S. illegally."

3.   H.R. 2202, Representative Lamar Smith's (R.–TX) "Immigration in the National Interest Act of 1996," is the immigration reform measure in the House. Senator Alan Simpson's (R.–WY) "Legal Immigration Reform Act of 1996" (S. 1665) and "Immigrant Control and Financial Responsibility Act" (S. 1664) are the legislative vehicles in the Senate. Together, these are the principal omnibus legislative packages threatening to overhaul our current immigration system.

4.   The Commission on Immigration Reform, originally chaired by the late, former Texas Congresswoman Barbara Jordan, made recommendations addressing issues of both undocumented and legal immigration reform. Included in its recommendations were sizable cuts in family-sponsored immigration.

5.   A Senate-passed antiterrorism bill (S. 735) authored by Senators Bob Dole (R.–KS) and Orrin Hatch (R.–UT) was reconciled with the Hyde counterterrorism bill (H.R. 1710) authored by Representative Henry Hyde (R.–IL) in conference committee before being signed into law by President Clinton

on the anniversary of the Oklahoma City bombing. Provisions in the antiterrorism law that are wholly unrelated to the counterterrorism issue establish procedures for summarily excluding would-be immigrants and asylum seekers from the United States. Despite serious concerns that many Democrats and a few Republicans had with those provisions, and the chilling effect they would have on the U.S.'s claim to be a human rights leader, the pressure on Congress to pass the bill by the anniversary of the Oklahoma City bombing prevented attempts to improve the bill from succeeding.

6. Rep. Bill Emerson's (R.–MO) "Language of Government Act" (H.R. 123), which is the primary English-only bill in the House, aims to make English the official language of government out of a fear that the federal government has propagated a dangerous breed of official multilingualism. During a congressional hearing on the topic held in October 1995, Rep. Dale Kildee (D.–MI) pointed out that according to the Government Accounting Office (GAO), only 265 out of 400,000 government documents (approximately six one-hundredths of one percent) were printed in languages in addition to English. Rep. Toby Roth's (R.–WI) "Declaration of Official Language Act" (H.R. 739) would not only make English the official language, it would also declare English to be the preferred language of communication *among citizens*.

7. On December 13, 1995, the House Judiciary Committees on Immigration and on the Constitution convened a hearing on a variety of bills introduced by several members of Congress that proposed to amend or reinterpret the Constitution in order to deny citizenship to the U.S.-born children of undocumented immigrants. Some of the proposals go so far as to actually call for the repeal of the Fourteenth Amendment to the Constitution, which guarantees citizenship to all persons born or naturalized in the U.S., in part as a draconian scheme for restricting the availability of public benefits.

8. Proposition 187, California's infamous statewide ballot initiative that strips basic rights and benefits from the undocumented population, is a prime example of the type of recriminatory backlash to which the immigrant community is susceptible in times of economic stagnation and concern over social ills, such as crime, moral decay, racial strife, and polarization between the rich and poor. Battles over similar state initiatives are currently being waged in Florida, Arizona, and Oregon.

9. An ironic highlight from the House Judiciary Committee's debate over H.R. 2202 serves to illustrate this point. An amendment to the bill was offered that reinstated a Diversity Visa program that benefits, in large part, European immigrants, such as the Irish. Several members of the committee, most notably Rep. John Bryant (D.–TX), attacked the restoration of the program and flatly accused it of being a white European amendment. The complaint was that virtually hundreds of thousands of Latin Americans with close family members in the U.S. would have the door shut in their faces, while white immigrants from Europe with absolutely no ties to this country would be welcomed in. Adding to the irony, Rep. Bryant is a cosponsor and strong supporter of the bill. His vocal opposition to this particular amendment was likely motivated out of fear that the inclusion of such obvious "pet" provisions to serve special interest groups could serve as a lightning rod for advocates trying to scuttle the bill.

10. The term "breathing space" was thought up by anti-immigrant lobbyists and adopted by both Rep. Lamar Smith (R.–TX) and Sen. Alan Simpson (R.–WY) in their speeches during the presentation of their respective immigration reform bills to help soften the perception of the drastic cuts in family and other visas that were actually being proposed.

11. Sen. Simpson, the author of S. 1394 (now divided into the two bills, S. 1664 and S. 1665), railed against Sen. Orrin Hatch (R.–UT), chairman of the Senate Judiciary Committee, and against Sen. Abraham in a surprisingly dramatic and personal fashion when the amendment to split the bill was first introduced. Sen. Simpson was hoping to postpone this effort to split his legislation until the very end of the markup process, by which point he estimated he would be able to peel off individual senators who were planning at the time to vote in favor of the amendment by giving them piecemeal concessions. Sen. Simpson pointedly reminded the chair that he had been a senator for 17 years, as opposed to Sen. Abraham's freshman status, and that he deserved special consideration as the chairman of the Immigration Subcommittee and author of the bill. He then invoked a somewhat obscure procedural tactic called a point of personal privilege to try to force the other senators on the committee to vote with

him and against Sen. Abraham on the question of when the amendment should be brought up. Sen. Hatch, who supported the amendment, shot back that he had been a senator for 20 years and reminded Sen. Simpson that he was the chairman of the full Judiciary Committee. Sen. Abraham, attempting to be diplomatic and not wishing to risk the fallout from a direct confrontation with a senior senator, delayed his amendment for two days, but did not relent on his assertion that separating legal immigration from undocumented immigration should be treated as a threshold issue.

12.   All family-sponsored immigrants need a sponsor to promise financial support sufficient to prevent the immigrant from becoming a "public charge" before the State Department grants a residency visa, or "green card," to the immigrant.

13.   The conference committee is a deliberative body composed of select members of both the House and the Senate whose task is to resolve and reconcile differences between the House and Senate versions of a bill on a given issue before sending a single bill back to both chambers for a final vote. From there the final bill, if approved by the House and Senate, is sent to the president's desk for signature.

14.   Senator Dianne Feinstein (D.–CA) and Rep. John Bryant (D.–TX) are just two examples of politicians, many from states affected heavily by immigration, who traded their traditional liberal allegiance to become rabid supporters of even the most extreme measures proposed by anti-immigrant conservatives.

15.   Various ideological segments of the Republican Party are strong defenders of legal immigration and were alarmed by some of the proposals included in their colleagues' immigration reform bills. For example, free-market Republicans, such as House Majority Leader Dick Armey (R.–TX), see immigration as a subset of the debate over free trade and prefer a relatively open policy on the issue. Libertarian Republicans wary of big government (such as Rep. Steve Chabot [R.–OH], who fought against H.R. 2202's national identification system, which was informally ridiculed as "1–800–BIG BROTHER"), also opposed many of the immigration reform bills' measures, which they saw as infringing on the rights and liberties of ordinary Americans.

16.   See Kristin A. Hansen and Amara Bachu, *Current Population Reports; The Foreign-Born Population: 1994* (Census Bureau, U.S. Department of Commerce, P20–486, August 1995). According to the report, the majority of immigrants in this country settle in California, New York, Florida, Texas, Illinois, and New Jersey. Although immigrants from Mexico represent the largest share of these newcomers at 45%, the list of countries contributing most heavily to our foreign-born population is quite diverse, including the Philippines, Cuba, El Salvador, Canada, Germany, China, the Dominican Republic, Korea, Vietnam, and India.

For an Immigration Policy Based on Human Rights

David Bacon

ROM THE INTRODUCTION OF THE ORIGINAL SIMPSON-MAZZOLI BILL IN THE MID-1970s, the key provisions of U.S. anti-immigrant legislation have been directed at undocumented immigrants. After one and one-half decades of repeated efforts, the Immigration Reform and Control Act of 1986 finally made employer sanctions, the heart of the act, part of federal law. This watershed action formalized and codified what has been national policy toward undocumented immigration — the creation of a special category of residents of the United States who have significantly fewer rights than the population as a whole, cannot legally work or receive social benefits, and can be apprehended, incarcerated, and deported at any time.

The creation of this special category has had widespread ramifications. It has influenced the wage levels and vulnerability of immigrant labor itself. It has spawned other proposals for the denial of rights, such as the right to education or medical care. The original premise that undocumented immigrants have no right to work or earn a living has been broadened to include the denial of rights to most other basic elements of normal life, including the right to be a part of a community and live in the U.S. at all. It has led to the demonizing and dehumanizing of undocumented immigrants in public debate and political life.

In the years following the passage of the Immigration Reform and Control Act, dozens of anti-immigrant bills were introduced, first into the California state legislature, and then into legislatures in other states (Bacon, 1993a). In 1994, California voters passed Proposition 187, an extreme measure to disqualify undocumented immigrants from education and health care services. Other states again took up similar measures.

Finally, in the spring of 1996 Congress debated and passed some of the most extensive and repressive immigration legislation in its history. A 187-like provision, an amendment introduced by Southern California Congress member Elton Gallegly to bar undocumented children from attending school, was included in the

DAVID BACON (1631 Channing Way, Berkeley, CA 94703, dbacon@igc.apc.org) is a West Coast writer and photographer who is documenting issues of labor, immigration, and international politics. He was a labor organizer for two decades and is a board member of the Northern California Coalition for Immigrant Rights. The coalition supports the views contained in this article.

bill as it was originally passed by the House of Representatives (*Los Angeles Times*, March 22, 1996). Predictably, what started as an attack against the most vulnerable group of immigrants, the undocumented, was broadened into a generalized campaign to cut legal immigration quotas and disqualify even permanent legal residents from a wide variety of social benefits.

Given this onslaught, groups that have traditionally defended the rights of immigrants in the U.S. have become divided over the need and ability to defend the rights of the undocumented. Faced with a Republican majority in Congress and Republican candidates who seek to whip up widespread anti-immigrant hysteria throughout the country, some organizations now advocate the defense of legal immigration, but also support many measures directed against undocumented immigrants.

This has generally been the strategy of the Democratic Party. It takes its cue from President Clinton, who in his State of the Union speech in January 1996 declared that "we are still a nation of immigrants" and called on the country to "go forward as one America, one nation working together." Yet behind the rhetoric of inclusion, the president called for cracking down on the undocumented. He proposed increased border enforcement, stiffer sanctions to punish undocumented workers applying for jobs and employers who hire them, and signed an order barring businesses that hire undocumented workers from receiving federal contracts.[1]

California Democratic Representative Howard Berman subsequently called the House's passage of a bill that had been stripped of many measures directed against legal immigrants a victory of hope over fear (*Ibid.*). Yet the bill also contained an amendment that would deny undocumented children the right to attend school and force schoolteachers to turn them in to the Immigration and Naturalization Service for deportation.

California Democratic Senator Barbara Boxer took the same approach in announcing that she would vote for the Senate bill, after provisions cutting legal immigration had been eliminated. Yet her speech on the floor of the Senate failed to condemn the brutal beating days earlier of an undocumented woman and man by Riverside County sheriffs, after they fled from the Border Patrol, or the death a week later of seven more undocumented workers at the end of a similar chase. Boxer proposed to make it a federal crime, punishable by prison and high fines, to flee from the INS at all.[2]

The essence of the distinction between legal and undocumented immigration, elaborated by these political leaders, was expressed succinctly by a Washington, D.C.-based lobbying organization in its guide for lobbying on the House and Senate bills, written at the end of 1995. It took the position that "legal immigration is not the same as illegal immigration," and that "the American people want the federal government to take decisive and effective action to control illegal immigration" (National Immigration Forum, 1995).

The "Problem" of "Illegal" Immigration

In making the distinction between legal and illegal immigration, proponents argue that although legal immigration has socially beneficial effects, the entry of undocumented people into the U.S. has a negative effect on society. Therefore, following this logic, government should control or halt it. This logic supports the view that undocumented immigration is out of control, or in danger of becoming so, and reduces the argument about undocumented immigration to one over tactics for suppressing it. Is it better to halt or control it by denying medical care and education for undocumented children, by prohibiting undocumented immigrants from working, by militarizing the border, or by increasing the number of Border Patrol raids and deportations?

This is, in fact, the terrain of debate between the Democratic administration and its Republican opponents. Republicans argue for the most extreme measures, including Proposition 187, and a national identification card and database that employers can use to screen job applicants. The administration instead beefs up the budget of the Border Patrol to its highest level in decades, sends soldiers to patrol the border as though we were at war with Mexico, or at least with Mexicans, and unleashes a wave of immigration raids and deportations in major cities from coast to coast.

Yet in what sense is undocumented immigration a problem? What kind of problem is it?

The Urban Institute estimated in its May 1994 report, *Immigration and Immigrants, Setting the Record Straight,* that the undocumented population in the U.S stood between 2.5 and 3.5 million people in 1980, and rose to between three and five million just before the passage of the Immigration Reform and Control Act. After IRCA's amnesty program, which allowed undocumented people to normalize their immigration status, the population fell to between 1.8 and three million, and had risen to 2.7 to 3.7 million by 1992, roughly the same level it had been 12 years earlier (Fix and Passel, 1994).

Despite much-publicized efforts that have as their announced purpose halting the flow of undocumented immigrants across the border, this is the description of a stable process and section of the U.S. population, both in terms of relative size and constancy. This undocumented population constitutes about one percent of the total population of the country (*Ibid.*).

According to the National Immigration Forum (1994), undocumented immigrants pay about $7 billion annually in taxes. Some taxes paid by the undocumented, including $2.7 billion annually to Social Security, and $168 million into state unemployment benefit funds, are direct subsidies to these systems, since undocumented workers cannot by law collect any benefits for their contributions.

In the State of California alone, which accounts for about 43% of the nation's undocumented population, undocumented immigrants pay an additional

$732 million in state and local taxes, in addition to federal payroll and social security taxes. The state, in turn, according to the Urban Institute, spends $1.3 billion on education for undocumented children, and $166 million for emergency medical care for their families (the only kind of state-provided medical care for which they qualify) (Fix and Passel, 1994).

Undocumented children are as much a resource of U.S. society as are any of its other children. They are part of its future work force and they will also become its leaders in all aspects of its social, cultural, and political life. Inasmuch as the state has an interest in investing in the future of any of its children (and there are certainly those political leaders now who question even this), it has an interest in all of its children. It has a similar public health interest in providing emergency medical care, preventing the spread of medical problems from immigrants to the rest of the population, and vice versa.

Yet leaving this argument aside, it is difficult to make the case that expenditures on the education of undocumented children, or on emergency medical care for their families, is a net economic drain, given the gross overpayment of benefits in many other areas. In fact, tax payments and payroll deductions by undocumented immigrants, for which they cannot collect services, subsidize the tax cuts promised by politicians to middle– and upper-class voters. Proposition 187 and similar federal proposals would shift the tax burden even further.

The creation and elaboration of the special status of undocumented immigrants are not economically neutral. According to a UCLA study, undocumented workers contribute approximately seven percent of the $900 billion gross economic product of the State of California, or $63 billion (North American Integration and Development Center, 1996). The Urban Institute estimates that California accounts for 43% of the nation's undocumented population, or about 1.4 million people (Fox and Passel, 1994). The gross economic contribution by each undocumented immigrant to the California economy is therefore about $45,000, including children, the unemployed, and those too old or ill to work. While no statistical surveys have determined the average wage of undocumented workers, their precarious status keeps their wages near, and sometimes even below, the legal minimum, which at $4.25 per hour equals an annual income of $8,840.

Clearly, the labor of undocumented workers not only pumps tens of billions of dollars into the state's economy, but the workers themselves also receive only a small percentage of it, a much smaller percentage of the value that they produce than that received by workers who are either citizens or legal residents. That difference in the rate of exploitation is a source of extra profit for those industries that are dependent on a work force made up largely of undocumented workers.

The industries are not difficult to identify. They include agriculture and food processing, land development (including the residential construction and building services industries), tourism (including the hotel and restaurant industries), garment production and light manufacturing, transportation, retail trade, health care, and domestic services.

Jorge Bustamante, the noted Mexican academic, argues that U.S. immigration law has historically been designed to drive down the price of Mexican labor in the U.S. Proposals for guestworker programs, put forward by agricultural and light manufacturing interests and the politicians who speak for them (who were especially vocal supporters of Proposition 187), show a clear economic self-interest. Yet Proposition 187 itself and similar proposals also have an economic, as well as a social, effect.

Although it is not difficult to see who suffers when immigrants are denied rights and social welfare, it is also important to see who benefits. In an economy in which whole industries depend on an abundant supply of immigrant labor, maintaining a subclass of undocumented workers with fewer rights and less access to benefits is an important source of profit. Moreover, when that work force is made more vulnerable by immigration legislation, it also becomes cheaper for employers.

An undocumented worker, for instance, considering whether to organize a union to win better wages, must take into account the possibility of being fired. Other workers also risk being fired in similar situations, an important obstacle to all union organizing efforts. Yet undocumented workers must also weigh employer sanctions in the balance. Sanctions make finding another job much more difficult and riskier. The period of unemployment is likely to be longer. Because sanctions also disqualify a fired worker from unemployment benefits, food stamps, or other sources of income, a fired worker will be forced to take whatever job is available, at whatever wage. Indeed, under National Labor Relations Board rulings, if an employer shows that a worker fired for union activity is undocumented, they are not obliged to rehire her or him.

This same set of choices also confronts undocumented workers who consider filing complaints about unpaid wages, unpaid overtime, wages below the minimum, violations of health and safety laws, sexual harassment, and violations of other basic legal protections for workers. Worker protection laws exist on the books, but it is difficult, often even impossible, for undocumented workers to enforce them.

All the legal measures that are designed to make life unpleasant for undocumented immigrants, who presumably are therefore encouraged to leave the country, also make them more vulnerable and socially isolated. When it becomes more difficult and riskier for them to make demands for social services, or to assert their rights at work or in the community, the social cost and the price of their labor drops.

In the eyes of immigrants themselves, these proposals are a product not only of anti-immigrant sentiment, but are also intended to maintain their second-class status. José Semperio, director of San Francisco's Comité de Trabajadores

Generales, a committee of day laborers who get their jobs on street corners every morning, points out that as the political storm over immigration has grown, undocumented communities have become increasingly marginalized. "San Francisco, Los Angeles, San Diego, and Orange County all eat because we work. But we have almost no chance to move upwards into better jobs, and to get out of the shadows," he says.[3]

Without immigrant janitors in the offices and business parks of Century City, without farm workers in California fields, with no electronics workers in the sweatshops of Santa Ana and Silicon Valley, without immigrant dishwashers and room cleaners in the luxury hotels of Newport Beach, and with no garment workers in downtown L.A. or San Francisco's Chinatown, the economy of California would crumble. The agricultural, electronics, and garment industries have always, since their inception, employed a work force in which immigrants made up the vast majority. Immigrants, especially undocumented immigrants, are indispensable to the economy of those areas where the cry for exclusion is strongest.

Communities and businesses that benefit heavily from low-wage immigrant labor have an economic interest in anti-immigrant proposals, Semperio says. He describes the high injury rate among construction day laborers, almost all of whom are undocumented. "When we have accidents, the contractor just drops us off at the emergency room parking lot. Now they even want to make it illegal for us to get medical care at all. This is really unjust. Our voice may not be loud, but they're going to have to hear it."[4]

Undocumented Workers — Not Content to Be Victims

In the last decade in California, immigrant workers have been the backbone of strike after strike, in some of the hardest-fought labor struggles since the farm workers' battles of the late 1960s. Over 20,000 immigrant workers have walked off their jobs, or participated in organizing campaigns, since 1990. Immigrant workers accuse their employers of maintaining sweatshop conditions and forcing them to accept a second-class status. These accusations, made repeatedly for years, are the foundation of a growing wave of labor unrest (Bacon, 1995).

Throughout the Southwest, factories and workplaces have become pressure cookers, waiting for something to blow. Indeed, something did blow for drywallers, framers, grape pickers, janitors, garment workers, electronics assemblers, foundry and metal workers, and others. Their strikes are signs of pressure building from below, as the growing dissatisfaction of immigrant workers meets an increasingly hard line taken by employers.

These job actions have rocked the foundation of those industries in the states that have grown dependent on immigrant labor. It is no accident that California's southland, the political home of Republican Governor Pete Wilson and the center of these strikes, has also been the source of the most repressive proposals for restricting the rights of undocumented workers and services to immigrant communities.

Anger among immigrant workers has been building up for years, over wages that are already depressed, and getting worse. Goetz Wolff, a professor at UCLA and lead researcher for the Los Angeles Manufacturing Action Project (a multi-union organizing project based among immigrant workers), documents falling wages among Los Angeles' immigrant industrial work force. In women's apparel, for instance, the average hourly wage fell from $6.37 to $5.62 between 1988 and 1993 (Wolff, 1994). UNITE (the Union of Needletrade, Industrial and Textile Employees — the newly merged combination of the old ILGWU and ACTWU) estimates that 120,000 people work in L.A.'s garment sweatshops, almost all of whom are immigrants, with a large percentage of undocumented.[5]

Falling wages are not just a problem for garment workers. Wages are falling in paper recycling, plastics manufacturing, and textiles and food processing — all industries with an immigrant, largely undocumented, work force. "Our wages and conditions are very bad no matter what industry we work in," says immigrant garment striker Sara Callejas.[6] By contrast, the average wage in aircraft production is over $20 per hour and is rising slightly despite layoffs and recession. Aerospace is still a major industry in the Los Angeles basin, employing a mostly unionized and native-born work force.

The history of the union struggles of immigrant workers in Los Angeles and Southern California is, by and large, a history of success. According to veteran union organizer Peter Olney, "fights involving immigrant workers are very militant. They force unions to discard tired old tactics, and make us relook at the whole question of how to organize, at what organizing means" (Bacon, 1995a). Joel Ochoa, an LAMAP staff organizer, says that "at this point the immigrant community is [looking for ties with] labor and not necessarily the other way around. People are coming here from Mexico and all over Latin America, with a tradition and culture that gives them a rich repertoire of tactics for fighting the companies."[7]

The city's labor movement is the home to many immigrant labor activists like Ochoa, with feet on both sides of the border. They include Ana Martínez, who came to Los Angeles from El Salvador, where she helped organize a general strike in a Texas Instruments plant in the early 1980s and wound up fleeing for her life. She became a Southern California strike organizer for the independent United Electrical Workers, and later for the hotel workers (Bacon, 1993b). Yanira Moreno also fled her native El Salvador as a young woman and activist. She was abducted and assaulted by supporters of the Salvadoran military junta in Los Angeles in the mid-1980s, and today is an organizer for the Laborers Union (Zachary, 1995). Their history is common to many immigrant union organizers. Like immigrant workers generally, they often arrive without papers and only normalize their status after living and working here for some time.

In 1990, one of the first battles in these immigrant labor wars broke out when Macario Camorlinga and a group of his work mates organized a rebellion in one of L.A.'s largest foundries, American Racing Equipment. Camorlinga and his coworkers had been imbued with the ideals of militant, democratic unionism through years of workplace and political activity in the Mexican city of Lázaro Cárdenas. In the end, they were blacklisted and had to leave Mexico to support their families.

At American Racing Equipment, Camorlinga and his friends found low wages and miserable working conditions. They also found a work force that, like themselves, had no legal status. Nevertheless, in the face of INS raids on the plant, they organized a movement that culminated in a strike of nearly 1,000 workers. Today, workers run a large, well-functioning local of the Machinists Union. A strong contract has made substantial improvements in wages and conditions.[8]

American Racing Equipment wasn't an isolated experience. The city's janitors' union, Service Employees Local 399, was rebuilt in a similar movement. In the mid-1980s, the union was driven out of the city's office buildings when janitorial contractors dumped their union workers and hired immigrants. Local 399, together with the national organizing department of the Service Employees International Union (SEIU), built a Justice for Janitors campaign in L.A. Immigrant janitors poured into the streets, confronting building owners and the L.A. Police Department, and eventually won contracts covering 4,000 workers.

The campaign became the union's national showpiece. When John Sweeney, then head of SEIU, successfully fought his way into the presidency of the AFL-CIO, he used the L.A. Justice for Janitors campaign as a symbol of his commitment to organizing immigrants, workers of color, and low-wage workers.

The most telling immigrant rebellion in Los Angeles was the yearlong strike by Southern California drywallers, who put up the interior walls in new homes. In 1992 and 1993, from the Mexican border all the way north to Santa Barbara, an area of 5,000 square miles, these mostly Mexican immigrants were able to stop all home construction. Their strike, followed by a similar strike of framers this past spring, electrified unions and workers across the Southwest and set new rules for successful labor battles. Workers ran their movement democratically, from the bottom up. They defied the police and the Border Patrol, blockading freeways when their car caravans were rousted as they traveled to construction sites.

Mass picketing broke the stereotypic image of a few strikers with picket signs standing beside a driveway, watching strikebreakers take their jobs. When the drywallers and framers picketed, their lines often numbered in the hundreds. They displayed an almost missionary zeal, not wasting their time hurling insults from outside the job. Instead, they walked onto the construction sites to talk nonstriking workers into putting down their tools.

In a world where workers and unions have become hamstrung following routine procedures on a playing field where only employers win, drywallers and framers did the unexpected. They had faith in the power of their own numbers, in direct action, and in the common culture of their immigrant communities. In

1992, they finally forced building contractors to sign the first agreements covering their work in decades — the first union contracts won by a grass-roots organizing effort in the building trades anywhere in the country since the 1930s (Bacon, 1995b).

In this labor upsurge, documented and undocumented workers participate on an equal basis, without distinctions based on legal status. In unions that are seeking to build their strength through an alliance with this movement, organizers must acquire a basic understanding of immigration law. They must know how to help workers defend themselves against it. Unions and community allies, for instance, often distribute business cards that advise workers on their rights if they are stopped by the Border Patrol. In union meetings, workers often ask questions about legal status, not only to get information, but also to test the union to see if it is really committed to defending undocumented as well as legal immigrants.

In this part of the labor movement, the defense of the rights of all immigrants, including the undocumented, has become a survival issue. Employers routinely use the threat of immigration raids to intimidate workers. Employer sanctions have provided companies with a legally unchallengable way of conducting mass firings when they are faced with organizing activity in their undocumented work force. The normal remedy, which calls for reinstatement and back pay for workers fired for organizing, cannot be meaningfully enforced for the undocumented.

Immigrant-based labor struggles have reinforced thinking within the labor movement that sees unions as social movements, as the United Farm Workers was at its height in the 1960s and 1970s. In the eyes of many active and progressive unionists, this upsurge contributes new ideas and tactics and an increased sense of militancy. It helps ground unions in local communities and is making them more democratic. Unions involved in this movement don't see the changing demographics in the work force as a cultural threat, but rather as a source of new traditions and new strength.

Experiences in organizing and representing undocumented immigrants first persuaded the two garment worker unions (since merged into the Union of Needletrades, Industrial and Textile Employees) to call for the repeal of employer sanctions in the late 1980s. The California Labor Federation later took the same position. They were followed by the Service Employees, whose past president, John Sweeney, was active in reformulating its position (Bacon, 1994). Sweeney is now president of the AFL-CIO.

Under its old leadership, the AFL-CIO supported employer sanctions during the debate over the 1986 Immigration Reform and Control Act. The federation's two historic concerns were protecting legal immigration, especially family reunification, and imposing restrictions on employers who want to bring workers into the country.

According to AFL-CIO Legislative Representative Jane O'Grady, "we've always said that our society can't tolerate large numbers of undocumented people, and that every humane effort should be made to stem the flow. The controversy has been over the method, particularly over employer sanctions."[9]

However, the direction of movement in the AFL-CIO is away from this position, toward defending the undocumented against rising anti-immigrant hysteria. California labor was a strong backer of the campaign against Proposition 187, especially financially. In many areas of the state, janitors' and garment workers' union halls became anti-187 campaign offices. Unions were some of the main organizers of the huge 150,000-strong march of immigrant workers in Los Angeles in the weeks before Proposition 187 passed.

Nevertheless, in the short term the effectiveness of the AFL-CIO seems to have been eroded by differences within its own ranks. During the recent debate in Congress, the federation urged "effective control of illegal immigration," including an additional 700 Border Patrol agents. It then objected to most of the omnibus bill's provisions, however, including the national ID card, unrestricted immigration raids in the fields, asylum restrictions, and the disqualification of legal immigrants from public benefits.[10] The AFL-CIO's position in the current debate over the immigration bills seems to be caught in the transition from the policies of its old leaders to those that might be expected from its new ones.

Immigration and the Global Economy

The U.S. border with Mexico has always been relatively permeable. Many Mexican immigrants in the U.S. describe a long period in which they came and went, to and from Mexico, relatively frequently. Despite the efforts to build fences, and now steel walls, along the border in major cities, vast sections of the border are still unfenced, and even unmarked, and have always been so. In small towns along the border, it is not uncommon to find families with members who live on both sides, passing back and forth every day. In the years before the current wave of anti-immigrant hysteria, only rarely were these described as the characteristics of a border "out of control."

In California's Imperial Valley, the vast bulk of the agricultural work force lives in the city of Mexicali, which lies just south of the border and now boasts over 600,000 inhabitants. By contrast, Imperial Valley towns are much smaller. Workers commute every morning across the border to their jobs in one of the most productive agricultural areas in the world and return home at night, during times of peak harvest. Workers prefer to live in Mexico, not only for cultural and historical reasons, but also because the cost of living is much less. On the other hand, a job in the U.S. pays much more than does a farm labor job in the Mexicali Valley. Increasing and militarizing border enforcement makes this flow more difficult, in essence trapping a growing number of people on the U.S. side.

Yet as the border becomes less permeable for people, it has become more permeable for the movement of capital, production, and commodities. The movement of money, goods, and production across borders, including that between the U.S. and Mexico, is part of the globalization of economic life, under the control of transnational corporations, international financial institutions, and government policies that support them.

The North American Free Trade Agreement accelerated and made easier the movement of goods and investment capital. On the other hand, its promised protections for workers and the environment proved to be toothless and ineffective. However, NAFTA is only a part of the growth of free-trade, neoliberal economic policies. These emphasize the creation of favorable conditions for private investment, usually at the cost of declining living standards for the vast majority of the population in the countries where they are imposed. It is no accident that the growth of the global system of free trade parallels a similar growth in the worldwide migration of the economically dispossessed. Mass human migration is a new international fact of life in an increasingly global economic system.

Almost all the political candidates who debate immigration hold that borders, while they must restrain people, must also allow free passage of capital, production, and material goods. In fact, free-trade philosophy holds that favorable conditions for investment must be created wherever U.S. influence can be extended. Creating these conditions is the responsibility of institutions like the U.S. Agency for International Development, the International Monetary Fund, the World Bank, and the General Agreement on Tariffs and Trade. For them, borders hardly exist.

For instance, in the Dominican Republic (a major source of immigrants to the U.S.), the connection is clear between immigration and U.S. government policies that encourage U.S. corporate investment. Between 1980 and 1992, U.S. aid to the Dominican Republic totaled $840 million. None of this money was spent on public health or education. Instead, 97% went to the private sector, most of it to assist the construction of free trade zones for U.S. companies and their Dominican partners.

Yet while the minimum cost of living in 1993 for a Dominican family of four was calculated at $276 per month by the Center for Economic Investigation of the Caribbean, the average wage paid by Westinghouse and other employers in the Dominican free trade zones was $99 per month. From 1980 to 1992, real wages declined 46% under austerity policies designed by the IMF and USAID.

Dominican workers met repression when they tried to organize unions to raise wages in the free trade zones. Some of those efforts were cooperative ones between Dominican unions and the U.S. Union of Needletrades, Industrial and Textile Employees. In February 1991, Westinghouse fired the leaders of a union that was trying to organize the company's Dominican plants.

In 1979, 17,000 Dominicans immigrated to the U.S. By 1992, the figure had grown to 41,000.[11]

In Mexico, the scale of the economic changes that seek to create favorable investment conditions for U.S. corporations dwarfs those taking place in the

Dominican Republic. The impact of those changes produces many times the number of immigrants than those arriving from the Caribbean.

In the 1970s, technocrats favoring foreign investment took over Mexico's ruling party, the PRI. Prior to that takeover, despite problems of corruption and lack of democracy, Mexican economic policies were based on protecting the country's economic independence from outside ownership, particularly U.S. interests. Big industries and banks were nationalized. Land reform created *ejidos*, where farmers held land in common. On paper, workers enjoyed extensive labor rights, including housing and health care, while practices like strike breaking were prohibited by law.

Under the impact of its rising foreign debt, owed mostly to U.S. banks, the Mexican government began to change these policies. Economic reforms were introduced to create attractive conditions for the investment of foreign capital. They included selling national enterprises to private investors, removing restrictions on foreign ownership, disbanding land reform, ending the subsidies on food and services for the poor, and restricting the rights of unions.

Austerity programs were designed by the World Bank and the IMF. Between 1980 and 1990, the average wage of Mexican workers lost 60% of its buying power. According to Alejandro Alvarez Bejar, an economist at the National Autonomous University in Mexico City, over 40% of Mexican workers earned less than the minimum wage of about $4 per day, even before the peso's devaluation in December 1994.[12] Since then, prices have skyrocketed, while wage increases have been held back. María Ibarra, a worker in the Maxcell factory in Tijuana, earns 38 pesos a day. It takes her half a day's labor to earn the 17.5 pesos needed to buy a gallon of milk.[13]

Negotiating NAFTA was a part of this package of reforms. Another was the *maquiladora* program, in which U.S. corporations set up hundreds of low-wage factories along the U.S.-Mexican border, employing over 900,000 workers. The population of border cities like Tijuana and Mexicali mushroomed, as they attracted workers in search of these jobs. Far from creating more prosperity and removing the incentive for immigration, these policies create wealth for the people at the top, but misery for those at the bottom. They also created a pool of surplus labor along the border.

Eduardo Badillo, general secretary of the Border Workers' Regional Support Committee in Tijuana, explains that "on the whole length of the border, they are building factories. Supposedly this brings us jobs, but many people look for a better life across the border. When they look at the jobs the transnationals are offering here, they see that for an eight-hour day they pay about $5.25 (U.S.). On the other side of the border, they pay $5.25 for just one hour. The whole situation is totally out of balance. That's why a lot of workers say these days that, despite all the mistreatment they know they'll receive on the other side, beaten and with their rights denied, they prefer to be beaten in dollars than in pesos."

The conditions that U.S. corporations, USAID, the IMF, and the World Bank require for investment make it impossible for many people to survive. Neither border enforcement nor the desperation of immigrants inside the U.S. have changed the reasons why people leave their countries of origin in the first place. "For them," Badillo says, "whether the U.S. puts up two or three fences, or a Berlin Wall, hunger and the desire for a better life will be stronger than all the walls they can put up."[14]

The growth of free trade policies has created a wave of immigration that has affected the industrialized countries of Europe and Japan as well. The migration of people has become a globalized phenomenon. According to the U.N., 75 to 80 million people across the globe have been forced to leave their countries of origin and live as immigrants elsewhere. Some 20 million are refugees. The rest have left home because of economic dislocation. The greatest number, 20 million, live in Europe, while 16 to 20 million live in Africa. North America comes in third, with 15 to 17 million. Immigrants constitute about 1.5% of the world's population (International Labor Organization, 1994).

According to a document on immigration prepared by the International Labor Organization, the International Organization for Migration, and the U.N. High Commission on Refugees, "international trade, investment, and aid policies have to target countries that produce refugees and migrants." Although international investment does flow toward areas of low wages, its goal is profitability, rather than development that improves the lives of the poor (*Ibid.*).

Without a radical reordering of the world's economic system, raising the standards of living from country to country and equalizing them at the highest level rather than the lowest, the movement of people will continue. Immigration policy, therefore, must not be examined in terms of which measure can halt the flow. None of them can. Their crucial effects are on people once they are here.

Immigration Policy Based on Respect for Human Rights

The consequences of continuing to reinforce and defend the distinction between legal and illegal immigrants are not difficult to predict. Making undocumented workers more socially vulnerable will produce both greater exploitation of workers themselves and greater social unrest as they challenge it. As authorities keep the lid on this unrest, repression will also increase.

Hysteria against the undocumented feeds a legacy of discrimination that affects immigrants and people of color in general. Susan Alva, an attorney for the Coalition for Humane Immigrant Rights in Los Angeles (CHIRLA), says that the tactics used in the fight against Proposition 187 actually contributed to the anti-immigrant climate. In television and other media advertising, some opponents of the proposition alleged that stopping illegal immigration was a necessary goal, but that the proposition was simply the wrong way to do it. "Once you say that illegal immigration is a problem, and only struggle over the means of solving it, you feed this hysteria," she says. "You have to tell the truth, even if it's not politically popular or runs against racist stereotypes."[15]

CHIRLA set up a hotline that documented over 1,000 discrimination cases in the 11 months after Proposition 187 passed. A Latino family's home was torched in Palmdale after being painted with racist graffiti. Chicano children were thrown out of amusement parks. Latino passengers were told to sit in the back of buses and were required to show identification to get meals in restaurants, cash checks, get medical care, or buy groceries. Hundreds of cases of racial insults were collected.

Many police officers stopped people for simply looking Latino and demanded immigration papers. "You're not an American citizen," a Chino Hills cop told a motorist he stopped. "Why don't you go back to Mexico?"

Proposition 187 "transformed everyday life for Latinos of every status," a CHIRLA report concluded, "including those born here, and many whose ancestors had lived in the U.S. for generations." Not only Latinos suffered. "There is abundant evidence of anti-Asian hate activity, which has been extensively documented," it added (Coalition for Humane Immigrant Rights, 1995).

The alternative to further anti-immigrant policies, especially those directed against the undocumented, must be a policy based on equal rights for all people who live in the U.S. Although this sounds very radical in terms of the context of the U.S. political debate, it is the direction of the thinking among immigrant rights activists internationally.

In 1994, after the U.N. world conference on population held in Cairo, a smaller gathering was convened by the U.N. and the World Council of Churches to analyze world migration. A document was prepared for the conference by the International Labor Organization and the U.N. High Commission for Refugees. It advocates increasing the opportunities for legal immigration to deal with the problem of illegal immigration. In addition, it calls for supplying immigrants with realistic information about conditions in destination countries, to counter myths and illusions about the kind of lives immigrant workers actually face. It proposes programs to support migrants who wish to return home voluntarily (International Labor Organization, 1994). The Cairo participants agreed that the U.N. International Convention on the Protection of the Rights of All Migrant Workers and Their Families was the starting point for protecting migrants' rights. It extends basic human rights without distinction to all migrant workers and members of their families, documented or undocumented. It supports the right of family reunification, establishes the principle of "equality of treatment" with citizens of the host country in relation to employment and education, protects migrants against collective deportation, and makes both sending and receiving countries responsible for protecting these rights (World Council of Churches, 1991).

Immigration is a relationship between countries, forged by people passing back and forth. The problems posed by this movement cannot be solved by the actions of one country alone. The Convention therefore starts by defining a set of rules that guides both countries. All countries still retain the right to determine who is admitted to their territories, and under what conditions people gain the right to work.

Predictably, countries that send immigrants favor the Convention, while countries that receive them, including the U.S., do not. Nevertheless, Jan Niessen, general secretary of the Committee on Migrants in Europe of the World Council of Churches, and Shirley Hune, a professor of urban planning at the University of California at Los Angeles, assert that "campaigning for ratification could change the debates in various countries on migration issues, where migrants are increasingly seen as people who are causing problems instead of people who contribute to society, but whose human rights are not fully secured" (Niessen and Hune, 1994).

The Convention clearly does not answer all the questions posed by immigration in the context of a world economic system. Yet it takes two basic steps forward, while the debate in the U.S. remains paralyzed. It recognizes the global scale of the migration of peoples and its permanence. Moreover, its starting point is the protection of the rights of people, especially those with the least power — immigrants themselves.

Ultimately, anti-immigrant hysteria, and repressive legislation based on it, cannot be fought in isolation from overall U.S. economic and social policies, both international and domestic.

To enable people to remain and survive in their countries of origin, the policies that impoverish them must be changed. Rather than supporting increased border enforcement, immigrant advocates in Washington must call for an end to U.S. government support for structural adjustment and austerity policies worldwide, especially in countries that are a source of immigration.

It is impossible to fight against the use of the undocumented as scapegoats for the problems of job flight and insecurity without calling for limitations on the ability of transnational corporations to move capital and production at will. Anti-immigrant domestic policies and free-trade policies abroad are interconnected and mutually supportive.

Similarly, immigrants are scapegoated for declining social services, rather than continual budget cuts. Fighting for immigrant rights must be connected to a fight to expand services. Competition over declining resources cannot be eliminated without demanding that all people share equal access to social benefits and that the cost of the benefits be paid through taxes on corporations and the wealthy.

Fighting against competition over jobs means fighting for a full employment economy, instead of one in which hundred of thousands lose their jobs in corporate downsizing and layoffs, and high levels of permanent unemployment are treated as normal and necessary, especially in black and brown communities. The struggle for immigrant rights is linked to efforts to attain a shorter workweek and governmental programs that create jobs. When the movement for jobs makes progress, both immigrants and non-immigrants benefit. Similarly, when workers fight for a higher minimum wage, or for increased labor rights, both immigrant and non-immigrant communities benefit.

The defense of the rights of immigrants is, in fact, part of a broader social struggle over the distribution of wealth, the protection of the rights of all working people and people of color, and the ending of all forms of social discrimination. It is a fight over political power — who holds it and in whose interest it is exercised. Finding that reality in the middle of the current wave of anti-immigrant hysteria is not easy. Yet the price for failure to recognize it will be very high.

In reality, the increasing movement of people on a global scale is a new phenomenon in the history of our world. It reflects the globalization of economic and social problems. These problems must find global solutions, based on social justice, a respect for the rights of all people, and a course of economic development that benefits the working people and poor of all countries.

NOTES

1. President Bill Clinton, State of the Union Address of the President (January 23, 1996).
2. Senator Barbara Boxer, Statement on S. 1664, The Immigration Control and Financial Responsibility Act of 1966 (April 24, 1996).
3. Interview with José Semperio, San Francisco (February 1993).
4. *Ibid.*
5. Interview with David Young, Organizing Director for the Western States Region, Union of Needletrades, Industrial and Textile Employees, Los Angeles (November 1995).
6. Interview with Sara Callejas, Los Angeles (November 1995).
7. Interview with Joel Ochoa, LAMAP staff organizer, New York (October 1995).
8. Interview with Macario Camorlinga, Los Angeles (December 1995).
9. Interview with Jane O'Grady, Washington, D.C. (February 1996).
10. Letter from Peggy Taylor, Director, Department of Legislation, AFL-CIO, to Senator Orrin Hatch, "AFL-CIO Legislative Alert" (March 6, 1996).
11. Charles Kernaghan, "Free Trade's Hidden Secrets," National Labor Committee Education Fund in Support of Worker and Human Rights in Central America. New York (November 1993).
12. Interview with Alejandro Alvarez Bejar, Mexico City (September 1992).
13. Interview with María Ibarra, Tijuana, B.C. (May 1996).
14. Interview with Eduardo Badillo, general secretary of the Border Workers' Regional Support Committee, Tijuana, B.C. (May 1996).
15. Interview with Susan Alva, Los Angeles (February 1996).

REFERENCES

Bacon, David
    1995a   "L.A. Labor — A New Militancy." The Nation (February 27).
    1995b   "Immigrant Carpenters Battle Contractors and the *'Migra.'* " LaborNotes
                (June).

1994	"California Unions Come Out for Immigrant Rights." Pacific News Service (September 26).
1993a	"California Lawmakers on Anti-Immigrant Binge." Pacific News Service (March 22).
1993b	"From Ilopango to Pomona — The Odyssey of Union Organizer Ana Martínez." Los Angeles Village View (October 1).

Coalition for Humane Immigrant Rights of Los Angeles
| 1995 | "Hate Unleashed: Los Angeles in the Aftermath of 187." Los Angeles, California (November). |

Fix, Michael and Jeffrey Passel
| 1994 | Immigration and Immigrants — Setting the Record Straight. The Urban Institute (May). |

International Labor Organization
| 1994 | "Migrants, Refugees, and International Cooperation." International Organization for Migration and the United Nations High Commission for Refugees, Cairo. |

National Immigration Forum
| 1995 | "Local Lobby Days to Defend Immigration" and "What's Wrong with the House Immigration Bill (HR 2202)" (November). |
| 1994 | "A Guide to Immigration Facts and Issues" (Fall). |

Niessen, Jan and Shirley Hune
| 1994 | "Ratifying the U.N. Migrant Workers Convention: Current Difficulties and Prospects." Committee on Migrants in Europe. |

North American Integration and Development Center
| 1996 | "Tracking the Economic Impacts of North American Integration: Trade, Capital, and Migration Flows." UCLA (forthcoming). |

Wolff, Goetz
| 1994 | "Manufacturing in Los Angeles: Opportunities for Organizing." Los Angeles Manufacturing Action Project (LAMAP) (September 22). |

World Council of Churches and Churches' Committee for Migrants in Europe
| 1991 | "Proclaiming Migrants Rights — The New International Convention on the Protection of the Rights of All Migrant Workers and Members of Their Families." Switzerland and Belgium (February). |

Zachary, G. Pascal
| 1995 | Wall Street Journal (November). |

Right-Wing Politics and
The Anti-Immigration Cause

Sara Diamond

I N 1994, CALIFORNIA GOVERNOR PETE WILSON REVIVED HIS FLOUNDERING REELEC-
tion campaign by hitching his sails to the cause against illegal immigration.
Both Wilson and the cause were big winners that year. California's Proposition 187, designed to deny many social services to undocumented immigrants, was
approved by a large majority of the state's voters. Turnout for the initiative was
credited with boosting the electoral victories of Republican candidates for
Congress and the state legislature.

Predictably, the initiative was challenged in court. One year after voters
approved Proposition 187, a federal judge struck down most of its provisions,
ruling that undocumented immigrants could not be denied public schooling, nor
could state health and welfare agencies withhold services by requiring applicants
to prove legal residency status (Holding, 1995). The swift passage and immediate
legal challenge to Proposition 187 were symptomatic of both the political utility
and liability of the anti-immigrant issue. In the short term, Pete Wilson and like-
minded politicians could make hay with strident rhetoric against "illegal" immigrants. Over the long term, however, the immigration issue was a challenge even
for those on the Right. Legally, Proposition 187 was unlikely to be upheld and
implemented in the form that had made the initiative so popular at the polls.
Politically, despite Wilson's smooth victory, immigration policy was the subject
of diverse viewpoints among activists and thinkers on the Right.

These differences were symptomatic of some persistent quandaries for the
Right in the 1990s. Among the unresolved questions were concerns about the
proper role of the state: in regulating the flow of cheap labor across borders, in
acting to redress economic inequality versus letting people fend for themselves,
and in preserving cultural homogeneity and the supremacy of white, native-born
citizens. For the Christian Right's large voting bloc in the 1990s, the anti-

SARA DIAMOND (P.O. Box 2439, Berkeley, CA 94702; e-mail: 102147.420@Compuserve.com) has
written about right-wing social movements for many years. She is the author of *Roads to Dominion:
Right-Wing Movements and Political Power in the United States* (Guilford Press, 1995); *Facing the
Wrath: Confronting the Right in Dangerous Times* (Common Courage Press, 1996); and *Spiritual
Warfare: The Politics of the Christian Right* (South End Press, 1989). She is a columnist for
Z Magazine. She holds a doctorate in sociology from the University of California at Berkeley and is
currently teaching sociology at California State University at Hayward.

immigration cause was a relatively low priority compared to the "family values" issues. For its own reasons, the Christian Right sought to integrate its ranks across racial lines and, therefore, a wholesale attack on immigrants of color did not fit the bill.

The anti-immigrant theme was expedient in electoral campaigns such as that of Governor Pete Wilson, and there was understandably a great deal of media attention accorded to the ways in which politicians sought to use the issue. Yet beneath the surface, and largely away from the media spotlight, the Right was not unified around the goal of making a priority of the anti-immigration issue. Empower America, a leading Republican think tank headed by Jack Kemp and William Bennett, opposed Proposition 187 and urged Republicans to embrace, not reject, ethnic diversity in party ranks. The Christian Coalition, the single largest and most influential right-wing movement organization in the country, was agnostic on the anti-immigration cause and instead waged a high-profile effort to recruit conservative religious African Americans and Latinos. Contrary to common perception, not everyone on the Right promoted the anti-immigration cause.

It was in the realm of high-profile electoral politics that the immigration issue received the most attention. Both in 1992 and in 1996, Republican presidential candidate Patrick Buchanan made opposition to illegal immigration central among his campaign themes. In his 1992 Republican convention speech, Buchanan named "illegal" immigration as one of the targets in his declaration of "a religious war that is going on for the soul of America." That year he called for the construction of a "Buchanan fence," a trench along the U.S.-Mexico border to stop illegal immigration (Dart, 1992; Dowd, 1992). In 1992 and 1996, Buchanan won about one-quarter to one-third of the GOP primary vote, with calls for a moratorium on immigration topping his agenda. Yet even Buchanan, the national politician most publicly identified with the anti-immigration cause, was careful to moderate his rhetoric between his first and second campaigns, focusing in the latter race more on the economic factors that lead Mexican workers to come across the border. At the 1995 convention of the Christian Coalition, Buchanan told the 4,000 activists assembled that the fault for "illegal" immigration lies not with the "hardworking" Mexican people, but with the "rotten regime" in Mexico City and the U.S. government that keeps it in power.[1] Buchanan's use of the anti-immigrant theme was crafty: he deployed it regularly as part of his fear-arousing arsenal, yet he sought to sidestep charges of crude and unbridled racism by blaming the problem on anonymous government agents.

Buchanan's use of the anti-immigration theme both exacerbated and reflected some of the ways in which the issue was a double-edged sword for the Right. The anti-immigrant theme could be used expediently by demagogues to mobilize fearful white voters. Yet for many Buchanan voters the immigration issue was far less salient than concerns about abortion and the economy. At a time when the strategy of the Republicans was to claim to represent the interests of the majority of Americans, there were those on the Right who sought to make common cause with conservative people of color. The anti-immigrant theme, when it was too overtly racist, ran counter to the Republicans' "big tent" theme of inclusiveness.

This is not meant to downplay the persistent salience of the anti-immigration cause, as one among many issues on which the Right endorsed racial and economic inequality while also simultaneously claiming to speak for a citizenry that is increasingly racially diverse and economically insecure. To the extent that immigration policy posed a conundrum for right-wing activists, it was a problem of their own making. Over a decade before Pete Wilson used the issue to win reelection, the electoral salience of the anti-immigration cause had been heavily promoted by a number of right-wing organizations and publishing outlets. Thus, it was an issue that caught the attention of many voters and politicians eager to attract them.

Organizing Against Immigrants

During the 1980s, a small number of right-wing intellectuals devoted them-selves to developing anti-immigration arguments. At the same time, two national lobbying organizations kept the issue alive for a larger constituency: those who subscribed to right-wing magazines and, therefore, also received direct mailings from the Federation for American Immigration Reform (FAIR) and the American Immigration Control Foundation (AICF). Only in the 1990s did scores of small grass-roots organizations mobilize, mostly in California and other border states, to fight local campaigns against immigrants.

Before immigration became a hot issue, and while most of the Right was fixated on the Communist "menace" abroad, the leading promoters of anti-immigration thinking were the self-identified "paleoconservatives" (Diamond, 1995). The paleoconservatives were a group of intellectuals who viewed them-selves as heirs to the Old Right, from the decades before the Cold War, when rightists advocated a non-interventionist role for the state in foreign affairs and the capitalist economy, combined with a "traditionalist" view of society as inherently unequal and undemocratic. Paleoconservatives, joined by Patrick Buchanan, opposed U.S. participation in United Nations-conducted wars (e.g., Iraq, 1991). They also opposed any kind of civil rights legislation to achieve racial and gender equality. While most right-wing activists of the 1980s, including Patrick Buchanan, were busy aiding and abetting anticommunist "freedom fighters" in Central America and elsewhere, the paleoconservatives fought a polemical campaign against their chief nemeses, the Cold War liberals, who by the 1980s had become neoconservatives and who, despite the rest of their reactionary agenda, neverthe-less viewed the United States as ideally an ethnically pluralistic society.

Unlike the libertarians who viewed lax immigration policies as a boon to employers of cheap labor, the paleoconservatives rejected economic arguments, one way or another, on immigration. The organizational headquarters for the paleoconservatives was the Illinois-based Rockford Institute, publisher of the monthly *Chronicles of Culture* magazine. This was the outlet to follow on the immigration issue during the 1980s. The paleoconservatives ignored the question of whether "illegal" immigrants take jobs away from U.S. citizens and instead focused on the threat to cultural homogeneity posed by the influx of nonwhite immigrant groups. In a decade's worth of articles, the paleoconservatives argued that ethnicity, not a shared belief in core American values, was what gave the nation its identity. Some of the *Chronicles* writers went further, claiming that liberal elites sought to use large numbers of immigrants from Third World countries to increase the power of the state, by creating a new "underclass" and increased social problems — crime, illiteracy, and interethnic conflict — that only a New Class of elite bureaucrats would then be able to solve (Francis, 1995).

The focus on cultural homogeneity was central to early anti-immigrant activity. The most successful project was U.S. English, which sponsored state ballot initiatives to outlaw the use of languages other than English in the public realm. U.S. English began as a Washington, D.C., lobby founded by California's retired U.S. Senator S.I. Hayakawa in 1983 (Crawford, 1992: 4). U.S. English seized on local conflicts brewing, especially in Southern California, over bilingual education and the rise of an Asian immigrant merchant class. (Many Chinese and Korean store owners posted signs only in their native languages.) Hayakawa's group organized meetings in Anglo-dominated areas to suggest an action plan for white citizens worried about the growth of communities of color in their neighborhoods. Then in 1986 California's Proposition 63, an Official English amendment to the state constitution, was approved by 73% of California voters (*Ibid.*: 15-16). Thereafter, Official English bills were introduced in the legislatures of 37 states, and by 1990, 17 states had passed laws or constitutional amendments declaring English their official language (*Ibid.*: 16).

In reality, the Official English measures were largely symbolic and advisory, with virtually no impact on policy. What caught the attention of politicians was the broad popularity of what were, essentially, public referenda on the supremacy of Anglo culture.

As an organization, U.S. English was on its way toward discrediting bi– and multilingualism in public services when a scandal ensued over Hayakawa's cofounder and the man who actually ran U.S. English from the start. Dr. John Tanton, a Michigan ophthalmologist, had also founded the Federation for American Immigration Reform (FAIR) in 1979, after he was unable to persuade the environmental and population control groups he worked with to take on his fight against illegal immigration (*Ibid.*: 151-152; Trombley, 1986). Shortly before the November 1988 elections, when Official English initiatives were on the ballots in three states, the *Arizona Republic* revealed the racist contents of a confidential 1986 memorandum Tanton had circulated among colleagues. In the memo, Tanton showed his true colors when he asked:

Will the present majority peaceably hand over its political power to a group that is simply more fertile? ...Does the fact that there will be no ethnic majority in California early in the next century mean that we will have minority coalition-type governments, with third parties? ...Can *homo contraceptivus* compete with *homo progenitiva* if borders aren't controlled?[2]

The Tanton memo provoked a storm of controversy. Linda Chavez, the former Reagan administration aide who had been selected to represent U.S. English as its president, felt compelled to resign, as did Walter Cronkite (Arocha, 1988; Crawford, 1992: 165).

Later, Tanton's most unsavory association would come to light. For years, Tanton tried to hide, and then downplay, the fact that one of FAIR's largest benefactors was the Pioneer Fund. This was a funding conduit founded in the 1930s to back research on eugenics and other population control measures inspired, literally, by the policies of Nazi Germany (Crawford, 1992: 159-161; Kuhl, 1994). By 1993, FAIR had received about one million dollars from the Pioneer Fund (Ferriss, 1993) and in 1994, opponents of California's Proposition 187 tried to make FAIR's connections to the Pioneer Fund an issue warranting a "no" vote on the initiative. By then, however, FAIR had developed an image as the most respectable of the anti-immigration groups. FAIR did this by restricting its publicly distributed literature to the topic of "illegal" immigration and by including on its board of advisors prominent "population control" liberals, including former Senator Eugene McCarthy, Anne Ehrlich, and Paul Ehrlich.

The other major anti-immigration organization, the American Immigration Control Foundation, is the publisher and distributor of the English translation of *Camp of the Saints*, a racist fantasy novel written by French xenophobe Jean Raspali, following France's defeat in Algeria. The book, circulated by both FAIR and AICF, portrays a voyage by dark-skinned hordes from India's Ganges River aboard the "Last Chance Armada" as they head toward France. In pornographic prose, Raspali describes subhuman creatures fornicating all over the ship, and burning their own excrement as cooking fuel while they watch their family members die like flies in the burning sun. The fantasy tale blames the coming invasion of France on treasonous government officials and conspiratorial religious bodies.

For spreading such inflammatory propaganda, FAIR and AICF have not been condemned by leading right-wing organizations. Yet neither have the big organizations on the Right elevated the anti-immigration cause to the top of their agenda. Instead, dozens of small, grass-roots groups have mobilized to fight local battles against "illegal" immigrants in their own neighborhoods. This trend has coincided with the rise of anti-immigrant sentiment among the general public and with the increased salience of the anti-immigration issue in elections.

A June 1993 New York Times/CBS poll reported that 61% of its sample favored a decrease in immigration rates; this was up from 1986, when 49% of a poll sample favored a decrease (Mydans, 1993). An August 1993 *Newsweek* poll found that 60% of its sample considered immigration a "bad thing for this country today," whereas 59% of the same sample responded that immigration was good for the country in the past (Morganthau, 1993). Politicians were quick to pander to the rising anti-immigration mood. They also inspired it. By 1994, there were 150 pieces of immigration control legislation pending in Congress or the Senate (Sandalow, 1994). Governor Pete Wilson, along with a slew of California Congress members and state legislators, staked their political futures on the anti-immigration cause, which grew more visible with the growth of a loose network of anti-immigrant activist groups.

The direct mail, recruitment, and fundraising undertaken for years by FAIR and AICF have paid off. Both national organizations have contributed logistical and moral support to several dozen grass-roots groups, mostly in California.[3] The existence of dozens of small anti-immigrant groups no doubt made a difference in the signature gathering campaign to place California's Proposition 187 on the ballot in 1994. In the end, sponsors of the "Save Our State" initiative had to hire a professional petition-gathering company to meet their deadline. However, the signature gathering effort drew volunteers from groups including the Federation for American Immigration Reform (FAIR), California Coalition for Immigration Control, and chapters of Ross Perot's United We Stand America. Reportedly, a corps of 8,000 volunteers collected more than a half million signatures in all 58 of the state's counties (Puente, 1994; Hernandez, 1994).

Racial Reconciliation

There were anecdotal reports that some of the Proposition 187 signature gathering took place in evangelical churches. There was a common misperception that the initiative drew strong support from the organized Christian Right. The evidence shows the opposite. In fact, it is safe to say that anti-immigrant activism in California and elsewhere would have been much more widespread and more virulent were it not for the Christian Right's relative neglect of the immigration issue. Because the Christian Right was incorrectly perceived to be organized around explicitly racist policy goals, progressive activists assumed heavy Christian Right involvement in the pro-187 campaign. Here is what actually happened.

Toward the end of the fall 1994 campaign season, a number of California-based Christian Right groups and media outlets endorsed Proposition 187 among their lists of voting recommendations.[4] Yet there was no high-profile, concerted effort to win support for the initiative. In the months leading up to the election, two articles in favor of fighting "illegal" immigration appeared in the bimonthly newspaper of the California Republican Assembly,[5] which is an organization of state GOP activists from every legislative district. For the past several years, CRA has been dominated by Christian Right activists and political candidates. It is an agenda-setting apparatus for the movement's work in electoral politics, yet it gave little official support for Proposition 187.

This was also true for the two major national Christian Right organizations, Focus on the Family and the Christian Coalition. Focus on the Family is radio psychologist Dr. James Dobson's multi-million dollar ministry, which broadcasts daily over about 1,400 Christian radio stations (Diamond, 1994b). Dobson sends his monthly letter on policy issues to more than two million supporters nationwide. During the 1990s, Focus has sponsored dozens of Community Impact Seminars and, with the coordination of the above-mentioned Capitol Resource Institute, has established about 100 community impact committees in evangelical churches in California. The Christian Coalition is the Christian Right's largest and most electorally focused organization, with an official membership of more than 1.5 million and a heavy concentration of local chapters in Southern California.

To document the conspicuous absence of the immigration issue in the literature of Focus on the Family and the Christian Coalition, I reviewed their leading publications during the time period in which the anti-immigration cause gained salience on the Right. Focus publishes a monthly political magazine, *The Citizen*. Each issue includes suggestions for action on the Christian Right's issue agenda, including opposing abortion, gay rights, sex education, public school condom distribution, etc. For issues of *The Citizen* from 1993 through mid-1996, there was one article titled "Now's the time to defend our borders" (August 1994), but this item was not about immigration. It was about boycotting pharmaceutical companies involved with the abortifacient RU-486 pill. For California subscribers, *The Citizen* includes a monthly insert newsletter from the Capitol Resource Institute. Two issues in 1994 featured favorable articles on Proposition 187; neither were wholehearted endorsements (Whitney, 1994a and 1994b). As an organization, Focus on the Family neither reported on nor took a position on immigration, legal or illegal, despite the high salience of the issue.

Similarly, the Christian Coalition did not take a stand. Between 1992 and mid-1996, the Coalition's *Christian American* magazine published only one article on the negative effects of immigration. This was a syndicated column by Phyllis Schlafly, whose writings are published regularly in the *Christian American*. In 1993, the California branch of the Christian Coalition began inserting its own four-page newsletter into the national newspaper. No issues of this California newsletter covered or referred to immigration, even though California's Proposition 187 was a major statewide controversy during the period reviewed.

Despite the Christian Coalition's eagerness to be involved in all forms of electoral politics, the organization issued no position, pro or con, on Proposition 187. The Coalition's California director, Sara Divito Hardman, acknowledged in an interview with *Christianity Today* magazine that "most of our members were definitely in support of it," but, she said, as a matter of legality, not morality (Zipperer, 1995: 42).

If we assume that most Christian Right constituents voted, along with a majority of California voters, in favor of Proposition 187, we must wonder why the movement's leading organizations have remained conspicuously inattentive to the anti-immigration cause. The answer has to do with the ways in which the anti-immigration issue poses liabilities for the rest of the Christian Right's agenda. Coinciding with the formation of dozens of small anti-immigration activist groups, the Christian Right grew in scope and influence as the only truly mass-based social movement on the Right and as a major faction of the Republican Party. Rooted in the evangelical subculture, the organized Christian Right was responsive to trends underway within the churches. Beginning in the late 1980s and early 1990s, one of these trends was called "racial reconciliation" (Diamond, 1994a). It was a drive led by white evangelical clergy to publicly repent for decades of institutional racism, the kind that led to the formation of racially segregated Baptist and Pentecostal churches in the first place.

During the 1990s, the evangelical press was full of reportage on interracial church events and editorials on the need to break down racial barriers and to build a more ethnically diverse body of believers. The National Association of Evangelicals and other prominent organizations built new, multiethnic church associations. Most of this activity went unreported by the mainstream press, perhaps because it challenged prevailing stereotypes linking "fundamentalists" to old-fashioned racial bigotry.

For Christian Right activists, racial reconciliation within the churches coincided with an imperative to defy the image that the Right is monolithically racist. Christian Right leaders saw conservative people of color as an untapped source of new members, new allies, and new voters. The Reverend Louis Sheldon mobilized African American pastors to lobby for the confirmation of Supreme Court Justice Clarence Thomas in 1991. Other prominent conservatives of color were useful spokespeople against the extension of civil rights protections for gays and lesbians. Just as a minority of people of color began to voice opposition to affirmative action policies, it became obvious that many people of color held conservative views on a range of social policy issues. In the fall of 1993, the Christian Coalition released the results of a poll it commissioned showing that large percentages of African Americans and Latinos opposed abortion, gay rights, welfare, and affirmative action. The validity of the poll data was dubious, but the purpose was clear. Christian Coalition executive director Ralph Reed pledged that his movement would no longer "concede the minority community to the political left," and he announced that the Coalition would begin recruiting from within Black and Latino churches.[6]

In recent years, the Coalition and other major Christian Right groups have invited prominent conservatives of color to speak at their conferences. This move looks like blatant tokenism, and it is. Few people of color are active within the Christian Right. But the racial reconciliation strategy has the potential to grow beyond rhetoric, to involve people of color in leadership roles.[7]

Leaders of the Christian Right understood the changing ethnic composition of the United States, and they saw that recent Latino immigrants were responsible for impressive growth in many evangelical churches (Tapia, 1995). Many people in the Christian Right have backgrounds in foreign missionary work. They are not interested in working for the economic interests of people of color, but they see them more as potential converts than as adversaries.

Here we see a split between two camps of rightists. Short-term opportunists, such as Governor Pete Wilson, use anti-immigrant themes to win support from fearful white voters. More farsighted pragmatists, such as Christian Right strategists, want to make common cause with conservative people of color. The pragmatists wish to claim to represent a majority of Americans. They seek to organize winning electoral coalitions around issues of traditional "morality," not around overt race-baiting.

This divergence of opinion among rightists was reflected in the limited debate that took place regarding Proposition 187. At the height of the campaign, when polls showed the initiative headed for victory, a major Republican think tank publicized its opposition. Empower America was founded by Jack Kemp, William Bennett, Jeane Kirkpatrick, and former Congress member Vin Weber on the heels of the 1992 presidential elections. Their goal was to solidify and represent a bloc of Republicans committed to Reaganite foreign, economic, and social policies, but opposed to the kind of ultra-nationalist rhetoric espoused by Patrick Buchanan (Diamond, 1993).

In 1994, Empower America tried to exert leadership on the immigration issue. Weeks before the election, Bennett and Kemp released a statement, summarized in a *Wall Street Journal* op-ed piece, calling on Republicans to retreat from a crusade against immigration. Bennett and Kemp stressed their support for curbing *illegal* immigration using existing laws. Yet they worried that "the legitimate concerns about illegal immigrants are broadening into an ugly antipathy toward all immigrants" (Bennett and Kemp, 1994). They argued that immigrants are a "net positive gain economically," and that immigrants come to the United States with the kind of "impressive energy and entrepreneurial spirit" and "a deeply rooted religious faith" that makes them ideal future citizens (*Ibid.*).

The nub of Bennett and Kemp's statement was that the anti-immigration cause, "perceived to bring short-term political advantage," was actually in the longer term "a loser for the GOP." They argued that the Republicans risked turning away potential new voters among growing Asian and Hispanic populations, nationwide and especially in California. Moreover, they argued that since immigration is opposed strongly by African Americans, unionists, and environmentalists — all key constituencies for the Democratic Party — the GOP ought to encourage the Democrats to be the ones associated with hostility toward new immigrants, while Republicans ought to "welcome" them (Bennett and Kemp, 1994). They cited an article in the Heritage Foundation's *Policy Review* magazine (Fall 1994) in which businessman and one-time California gubernatorial candidate Ron Unz argued that "if used properly, immigration could serve as the issue that breaks the Democratic Party and forges a new and dominant conservative/ Republican governing coalition" (Unz, 1994: 37).

The Bennett-Kemp statement received minimal play in the mainstream press, which was focused on reporting poll data showing Proposition 187 headed for a big victory. On the Right, the Bennett-Kemp statement went over like a lead balloon. *Human Events* newspaper reported that California Republicans were "furious" and determined to sink any hopes Kemp had of running for president (*Human Events*, 1994). *National Review* magazine responded with a cover article, "Why Kemp and Bennett Are Wrong on Immigration." In it, William F. Buckley, Jr., acknowledged that with California's growing Asian and Hispanic populations, initiatives such as 187 could "evolve into massive anti-GOP resentments by the majority of Californians." Yet Buckley supported the proposition on grounds that Californians should not have to pay for social services for immigrants (Buckley, 1994: 78).

National Review editor John O'Sullivan, like the paleoconservative writers who had spent years honing anti-immigration arguments, tried to shift the debate away from either economic or electoral considerations. The issue for O'Sullivan boiled down to a single theme: for too long, liberals have claimed that America is an idea, rather than a nation, and that what unifies Americans are not blood ties, but ideals of liberty and equality. For O'Sullivan the reverse was true. What unifies and ought to unify the nation is a shared (Anglo) ethnicity and culture. To link national identity to a philosophy of cultural pluralism is, O'Sullivan wrote, to strengthen the welfare state, particularly in its role as distributor of benefits to particular aggrieved groups (O'Sullivan, 1994: 36-45, 76).

A State of Alienation

The "ethno-cultural" argument was a bridge linking rhetorical campaigns against *illegal* and *legal* immigration. Well before anti-immigration groups placed Proposition 187 on the California ballot, rightist intellectuals had their sights set further on legal immigration. In 1992, *National Review* editor John O'Sullivan published a cover story by fellow English immigrant Peter Brimelow, a senior editor at both *National Review* and *Forbes* magazine. In "Time to Rethink Immigration?" Brimelow introduced the anti-immigration arguments he later elaborated in *Alien Nation: Common Sense About America's Immigration Disaster*, published by Random House in 1995. Ideas once confined to movement magazines of the Right were now deemed marketable to mainstream readerships.

Alien Nation is startling in its candor. Brimelow takes aim at the 1965 Immigration Act, which rescinded the old quotas that for decades gave most openings to immigrants from northern and western Europe. The 1965 act made family reunification, as well as job skills, the criteria for legal immigration from all over the world. Since 1965, most immigrants have come from Asia and Latin America — a trend that just might have something to do with the end results of U.S. foreign policy since the 1960s, but Brimelow does not see that. After an immediate cutoff of all immigration for three to five years, Brimelow proposes a permanent two-thirds reduction in immigration rates and a reinstatement of country-of-origin quotas.

His reasoning is demographic and racist. He claims that immigration is threatening to break the "racial hegemony of white Americans" (p. 122) and he constructs a Pincer Chart to demonstrate how whites are caught between the tentacles of a growing African American population, combined with an influx of immigrants from Asia and Latin America. By the year 2050, he projects, whites will be on the verge of becoming a minority in the United States (p. 62). This population shift is automatically assumed to be undesirable.

To heighten the immediacy of the crisis, Brimelow arrays data to the effect that post-1965 immigrant cohorts are, on average, less skilled, less educated, more likely to become dependent on welfare, and more likely to become criminals and to carry infectious diseases (pp. 142-186). If that were not enough, these new minorities have "different values" than whites, including "their more radical feeling of alienation from white American society" (p. 196).

Finally, Brimelow claims that immigration is a threat to the nation-state as we know it. He defines a nation as "the interlacing of ethnicity and culture" and the nation-state as its "political expression" (p. 222). The stability of the ethnicity and culture-based nation-state is threatened not just by unwitting immigrants of color, but by a "contemporary campaign" led by a rising New Class. The term "New Class" was first coined by neoconservative thinker Irving Kristol, in the 1970s, to describe a professional elite who, as Brimelow puts it, "run and benefit from the state (...polity) and its power to tax: the government bureaucracy; the educational establishment; the media, which interlocks with both; and all their various client constituencies, to whom they channel tax monies" (Brimelow, 1995: 230).

The critique of this New Class is more than just another right-wing conspiracy theory. It is a recognition that the state, in its capacity to actively distribute resources downward into society, i.e., out of the hands of a tiny corporate elite, is a real or potential threat to runaway capitalism. Brimelow explains the relationship differently. He writes that the New Class dislikes both the ethnic nation-state and the "free market" because "both are machines that run of themselves with no need for New Class-directed government intervention" (p. 230).

Unrestrained capitalism, wedded to a homogenous culture with its attendant social controls, is a formula favored by the Right. The New Class, representing the welfare state, poses a threatening, alternative model. Here, theoretically, the state defends the rights of individuals equally before the law regardless of race while also — recently and very tentatively — protecting the rights of subordinate groups (women, racial and ethnic minorities) from abuses by the dominant few.

Anti-immigration conservatives, including John O'Sullivan and Peter Brimelow, have no inherent problem with individualism. Yet they desperately fear the consequences of a state organized, to any degree, on behalf of non-elite groups. The real question is not whether there will continue to be a nation-state. What is at stake are the central social divisions around which the state will be organized. Will the state be organized to the advantage of a particular ethno-cultural group, dominant by virtue of "tradition"? Or will state agencies and resources be deployed to defend and extend political-economic rights to a multiplicity of groups, all eager for a share of the pie? Policy controversies on affirmative action, welfare, and immigration all press this quandary over the role of the state.

For decades the priority of anticommunism set the parameters on who was and who was not a "real American." Now the dividing lines have less to do with foreign militarism and more to do with the distribution of scarce economic resources at home. Agencies of the state waged anticommunist wars and kept domestic dissidents in check. Now, after Communism, the future role of the state is less determinate. Brimelow, O'Sullivan, and the paleoconservative writers at the Rockford Institute wish to make cultural nationalism the new central organizing principle for a state that is advantageous to the white race.

They are hindered by those on the Right who have other agendas. In electoral politics, the anti-immigration cause may not always cut neatly. It worked for Governor Pete Wilson, but it may not work for others. In 1994, *National Review* published the results of a Republican National Committee survey of party activists and possible presidential contenders. By a five to one margin, party activists said they thought immigration levels were too high. Yet only two of the then likely presidential candidates, Bob Dole and Patrick Buchanan, were willing to favor reductions in legal immigration. Jack Kemp and Phil Gramm said they would oppose cutting legal immigration. Six other Republican leaders (William Bennett, Dick Cheney, Dan Quayle, Pat Robertson, William Weld, and Pete Wilson) would not take a position on cutting legal immigration (Beck, 1994).

The party wasn't any more unified a year later. Buchanan launched his 1996 presidential campaign with calls for a five-year moratorium on most legal immi-gration. He was immediately opposed by Republican House Majority leader Dick Armey (R.-TX), who gave a pro-immigration speech following Buchanan's an-nouncement (Brownstein, 1994). The party was unified only against the provision of social services to "illegal" immigrants. It was the Clinton administration that proposed reductions in legal immigration. Apart from the anti-immigration activist groups such as FAIR and AICF, and the campaign of Patrick Buchanan, the organized Right did not promote reductions as a top 1996 presidential campaign issue. (Of course, this does not mean that the Right was eager to welcome more immigrants of color.)

To win power through elections, a party must appeal to as broad a base as possible. The Christian Right, representing a broad evangelical subculture shared by millions, was focused on expanding its numbers, to win elections and to lobby on social policy issues: against abortion and gay rights, and for "welfare reform" and school prayer. The Christian Right's game plan involved recruiting, not alienating, people of color, including immigrants. At the national and local levels, the Republican Party was responsive to the Christian Right's agenda, and here immigration was granted little priority.

Still, the immigration issue — particularly when used to rally economically insecure white voters — was likely to remain expedient for some politicians and, therefore, it would be incumbent upon leaders of the Right to stake out their positions on the issue. In the short run, anti-immigrant themes, especially when focused on "illegal" immigration, were likely to remain advantageous at the polls. Yet right-wing organizers needed to be careful to contain anti-immigrant fervor, lest it appear to be too stridently racist. Apart from election campaigns, anti-immigrant rhetoric would be most useful to the Right as part of a long-term project to roll back or prevent government intervention on behalf of racial minorities and poor people generally.

NOTES

1. Author's attendance at Patrick Buchanan's keynote banquet speech at the Christian Coalition's September 1995 "Road to Victory" conference, Washington, D.C.

2. This quotation comes from John Tanton, October 10, 1986, Memorandum, author's collection. The memo is also excerpted in Crawford (1992: 151).

3. The scope and size of the anti-immigrant groups are not known. On May 8 and 10, 1995, two advertisements appeared in the *Washington Times* newspaper. In the form of open letters to President Clinton and Congress, they called for a moratorium on legal immigration and an end to social services for immigrants residing in the United States illegally. The letters were signed by two overlapping lists of 56 and 25 groups from Alabama, Arizona, Florida, Kentucky, Virginia, and Washington State. Some of these groups report their local anti-immigrant activities to others in their movement through the *Border Watch* newsletter of the American Immigration Control Foundation, which claims a circulation of 100,000.

4. Among groups and outlets I monitored, Louis Sheldon's Traditional Values Coalition included a pro-187 position in his November 1994 California Voter's Guide. The Capitol Resource Institute, a Sacramento-based Christian Right think tank and lobby, included an endorsement of 187 in its October 1994 mailer to supporters. California's independent Christian Right monthly newspapers (*The Forum* in Santa Cruz, *The Southern California Christian Times,* and *Good News* in San Diego County) endorsed 187 in their respective voter guides. All sources from author's collection.

5. *The California Republican* (November-December 1993; March-April 1994); from the author's collection.

6. "Minority Myths Exploded," *Christian American* (October 1993), author's collection.

7.   In 1995, for example, the Coalition appointed Stephan Brown, a young African American man from Southern California, as western regional coordinator for the organization. His job was to recruit Coalition chapter leaders in urban areas and to organize them for the 1996 elections. See "New Regional Coordinator Named" (*California Christian*, January 1995: 3). This was the newsletter of the California branch of the Christian Coalition.

REFERENCES

Arocha, Zita
    1988   "Chavez Quits U.S. English Organization." Washington Post (October 20).
Beck, Roy
    1994   "Right of Silence?" National Review (July 11).
Bennett, William
    1994   "A Statement on Immigration." Distributed by William Bennett and Jack
                  Kemp, Empower America, Washington, D.C. Undated.
Bennett, William and Jack Kemp
    1994   "The Fortress Party?" Wall Street Journal (October 21).
Brimelow, Peter
    1995   Alien Nation: Common Sense About America's Immigration Disaster. New
                  York: Random House.
    1992   "Time to Rethink Immigration?" National Review (June 22).
Brownstein, Ronald
    1994   "Immigration Debate Roils GOP Presidential Contest." Los Angeles Times
                  (May 14).
Buckley, William F., Jr.
    1994   "Kemp/Bennett vs. the Right." National Review (November 21).
Crawford, James
    1992   Hold Your Tongue: Bilingualism and the Politics of "English Only." Reading,
                  Mass.: Addison-Wesley.
Dart, John
    1992   "Buchanan Calls Riots Part of War for Soul of U.S." Los Angeles Times
                  (May 8).
Diamond, Sara
    1995   Roads to Dominion: Right-Wing Movements and Political Power in the United
                  States. New York: Guilford Press.
    1994a   "Change in Strategy." The Humanist (January-February).
    1994b   "Focus on Some Families." Z Magazine (July-August).
    1993   "Shifting Alliances on the Right." Z Magazine (November).
Dowd, Maureen
    1992   "Buchanan's Alternative: Not Kind and Gentle." New York Times (Janu-
                  ary 15).
Ferriss, Susan
    1993   "FAIR: Mounting Campaign to Keep Immigrants Out." San Francisco
                  Examiner (December 12).
Francis, Samuel
    1995   "The Transnational Elite." In Immigration and the American Identity,
                  Selections from Chronicles: A Magazine of American Culture, 1985-1995.
                  Rockford, Illinois: The Rockford Institute.
Hernandez, Rosalva
    1994   "On the Border." Orange County Register (May 12).
Holding, Reynolds
    1995   "Prop. 187 Ruled Mostly Illegal." San Francisco Chronicle (November 21).

Human Events
1994   "California Conservatives Fire Back at Kemp and Bennett" (November 4).
Kuhl, Stefan
1994   The Nazi Connection: Eugenics, American Racism, and German National Socialism. New York: Oxford University Press.
Morganthau, Tom
1993   "America: Still a Melting Pot?" Newsweek (August 9).
Mydans, Seth
1993   "A New Tide of Immigration Brings Hostility to the Surface, Poll Finds." New York Times (June 27).
O'Sullivan, John
1994   "America's Identity Crisis." National Review (November 21).
Puente, Teresa
1994   "Save Our State Group Turns in Petitions." Orange County Register (May 17).
Sandalow, Marc
1994   "Politicians Paying Attention to Uproar over Immigration." San Francisco Chronicle (March 31).
Tapia, Andres
1995   "Growing Pains." Christianity Today (February 6).
Trombley, W.
1986   "Prop. 63 Roots Traced to Small Michigan City." Los Angeles Times (October 20).
Unz, Ron K.
1994   "Immigration or the Welfare State." Policy Review (Fall).
Whitney, Bob
1994a   "The Cost of Illegal Aliens." California Citizen (April).
1994b   "Prop. 187: Illegal Aliens." California Citizen (October).
Zipperer, John
1995   "Immigration Debate Divides Christians." Christianity Today (February 6).

The Immigration Crisis: Detention as an Emerging Mechanism of Social Control

Michael Welch

Introduction

A S A RESULT OF WORLDWIDE POLITICAL AND ECONOMIC SHIFTS, IMMIGRATION HAS emerged as an international problem affecting most Western nations. Indeed, immigration in the United States has increasingly become politicized at the national and local levels of government. Making matters worse, political leaders have yet to define and adequately implement a singular national immigration policy. Subsequently, government officials tentatively initiate one set of policies, only to abruptly reverse their position in favor of more repressive measures.

Historically, immigration has always met formidable resistance from mainstream citizens. Similarly, in recent times, immigration has become a lightning rod for mounting anger, and this outrage has taken on many forms. Immigration has contributed to a renewed sense of nativism, nationalism, and political isolationism, as well as to institutionalized racism. This antagonism is largely fueled by economic tensions, insofar as immigrants and undocumented immigrants ("illegal aliens") serve as convenient scapegoats — viewed as threats to scarce employment opportunities and blamed for draining public resources and social services.

Problems concerning immigration are as numerous as they are complex. Indeed, the complexity of the problems affects all aspects of immigration control, including immigration law, asylum hearings, border patrol, and parole. This article, however, concentrates on one particular mechanism in the control of immigration — the *detention* of undocumented immigrants. Although most illegal

MICHAEL WELCH, Ph.D., is an Associate Professor in the Administration of Justice Program at Rutgers University, 43 Mine Street, New Brunswick, New Jersey 08903, (201) 216–0294. The author also has correctional experience at the federal, state, and local levels. His research interests include corrections and social control, and he is the author of the forthcoming textbook, *Corrections: A Critical Approach* (New York: McGraw-Hill). A version of this article was presented at the annual meeting of the American Society of Criminology, Miami, 1994. The author gratefully acknowledges Carrissa Griffing, Marie Mark, Judy Rabinovitz of the ACLU Immigrants' Rights Project, Stephanie Marks of the Lawyers Committee for Human Rights, and Mark Dow for their valuable assistance in preparing this article.

immigration takes place at the Mexican border (the Border Patrol reports apprehending and returning 1,000 aliens to Mexico each day [*The New York Times*, 1995]), there are more than 6,000 undocumented immigrants currently detained by the Immigration and Naturalization Service (INS) (ACLU Immigrants' Rights Project, 1993). Yet, even a cursory examination of INS operations indicates that detention policy is often ambiguous and contradictory as current immigration policy itself.

Recent investigations of INS policy have revealed major problems in the detention of undocumented immigrants. For instance, the American Civil Liberties Union Immigrants' Rights Project (1993) inspected INS detention centers in New York City and documented numerous institutional problems, as well as allegations of human rights violations. Moreover, similar institutional problems and human rights violations have been reported at several other INS detention centers (Welch, 1995; 1994a; 1994b; 1993; 1991). The objective of this article is to explore institutional problems facing INS detention centers. Additionally, INS detention policy is also discussed in the context of the new penology (Feeley and Simon, 1992), thereby conceptualizing detention as an emerging mechanism of social control.

INS Detention as an Emerging Mechanism of Social Control

Detaining large numbers of undocumented immigrants marks a relatively recent development in INS policy. "For twenty-five years prior to the 1980s, the I.N.S. maintained a policy of detaining only those individuals deemed likely to abscond or who posed a security risk" (Marks and Levy, 1994: 2). Policy shifts during the early Reagan administration marked a significant change in immigration and detention. With the arrival of the Mariel Cubans and the Haitian boat people, widespread detention was used as a deterrent to illegal immigration. Under this policy, all "excludable" aliens were detained for further inquiry. In July 1982, this policy was further formalized as an interim rule in the Federal Register, later codified in 8 C.F.R. SS 212.5, 235.3. "Under these rules, which are still in effect, all aliens arriving without proper travel documents are detained pending a determination of their status, unless they are considered eligible for parole for 'emergent reasons' or reasons 'strictly in the public interest' " (Marks and Levy, 1994: 2; see 8 C.F.R. S 212.5 (a) [1993]).

As a result of the shift in immigration policy, the use of detention by the INS grew significantly during the 1980s. According to the American Civil Liberties Union Immigrants' Rights Project, "in 1981, the average stay in an INS detention facility was less than four days. By 1990, it had grown to 23 days, with many individuals detained for more than a year" (ACLU, 1993: 1; see U.S. GAO, 1992). The General Accounting Office (U.S. GAO, 1992) reports that during the 1980s, the INS detention budget grew from $15.7 million to more than $149 million, thereby expanding the detention capacity to hold more than 6,000 persons. The estimated daily cost to taxpayers is approximately $50 per detainee.

Since the 1980s, more than 26 INS detention centers have opened; currently, more than 6,000 undocumented persons are detained, most of whom are people of color. Indeed, allegations of Eurocentrism and racism in U.S. immigration policy have surfaced. Critics argue that whites seeking asylum in the United States have encountered much less resistance and generally are not detained for indefinite periods of time. However, persons of color are typically detained while they apply for residency. Among those persons most commonly detained are Cubans, Haitians, Central Americans, and Nigerians. Many of these refugees seek political asylum in the United States because they fear persecution in their homelands (Marks and Levy, 1994; Welch, 1995, 1991; Arp, Dantico, and Zatz, 1990; see also Cook, 1993). Although the INS claims that they do not keep records on the nationality of detainees, immigration and human rights lawyers who visit detention centers report that the vast majority of detainees are people of color (Marks, 1995).

In 1986, Congress passed the Immigration Reform and Control Act (IRCA, also known as the Simpson-Rodino law), requiring all employees to document their citizenship. A major consequence of IRCA has been the emergence of repressive measures against undocumented immigrants. For example, before 1980, INS detention was the exception. During the 1980s, however, "INS policy changed significantly. As a result, many individuals previously eligible for release are now subject to mandatory detention" (ACLU, 1993: 3). Other detainees, though not subjected to mandatory detention, also are held because they cannot meet the excessively high bonds demanded for their release.

The ACLU Immigrants' Rights Project and the
Varick Street Investigation, New York City, 1993

As a result of the increased use of detention, institutional problems plaguing INS detention centers have become significantly compounded, including poor staffing, obstructed access to counsel and the courts, inhumane living conditions, and inadequate medical care. Furthermore, allegations of human rights violations, such as physical and sexual assault by staff, also are reported.

One reason why the institutional problems evident in INS detention centers have remained concealed is attributable to the lack of systematic inspections and routine monitoring. However, one of the few comprehensive investigations of an INS detention facility was coordinated by Judy Rabinovitz, staff counsel of the American Civil Liberties Union (ACLU) Immigrants' Rights Project. This project engages in litigation, public education, and advocacy and professional training to protect immigrants against discrimination and exploitation, and to enforce the fundamental safeguards of due process and equal protection (ACLU Immigrants' Rights Project, 1993).

In its report, *Justice Detained*, the ACLU Immigrants' Rights Project summarizes a two-year investigation of the INS' Varick Street detention facility in New York City (*Ibid.*; see also Sontag, 1993a, 1993b). In addition to documenting the substandard conditions at Varick Street, the investigation also exposed egregious errors by the INS. For example, U.S. citizens have occasionally been mistakenly detained by INS. In fact, during the ACLU study, researchers assisted the release of a detainee who had been held for 14 months, long beyond the statutory release period. In this case, the detainee was being held despite uncontroverted evidence of U.S. citizenship. Also during the investigation, two other detainees were in the process of verifying their U.S. citizenship.

The report confirms that many detainees at Varick Street are legal permanent residents with long-standing ties to this country, with family members who are United States citizens, and with bona fide legal claims to remain in this country. Moreover, the report reveals that INS detention policies and practices subject detainees to lengthy periods of confinement in a facility that was designed solely for short-term detention. At Varick Street, detention averages six months, and sometimes lasts as long as three years.

According to Lucas Guttentag, director of the ACLU Immigrants' Rights Project, "immigrants awaiting administrative hearings are being detained in conditions that would be unacceptable at prisons for criminal offenders" (Sontag, 1993a). In addition to the lengthy periods of confinement, the report reveals that the Varick Street facility is characterized by inhumane living conditions, including overcrowding, staffing problems, substandard sanitation leading to poor hygiene among detainees, lack of fresh air and sunlight, inadequate food, medical, and legal services, arbitrary and punitive use of segregation, and lack of grievance mechanisms. Even when detainees are ruled deportable, often they are held for several more months or years, because the INS fails to promptly arrange travel and execute their departures (ACLU Immigrants' Rights Project, 1993).

Complaints over conditions at INS facilities in New York are not new. During the 1980s, the INS was sued twice. In fact, the facility at Varick Street was opened in the wake of one of the previous lawsuits — yet, more problems followed. In 1986, the U.S. General Accounting Office (U.S. GAO, 1986) issued a report that also criticized the Varick Street facility for, among other things, the lack of outdoor exercise facilities and poor quality staffing.

The investigation of the conditions at the Varick Street facility further disclosed an important characteristic of the detainee population: "Virtually all of the detainees we spoke with had close family members who were either U.S. citizens or legal permanent residents" (ACLU Immigrants' Rights Project, 1993: 10):

- • Mr. D had lived in the United States for 27 years, 25 as a legal permanent resident. Almost all of his relatives reside in the United States.

- Mr. C had lived in the United States almost 10 years after fleeing from Bangladesh as a political refugee. His wife is a legal permanent resident of the United States and his three children are U.S. citizens.

- Ms. A had lived in the United States for 22 years, 17 as a legal permanent resident. Her two children are U.S. citizens.

- Ms. M had been a legal permanent resident for 18 years, immigrating from Haiti with her family at the age of seven. All of her immediate family members live in the U.S., including her nine-month-old U.S. citizen daughter.

In light of these cases, serious questions remain concerning the usefulness and fairness of current INS detention policy. Clearly, these detainees do not meet the most basic justification for mandatory detention because they do not pose a security risk. Moreover, their risk of absconding is minimal since they have family and relatives in the United States. Because detention interferes with the ability of detainees to pursue their legal claims, it is recommended that current INS detention policy be reexamined. Beyond the inhumane conditions at the detention centers, INS detention practices are costly, unnecessary, and unjust for most undocumented immigrants.

Problems Affecting Other INS Detention Centers, Queens, New York

The problems at the Varick Street facility are generally representative of several other INS detention centers. In fact, similar problems are associated with INS detention practices nearby in Queens, New York. At Kennedy Airport, INS officials confront numerous travelers without visas (TWOV); however, the detention practice employed features a double standard.

INS has forced airlines to act as jailers for the TWOVs, even though the agency lets most political asylum applicants enter the country without much fuss. Applicants are simply told to show up months later when their case is called. But the INS has decided any TWOV who requests asylum should get different treatment. All TWOVs must be detained by the air carrier that ferried them into the country — at the airline's expense (*New York Newsday*, 1993: 3).

The INS detention policy costs the airline industry eight million dollars per year, including the expense of detaining TWOVs in neighboring motels — nicknamed "Motel Kafkas." Indeed, such detention is quite Kafkaesque. Private guards are hired by the airlines to serve as detention officers, but these officers do not answer to the government. Moreover, while being held in a motel room for months, detainees are deprived of fresh air, telephones, and, in some cases, are shackled and sexually abused. The following cases further illuminate problems with current INS detention policy:

In August [1993], three teenagers — two boys and a girl — from Sri Lanka arrived at Kennedy Airport on a Northwest Airlines flight and requested asylum. Northwest detained them for about two months, footing the motel and security guard bills until the airline persuaded the city to arrange for foster care. During those two months, the teenagers' lawyer never knew where they were being held. And the young people weren't allowed to call him. They told him that they only were fed twice a day because the guard said there wasn't enough money for three meals (*Ibid.*).

In May 1992, Delta Airlines found itself with 13 TWOV passengers from China who requested asylum. Two escaped, a pregnant woman was paroled, and Delta ended up housing, feeding, and guarding the remaining 10 until August when INS arranged for them to get an asylum hearing. Delta shelled out $181,000, which included $9,800 in medical bills for a woman who broke her arm when she leapt from her hotel room in an attempt to escape (*Ibid.*; see also Hartocollis, 1990).

However, recent court decisions have significantly affected INS detention policy, especially as it relates to owners of ships and airplanes carrying stowaways. In June 1994, the Federal Court of Appeals for the Third Circuit in Philadelphia overturned an INS policy that required the owners of ships and airplanes to pay the cost of detaining stowaways while awaiting asylum proceedings. The court ruled that the INS had violated federal guidelines in establishing its detention policy. The decision marks the "first blow against rules that human rights advocates have long attacked for forcing owners of ships and airplanes into the expensive and unwarranted role of jailing stowaways" (Levy, 1994: B–1).

The case referred to an incident in which 20 Rumanian stowaways arrived in Boston by hiding in huge metal cargo containers loaded on a freighter in France. The INS required that the shipping company, Sea Land Service, detain the stowaways. Consequently, the Rumanians were detained in hotels in Newark, New Jersey — shackled together by leg irons. Later, the detainees were transferred to a county jail in Pennsylvania, but the INS still required Sea Land Service to pay for the use of jail space (*Ibid.*).

As a result of the ruling, shipping companies could sue the federal government for the costs of detaining stowaways for the last six years — the statute of limitations. Companies in other states are expected to file similar lawsuits. "I am quite pleased by the decision," said Stephanie Marks, coordinator of the asylum program for the Lawyers Committee for Human Rights. "I would hope now that the I.N.S. would see the error of this policy of requiring shipping companies to act as jailers" (*Ibid.*: B–8). (Also see the Immigration and Nationality Technical Corrections Act of 1994 [INTCA] as published in the Congressional Record — Senate, October 17, 1994: Appendix I, pp. 1387–1392.)

Krome Detention Center, Miami

Major problems at INS detention centers are not confined to New York. During the past several years, the Krome Detention Center in Miami has been plagued with numerous institutional problems, including complaints of sexual harassment and physical abuse. Moreover, the controversy surrounding Krome heightened in 1990 when three educational contract employees working at the detention center were dismissed. Each of them was a whistle blower who had complained of the mistreatment of the detainees (mostly Haitian). INS officials concede that there are institutional problems at Krome, but point to understaffing as a major source of their difficulties (LeMoyne, 1990).

At Krome, detainees "wear orange uniforms, and the guards on the grounds are armed, and the intimidating sound of gunfire can echo through the camp from a nearby target range where I.N.S. officers practice" (Rohter, 1992: E–18). Richard Smith, the immigration service regional director, has been asked why Krome looks so much like a jail. "That's because it is a jail, albeit a minimum security jail. The sign outside may say that it's a processing center, but that's just semantics" (*Ibid.*).

Though Krome was designed for short-term detention, many detainees spend more than 90 days there. Another point of controversy concerns the detention of minors, who by INS regulations are not to be held in the same facility with adults. According to Joan Friedland, an immigration lawyer at Krome, "the basic problem is that there are no rules.... Everything is discretionary" (*Ibid.*).

INS officials at Krome deny allegations of violence and human rights abuses. Constance K. Weiss, an INS administrator at Krome, argued: "Why would we want to run a place where we beat the hell out of people?" To this, refugee advocates reply with a two-part answer: "to discourage other potential refugees and because it is easy to get away with. Detained immigrants are a powerless group...without recourse to normal political or legal channels" (*Ibid.*; see also DePalma, 1992).

A key decision by the Clinton administration announced August 19, 1994, has greatly affected the INS detention center at Krome, as well as other detention centers such as Port Isabel, Texas. As outlined in an INS memorandum from the Office of the Deputy Commissioner to District Directors, the new directive marks a reversal from a previous position allowing nearly all Cuban immigrants to be granted political asylum: "Due to the situation confronting the Service in August 1994 relative to a massive flow of Cuban migrants to the United States, the Attorney General decided that all excludable Cubans arriving in the United States should be detained" (memorandum dated September 14, 1994). (Note that the memorandum also specifies that unaccompanied children and other persons presenting compelling humanitarian concerns be paroled.)

Between August 5 and September 13, 1994, the Coast Guard picked up 32,051 Cuban refugees. At Guantanamo Bay, the U.S. has detained 28,266 Cubans and

14,181 Haitians. An additional 2,851 Cubans are held on Coast Guard and Navy ships; 607 Cubans are detained at Krome detention center; 1,102 Cubans are detained in Panama and Texas (Silver, 1994).

The INS detention policy pertaining to Cubans parallels recent initiatives to control immigration in California. On September 18, 1994, Attorney General Janet Reno announced that the new immigration directive targeting Mexicans would "shut the door on illegal immigration" (*The New York Times*, September 18, 1994: 40). The Justice Department refers to the new initiative as "Operation Gatekeeper," which brings more federal personnel and money to California. The political valence in California, Florida, and Texas ought not be overlooked since the immigration issue profoundly shapes state and local politics.

Forced Tranquilizing, Deportation, and Human Rights Violations: The Case of Tony Ekpen Ebibillo (1993)

INS detention practices recently drew additional controversy when a detainee was forcibly tranquilized and deported. On three occasions, the INS tried and failed to deport Tony Ekpen Ebibillo — an asylum seeker from Nigeria. Ebibillo resisted his deportation and allegedly fought and bit INS officers. On the third attempt, INS staff forcibly drugged Ebibillo at Krome detention center, placed him into a straightjacket and leg weights, and transported him to the airport. "Gagged, groaning, and surrounded by four officers, one with a syringe, the Nigerian had been drugged at the direction of immigration authorities" (Booth, 1993: A–1). Yet, the airline captain would not allow the INS to board Ebibillo while in such condition. Finally, the INS quietly chartered another airplane and deported Ebibillo and 77 other Nigerian deportees on December 15, 1993 (Viglucci, 1994: 2B).

Amnesty International (AI) intervened, but its efforts came too late. The INS deported Ebibillo before AI representatives could negotiate for a fair asylum hearing. "Had I known his deportation was in the works, we would have asked them not to do this," said Nick Rizzo, refugee coordinator for the U.S. section of Amnesty International in San Francisco. "I think he probably had a case for asylum. He seemed credible. And the facts hung together" (*Ibid.*). Indeed, supporters of Ebibillo suspect that the INS quietly deported him because they were aware that AI was looking into the case. Public interest lawyer Cheryl Little, who advocated for Ebibillo's asylum, concluded "that Tony was deprived of his day in court" (*Ibid.*). INS officials deny doing anything improper in deporting Ebibillo, noting that a judge ordered him expelled from the country two years earlier. Ebibillo had requested political asylum after entering the country illegally, claiming that he was a prodemocracy activist fleeing persecution by Nigeria's military. Ebibillo had no criminal convictions.

Ebibillo had been detained by the INS since December 18, 1990. To ensure his deportation, INS staff at the clinic at Krome placed Ebibillo in restraints for

48 hours while Public Health Service physicians drugged him with Thorazine (a powerful anti-psychotic medication). INS officials defended the forced drugging by arguing that Ebibillo was passive-aggressive (a personality disorder). Though medical records show that Ebibillo had not been diagnosed as psychotic, he was medicated "apparently to control him during deportation" (Booth, 1993: A–1; see also Ezem, 1991).

> Government policy allows the use of drugs for detainees who are mentally ill or dangerous. It bars the use of drugs for the purpose of deporting people who offer physical resistance.
> Ebibillo was apparently never diagnosed as having a mental illness. But government doctors said the use of drugs was justified because Ebibillo was acting aggressively and posed a threat to himself and others (Viglucci, 1994: 2B).

Questions persist as to the extent to which deportees are involuntarily drugged for the purposes of facilitating their departure. "I am aware that it was a practice for very difficult deportees," said a former INS official at Krome who asked not to be named. "It wasn't the practice in every case, but they did use drugs for the purpose of getting somebody quietly on a plane" (Booth, 1993: A–20).

According to Gregg Bloch, a psychiatrist and associate professor at Georgetown University Law Center and specialist in medical ethics, "it sounds as if they are transparently using the medication for police purposes, and that is a violation of medical ethics and tort law" (*Ibid.*). Bloch elaborates:

> It is not even a gray area. It is not ethical or legal to take difficult-to-handle people, even violent criminals, and drug them to make them less violent. It would be like a doctor riding around with the police and injecting violent offenders (*Ibid.*).

Arthur Helton, director of the Refugee Project for the Lawyers Committee for Human Rights in New York added: "This sounds like an extraordinary procedure, and it seems there must be some kind of review process so the use of drugs is not abused by local enforcement personnel" (*Ibid.*).

For nearly a year, supporters of Ebibillo continued their efforts to locate him with the help of human rights groups (i.e., Human Rights Watch/Africa) in Lagos, Nigeria. Upon his arrival in Lagos, he was reportedly arrested (along with other deportees facing drug charges) by the Security Service (Dow, 1993).

In December 1994, a year after being forcibly deported, Cheryl Little received a letter from Ebibillo. In the letter, Ebibillo reports being in satisfactory physical condition; however, he faces criminal charges in Nigeria. (It is unknown what he is charged with, although it is suspected that he is being detained for his prodemocracy activism against the military regime.) Ebibillo alleges additional human rights violations by the INS, including physical abuse and psychological manipulation. For instance, Ebibillo claims being told that he was being transported to a court hearing when, in fact, he was being driven to the airport for deportation (Dow, 1994).

Undocumented Immigrant Children

Another aspect of INS policy that remains controversial is the detention of undocumented immigrant children. Whereas some undocumented adults are eligible for release to await their hearings, undocumented children are detained if they lack a close relative or legal guardian in the United States. In 1993, the United States Supreme Court (*Reno* v. *Flores*, No. 91–905) upheld this INS detention policy. However, an earlier decision by the U.S. Court of Appeals for the Ninth Circuit in San Francisco held that the policy had violated the children's constitutional right to due process. The appeals court ruled that children are entitled to a hearing, including an inquiry into whether an unrelated adult was available to care for the child during the deportation hearing.

Each year, thousands of children are arrested on suspicion of being deportable aliens. Of the 8,500 arrested in 1990, 70% were not accompanied by adults. Most of these youths are teenage boys from Mexico and Central America. Currently, the INS holds more than 2,000 undocumented youth. The INS reports that it has neither the resources nor the expertise to conduct thousands of hearings to approve suitable caretakers.

Justice Stevens, in a dissenting opinion of the 1993 decision, argued that the Constitution requires that the INS demonstrate in each case why detention was better than being released to an unrelated adult. The conditions of confinement also have been challenged in several lawsuits concerning the detention of undocumented children. In 1987, a consent decree ordered the INS to improve such conditions (Greenhouse, 1993; Johnson, 1992).

Detention, Social Control, and the New Penology

The prevailing response to the immigration crisis has encouraged government officials to resort to detention. In this sense, detention has emerged as a mechanism of social control for unpopular and powerless persons — namely, undocumented immigrants of color. Since the 1980s, detention has become a practice widely used to control and deter undocumented immigrants. Currently, such policies persist despite the recommendations of immigration experts who argue that the existing detention policy is costly, unnecessary, and unjust for most undocumented immigrants (ACLU Immigrants' Rights Project, 1993; Marks and Levy, 1994).

In light of these developments, the popularity of detaining undocumented immigrants mirrors the practice of incarcerating increasing numbers of offenders in the criminal justice system. Certainly, incarceration continues to enjoy considerable ideological popularity among political leaders and mainstream citizens —

in 1994, the prison population in the United States surpassed the one million mark. In explaining the prevailing trend in incarceration, Feeley and Simon (1992) present an alternative view of correctional policy that they call the *new penology*. Feeley and Simon contend that a new set of terms, concepts, and strategies have begun to replace those of traditional penology. Whereas the traditional penology stems from criminal law and criminology, with their emphasis on punishing and correcting individual offenders, the new penology adopts an actuarial approach in which *specialists* assess the risks of specific criminal subpopulations (e.g., drug offenders) and recommends strategies that attempt to control these *aggregates*. The main objective of the new penology is to improve social control measures for high-risk and dangerous groups, thereby establishing a greater reliance on imprisonment — that is, correctional "warehousing" (Welch, 1996).

Since the new penology represents a strikingly different course for the future direction of correctional policy, there are several areas of concern. For instance, the new penology does not set out to intervene or respond to either the individual offender or adverse societal conditions that serve as the root causes of many forms of street crime. "It does not speak of impaired persons in need of treatment or of morally irresponsible persons who need to be held accountable for their actions" (Feeley and Simon, 1992: 452). Rather, the new penology concentrates on maximizing social control — utilizing prediction tables and population projections to streamline the criminal justice system.

Because the new penology takes an actuarial approach, it emphasizes efficiency, management, and control instead of individualized justice and reform attempts. Simply put, the criminal justice system recycles human beings from one form of custodial management to another without attempting to impose justice or reintegrate offenders into society (Feeley and Simon, 1992; see also Gordon, 1991; Platt, 1994).

Perhaps the most distressing contradiction of the new penology is that its actuarial approach strives to improve public safety without attempting to reduce crime. According to Feeley and Simon (1992: 455):

> The new penology is neither about punishing nor about rehabilitating individuals. It is about identifying and managing unruly groups. It is concerned with the rationality not of individual behavior or even community organization, but of managerial process. Its goal is not to eliminate crime, but to make it more tolerable through systemic coordination.

The new penology also has implications for poverty and the underclass — a segment of society, typically African American and Hispanic, that is permanently marginalized economically and otherwise removed from America's mainstream. Since members of the underclass as a whole are unemployed, uneducated, and possess few or no work skills, they are generally characterized as posing a threat to society, and are depicted as constituting a dangerous class. According to the new penology, this so-called dangerous and high-risk group must be controlled and managed by the criminal justice system. For decades, a clear trend of incarcerating impoverished and minority offenders has been emerging. Mauer (1990) documents this trend by noting that approximately one in every four young (between the ages of 20 and 29) African American males are either in prison, in jail, or on probation or parole.

As the imprisonment trend continues, the actuarial impetus of the new penology becomes evident — that is, social management and social sanitation override individualized justice (Welch, 1994b; see also Welch, 1996; Adler, 1994; Irwin, 1985; Spitzer, 1975). Unfortunately, the prospects for the future remain bleak, since both poverty and imprisonment continue to escalate. Feeley and Simon conclude: "This, in turn, can push corrections even further toward a self-understanding based on the imperative of herding a specific population that cannot be disaggregated and transformed, but only maintained — a kind of waste management function" (1992: 469–470).

Comparing the new penology to prevailing INS detention policy further illuminates the emerging form of social control within the immigration crisis. Indeed, the practice of INS detention mirrors the new penology. For example, instead of reviewing individualized cases of asylum and applications for citizenship, the INS tends to resort to the processing of large aggregates — groups of specific nationalities, namely, Cubans, Haitians, Central Americans, and Nigerians. Similarly, a recent executive order has instructed the INS to detain all excludable Cubans arriving in the United States effective September 14, 1994 (Sale, 1994). Moreover, during the 1980s the U.S. Attorney General targeted Salvadorans by granting the INS the authority to make arrests without warrants, leading to the detention of hundreds of Salvadorans (see *Orantes-Hernandez* v. *Thornburgh* and *Orantes-Hernandez* v. *Meese*).

The actuarial approach further complements a detention policy that emphasizes efficiency, management, and control. The actuarial approach in INS detention is clearly evident since the agency functions according to bureaucratic and rational-legal procedures. For instance, the INS relies on specialists, experts, and technicians to *classify* aliens (i.e., excludable and deportable aliens) as well as *predict* and *forecast* immigration trends. In doing so, immigration specialists apply actuarial methods to determine the costs of immigration (e.g., establishing financial estimates related to health care, education, and other social services). From the perspective of the new penology, INS specialists are given the task of managing aggregates — insofar as groups, not individuals, are the unit of analysis. The emphasis here is on managing categories, rather than on accommodation, equity, and significant social transformation.

Similarly, the current INS detention policy does not endeavor to reintegrate undocumented immigrants into the community. In fact, it often resists and opposes such reintegration. A case in point is the controversy surrounding the Asylum Pre-Screening Officer (APSO) Program, which was designed to use detention space more judiciously and to expand the use of the Pilot Parole Project.[1] Though the Pilot Parole Project has been found to create a more rational and economic detention policy and is supported by officials from the United Nations High Commissioner for Refugees, the Department of Justice, Amnesty International, and the Lawyers Committee for Human Rights, there are reports of noncompliance in certain districts. Marks and Levy (1994: 10) found "that the district directors in Harlingen and New York have rejected a significant number of positive parole recommendations."

Marks and Levy (*Ibid.*: 11) also find "the New York district director's action in this regard particularly troubling in light of evidence that aliens are denied parole in New York solely because of national origin. In particular, we are concerned about reports that Nigerian asylum seekers face a presumption against parole solely because they are Nigerian." In response to these findings, the allegation of discrimination and institutionalized racism in the New York district has been brought to the attention of the New York City Commission on Human Rights, which issued a letter of concern to the INS district director.

Finally, whereas the new penology addresses the social control of the impoverished people of color in the nation, INS detention policy also targets unpopular immigrants of color.

Conclusion

The purpose of this article is to identify and describe the problems surrounding INS detention policy, as well as to acknowledge the poor institutional conditions and services that exist at many of the INS detention centers. In sum, immigration lawyers emphasize that INS detention practices are costly, unnecessary, and unjust for most undocumented immigrants (ACLU Immigrants' Rights Project, 1993; Marks and Levy, 1994). Yet, an important thrust of this article is to present INS detention policy in a broader social context, in particular, to demonstrate how detention policy has emerged as a more repressive mechanism of social control. The immigration crisis has fueled a renewed sense of nativism, nationalism, political isolationism, and institutional racism. Due to the political valence that resists immigration, INS detention is used as a form of deterrence and social control of select racial and ethnic groups.

The new penology (Feeley and Simon, 1992) is applicable to INS detention policy for several reasons. First, the new penology is based on an actuarial model to control large aggregates by emphasizing efficiency and management. The actuarial approach facilitates INS detention policy since it rests on bureaucratic and rational-legal procedures. Second, both the new penology and INS detention policy resist efforts to reintegrate certain groups into the community, especially the impoverished people of color and undocumented immigrants of color. Finally, critiques of the new penology point out that imprisonment, as a mechanism of social control, is likely to escalate — paralleling a similar trend among undocumented immigrants.

NOTES

1.   The Pilot Parole Project was initiated in 1990 by the INS Commissioner in an effort to create a more rational and economic detention policy. According to the project, INS district directors were instructed to take into account a number of criteria (e.g., certainty of true identity and strength of the asylum claim) in making parole decisions. A final assessment of the Pilot Parole Project, which concluded in October 1991, demonstrated the desirability of a durable release authority (see Marks and Levy, 1994: 5–6).

REFERENCES

Adler, Jeffrey S.
     1994   "The Dynamite, Wreckage, and Scum in Our Cities: The Social Construction
                     of Deviance in Industrial America." Justice Quarterly 11,1: 7–32.
American Civil Liberties Union (ACLU) Immigrants' Rights Project
     1993   Justice Detained: Conditions at the Varick Street Immigration Detention
                     Center, A Report by the ACLU Immigrants' Rights Project. New York:
                     ACLU.
Arp, William, Marilyn K. Dantico, and Marjorie S. Zatz
     1990   "The Immigration Reform and Control Act of 1986: Differential Impacts on
                     Women?" Social Justice: A Journal of Crime, Conflict and World Order 17,2:
                     23–39.
Booth, William
     1993   "U.S. Accused of Sedating Deportees: Tranquilizers Given to Those Who
                     Resist." The Washington Post (October 7): A–1, A–20.
Cook, Dee
     1993   "Racism, Citizenship, and Exclusion." Dee Cook and Barbara Hudson (eds.),
                     Racism and Criminology. London: Sage Publications.
DePalma, Anthony
     1992   "Winds Free 40 Aliens, Stirring Second Storm." The New York Times
                     (September 21): A–10.
Dow, Mark
     1994   A letter of correspondence regarding Tony Ebibillo. December 20.
     1993   "United States of America vs. Tony Ebibillo." August.
Ezem, Nwachukwu
     1991   "Nigerian Arrested After 10 Years in Miami Accuses INS of Mistreatment."
                     The Miami Times (December 19): 1–A, 2–A.
Feeley, Malcolm M. and Jonathan Simon
     1992   "The New Penology: Notes on the Emerging Strategy of Corrections and Its
                     Implications." Criminology 30,4: 449–474.
Gordon, Diana R.
     1991   The Justice Juggernaut: Fighting Street Crime, Controlling Citizens. New
                     Brunswick, NJ: Rutgers University Press.
Greenhouse, Linda
     1993   "Detention Upheld on Alien Children: Justices Affirm a U.S. Policy on
                     Deportation Hearings." The New York Times (March 24): A–19.

Hartocollis, Anemona
    1990   "A Woman Without a Country." New York Newsday (July 25): Part II, 8–9.
Irwin, John
    1985   The Jail: Managing the Underclass in American Society. Berkeley: University of California Press.
Johnson, Dirk
    1992   "Choice of Young Illegal Aliens: Long Detentions or Deportation." The New York Times (November 30): A–1, A–12.
LeMoyne, James
    1990   "Florida Center Holding Aliens Is Under Inquiry: Additional Complaints Made of Abuse." The New York Times (May 16): A–16.
Levy, Clifford J.
    1994   "Court Upsets Law on Costs of Stowaways: Companies Had to Pay Expenses for Detention." The New York Times (June 30): B–1, B–8.
Marks, Stephanie
    1995   Personal communication, Lawyers Committee for Human Rights (March 1).
Marks, Stephanie and Jack Levy
    1994   "Detention of Refugees: Problems in Implementation of the Asylum Pre-Screening Officer Program." A Briefing Paper issued by the Lawyers Committee for Human Rights (September). New York, New York.
Mauer, Marc
    1990   "Young Black Men and the Criminal Justice System: A Growing National Problem." Washington, D.C.: The Sentencing Project.
New York Newsday
    1993   "Motel Kafka." New York Newsday Editorial (October 24): 2–3.
Platt, Anthony M.
    1994   "Rethinking and Unthinking 'Social Control.'" George S. Bridges and Martha A. Myers (eds.), Inequality, Crime, and Social Control. Boulder, Col.: Westview Press.
Rohter, Larry
    1992   "'Processing' for Haitians Is Time in a Rural Prison." The New York Times (June 21): E–18.
Sale, Chris
    1994   INS Memorandum from Office of the Deputy Commissioner to District Directors, Subject: Parole Authorization (September 14).
Silver, Vernon
    1994   "Some Cubans Are Released from Detention in Florida." The New York Times (September 14): A–6.
Sontag, Deborah
    1993a   "Report Cites Mistreatment of Immigrants: A.C.L.U. Says Aliens Are Detained Too Long." The New York Times (August 12): B1, B8.
    1993b   "New York City Rights Chief Investigating U.S. Immigration Centers." The New York Times (September 21): B3.
Spitzer, S.
    1975   "Toward a Marxian Theory of Deviance." Social Problems 22 (June): 638–651.
The New York Times
    1995   "62 New Guards Will Reinforce Arizona Border." February 6: A–12.
    1994   "Reno Initiative Aims to Control Immigration." September 18: 40.
U.S. General Accounting Office (GAO)
    1992   Immigration Control: Immigration Policies Affect INS Detention Efforts. Washington, D.C.: U.S. Government Printing.
    1986   Criminal Aliens: INS Detention and Deportation Activities in the New York Area. Washington, D.C.: U.S. Government Printing.
Viglucci, Andres
    1994   "INS Deports Nigerian Without Telling Lawyers." Miami Herald (January 12): 2–B.

Welch, Michael
1996   Corrections: A Critical Approach. New York: McGraw-Hill.
1995   "Problems Facing Immigration and Naturalization Service (INS) Detention
            Centers: Policies, Procedures, and Allegations of Human Rights Violations."
            Rosemary L. Gido and Ted Alleman (eds.), Turnstile Justice: The Practice of
            Institutional Punishment. Englewood Cliffs, NJ: Prentice-Hall.
1994a   "Detention Practices in Immigration and Naturalization Service (INS)
            Facilities: Policies, Procedures, and Allegations of Human Rights Violations."
            A Paper Presented at the Annual Meeting of the Academy of Criminal Justice
            Sciences, Chicago.
1994b   "Jail Overcrowding: Social Sanitation and the Warehousing of the Urban
            Underclass." Albert R. Roberts (ed.), Critical Issues in Crime and Justice.
            Thousand Oaks, Cal.: Sage.
1993   A Summary Report on INS Detention Practices. Submitted to the ACLU
            Immigrants' Rights Project, New York.
1991   "Social Class, Special Populations, and Other Unpopular Issues: Setting the
            Jail Research Agenda for the 1990s." G. Larry Mays (ed.), Setting the Jail
            Research Agenda for the 1990s: Proceedings from a Special Meeting.
            Washington, D.C.: U.S. Department of Justice, National Institute of
            Corrections.

CASES

Orantes-Hernandez v. *Meese*, 685 F. Supp. 1488 (C.D.Cal. 1988).
Orantes-Hernandez v. *Thornburgh*, 919 F. 2d 549 (9th Cir. 1990).